DATE DUE

Implementing E-Commerce Strategies

Implementing E-Commerce Strategies

A Guide to Corporate Success after the Dot.Com Bust

MARC J. EPSTEIN

PRAEGER

Westport, Connecticut
London

Library of Congress Cataloging-in-Publication Data

Epstein, Marc J.
 Implementing e-commerce strategies : a guide to corporate success after the dot.com bust / Marc J. Epstein
  p. cm.
 Includes bibliographical references and index.
 ISBN 0–275–98463–X
 1. Electronic commerce. 2. Strategic planning. 3. Business enterprises—Computer networks—Planning. 4. Electronic commerce—Case studies. I. Title: Implementing e-commerce strategies. II. Title.
 HF5548.32.E67 2004
 658.8'72—dc22 2004049568

British Library Cataloguing in Publication Data is available.

Library of Congress Catalog Card Number: 2004049568
ISBN: 0–275–98463–X

First published in 2004

Praeger Publishers, 88 Post Road West, Westport, CT 06881
An imprint of Greenwood Publishing Group, Inc.
www.praeger.com

Printed in the United States of America

The paper used in this book complies with the Permanent Paper Standard issued by the National Information Standards Organization (Z39.48-1984).

10 9 8 7 6 5 4 3 2 1

Contents

Companies Profiled

Sector: Retail

Industry: Bookstores
   Amazon
   Barnes and Noble
   Borders

Industry: Discount Retail
   Wal-Mart
   Kmart
   Target

Industry: Luxury Retail
   Nordstrom
   Neiman Marcus
   Ashford.com

Industry: Grocers
   Tesco
   Webvan and Homegrocer
   D'Agostino's-MWG

Industry: Office Supplies
   Office Depot
   Staples

Sector: Services

  Industry: Stockbrokers
    Charles Schwab
    Merrill Lynch
    E*Trade

  Industry: Consumer Banks
    Wells Fargo
    Bank of America
    Bank One-Wingspan

  Industry: Pharmacies
    CVS
    Walgreens
    Rite Aid-Drugstore.com

  Industry: Postal Services
    UPS
    Federal Express

Sector: B2B

  Industry: Computers
    Dell
    Compaq/HP

  Industry: Networking
    Cisco
    Lucent

  Industry: Plastics
    GE Plastics
    Omnexus
    PlasticsNet.com

Preface

With the growth of the Internet, corporations have struggled with the determination of the appropriate level of investment in the new technology. CEOs faced the quandary of whether to fully commit or wait and watch. Academics devoted effort to determining ways to formulate e-commerce strategies. But, little research has focused on how to choose among alternative strategies or how to execute an e-commerce strategy.

This book relies on extensive analysis of academic and managerial research, along with a review of company successes and failures during the foundation and short history of e-commerce. It provides industry and company cases and specific recommendations for actions that managers can take to improve e-commerce success. It provides a framework for measuring the benefits and costs of potential e-commerce investments that can aid in deciding how much to invest and how to achieve the greatest potential payoffs. It places e-commerce in a value creation frame, so that corporate and business unit managers can more effectively evaluate the possibilities and trade-offs. The author hopes that lessons learned can guide managers to effectively formulate, evaluate, and implement an e-commerce strategy.

This book could not have been completed without the important contributions of research assistants Todd Makse, Steve Wilbur, Kirby Brendsel, and Pranika Uppal. The dedication of faculty assistant Karen Lavelle has been critical in managing all of the documents related to the preparation of this book. I also thank Nick Philipson, senior editor at

Praeger, for his support, guidance, and friendship over the years of our association. Finally, I acknowledge my colleague and friend, Al Napier, who was an important inspiration to this project and provided significant input throughout the project.

The book is dedicated to the many managers whom I have worked with who have asked about evaluating both potential e-commerce investments and e-commerce success. The lessons we learn from prior successes and failures and the frameworks presented here are intended to help senior general managers to better develop, evaluate, and implement e-commerce strategies. IT managers should be aided to better analyze the value creation potential of investing additional resources in e-commerce initiatives. I hope also that for students and researchers this book pulls together the managerial experiences and academic literature on the formulation, implementation, and evaluation of e-commerce strategies and that it adds to the understanding of management control and performance measurement in corporations. If some find its synthesis, frameworks, and guidance useful, this book will be a success.

Marc J. Epstein

PART I

Increasing the Return
on E-Commerce Investments

CHAPTER 1

Characteristics of E-Commerce Success

What is the CEO to do today about e-commerce? Clearly, the dot.coms were a bust. The stock market took values from nothing to billions in the late 1990s. Some investors made hundreds of millions of dollars. In early 2000, the dot.com bubble burst, and many investors lost their dollars just as quickly. Now that the hype is over, we can look back to see what worked and what didn't—and also apply what we know about business, about management, about information technology (IT). What we know is that the Internet does require some special considerations, but also that many principles that apply to business in general have not been generally applied to e-commerce. For example, revenues, costs, and profits do count—not just Web site hits!

What is the CEO to do today? What do senior managers need to know and do when considering their companies' involvement in e-commerce? Specifically, what actions should senior managers take to successfully formulate and implement an e-commerce strategy? They must consider alternative choices related to leadership, strategy, structure, and systems and decide among them.

The study of e-commerce has unfolded in much the same way that e-commerce thrust itself on the business world—with a great deal of overstatement. After a long period of treating the topic of e-commerce with awe and confusion, we can now discuss the subject more objectively.

Most companies have ventured into e-commerce, and many of these attempts have not met expectations. For example, the acknowledged technology leader in the retail industry, Wal-Mart, has gone through several redesigns and sales strategies in its online activities and an outright suspension of its Web site. Because of the poor showing of its e-commerce activities, Borders eventually outsourced its Internet sales activities to Amazon. Bank One dissolved its online banking entity, Wingspan, and integrated its online operations into the bank.

Some companies had inept strategies and reacted slowly as other companies in their industry succeeded at using the Internet. After Amazon initiated its business activities, Barnes and Noble imperiled its future by attempting to imitate Amazon, by creating a separate company that did not take advantage of the company's "brick-and-mortar" presence and existing logistical systems. Compaq was eventually purchased by Hewlett-Packard because it could not match Dell's Internet sales prowess and superior Internet-based supply-chain operations, which provided significant cost advantages.

We now can examine the e-commerce records of numerous companies to ascertain the characteristics of success and failure in e-commerce activities. This book offers a complete model of the choices that exist for e-commerce leadership, strategy, structure, and systems—and how to go about making those choices. This includes what to do (strategy), who needs to be involved (leadership), how to organize the company to do e-commerce (structure), and how to operationalize and implement e-commerce in corporations (systems).

An extensive framework and analysis by which to measure the effectiveness and benefits (payoffs) of an e-commerce initiative includes a careful analysis of the causal relationships and the impact of potential managerial actions in e-commerce on long-term corporate profitability. It also includes an extensive listing of potential measures of inputs, processes, outputs, and outcomes. As companies consider beginning or broadening e-commerce initiatives, a clearer understanding of the benefits and costs is critical. To obtain adequate resources, CIOs must justify the potential payoffs from an e-commerce investment and calculate the return on investment. This book provides the objectives, drivers, and measures of e-commerce success.

From a perspective that we didn't have a few years ago, we can now analyze why certain approaches to e-commerce were destined to fail. The twelve industry cases provide an opportunity to examine both successes and failures and identify specific lessons learned.

The guidelines set out here characterize the most successful actions of established e-commerce leaders, providing pertinent advice to senior managers in all segments, industries, and stages of e-commerce.

The dynamic model centered on these guidelines focuses on the key factors for corporate success in e-commerce integration. It includes the critical inputs and processes that lead to success in e-commerce (outputs), as measured by its contribution to overall corporate profitability (outcome). We see how a company that lacks significant e-commerce operations can become a company that uses e-commerce operations to significantly enhance its profitability.

A company's existing strategy, structure, and systems represent important inputs to the model, leading to processes through which a strong leader can transform all three to achieve e-commerce success. This book is grounded both in the latest academic and managerial research and in extensive research on company activities and experiences (Exhibit 1.1).

This book is written for the many large corporations that are reexamining the formulation and the implementation of e-commerce strategies and their level of investment in e-commerce. Its target is the large manufacturing, distribution, and service firms that would like to improve their return on e-commerce investments.

The processes begin with leadership in the formulation and implementation of a successful e-commerce initiative. Leadership starts with a commitment by the CEO and other senior managers to consider a significant role for e-commerce in the organization. The CEO should initiate a dialogue within the company on the changes necessary for a full-scale e-commerce effort. The CEO, along with other key executives, must examine the emerging role of e-commerce within the company's

Exhibit 1.1
Antecedents and Consequences of E-Commerce Success

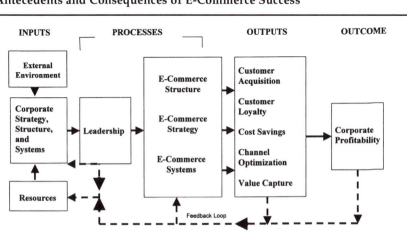

industry, ascertain its current position with respect to its competitors, and determine an appropriate level of investment.

Next, proven guidelines for e-commerce strategies permit the company to build on its position and quickly increase its online business activities. Though these strategies do represent some different options, successful e-commerce operations will likely incorporate all of them into its activities.

Senior managers must decide how to organize, finance, manage, and provide IT solutions for e-commerce. I encourage a perspective that looks at the various alternatives and generally propose a structure that leads to full integration of e-commerce throughout the fabric of the organization. The company should avoid the temptation of small benefits in one company segment in favor of the larger benefits of total or near-total integration.

Appropriate systems must also be implemented to ensure the successful integration of e-commerce. Corporate culture, performance and operational measures, and compensation systems must all be considered unique challenges. Customer data management and demand and supply chain management are vital to maximizing the value of e-commerce. The introduction of changes to these systems may not have any deleterious effect on traditional commerce, but systems designed for traditional commerce may fail to provide proper management control for e-commerce.

Finally, the outcomes detailed in the model are not vague goals. Chapter 6 presents a detailed approach to measuring the payoffs of e-commerce investments, to better understand causal relationships and which specific actions lead to improved profitability.

Chapter 1 provides an executive summary of findings and articulates sixteen characteristics of successful e-commerce firms. Without examining all of the industry specifics or examining the full dynamics of the measurement systems for the payoffs of e-commerce, it is a blueprint that will clearly guide companies in the right direction.

LEADERSHIP

To move forward with e-commerce, the CEO and other senior managers must pursue several initial activities. Leadership comprises words and deeds, explicit and implicit behavior, control of purse-strings, and leadership by example. Successful e-commerce leadership has four main characteristics (Exhibit 1.2), which can be implemented as follows.

1. Commitment at the Top: The CEO and Other Senior Managers Must Embrace E-Commerce. Implementing an e-commerce plan requires strong leadership at the top of the organization. The CEO and other senior managers must understand the issues surrounding e-commerce well enough to evaluate the organization's strengths and weaknesses

Exhibit 1.2
Leadership

1. Commitment at the top
2. Thorough competitive analysis
3. Significant financial investment
4. Cultural transformation

and make appropriate decisions on strategy, structure, and systems. The CEO must view IT and its applications as a vital component of the company's strategy and publicly demonstrate this belief through words and actions. The CEO must also adopt the attitude that e-commerce is not optional. The company may decide to have a larger or smaller role for e-commerce and may develop that role quickly or slowly, and it may sell directly to customers or limit its major initiative to the back-end systems, but it cannot ignore e-commerce entirely.

Many CEOs have become e-commerce believers by discussing the topic with more experienced executives at other companies. For example, a conversation with Michael Dell of Dell Computer led Jack Welch at GE to hasten his company's movement into large scale e-commerce activities. Others, such as Howard Lester at Williams-Sonoma, have been convinced by believers within their own firm through some positive pilot e-commerce projects. In any case, the CEO should begin an earnest dialogue with people who understand e-commerce to learn about its successes and failures in relevant industries.

Other leadership roles are also important. The CIO must be a proactive member of the senior management team who communicates well with the CEO about the usefulness of IT applications. Rather than serving strictly as a technologist, the CIO must also be a strategist. The CIO should serve in a leadership role in cross-functional teams that combine business units, IT, and e-commerce. The CFO needs to understand the strategic role of IT in the business and consider its ramifications in funding decisions. Other members of the senior management team should have an active role in e-commerce, in a direct advisory role when it relates to specific relevant areas of responsibility and in a support role for other areas of the company. If possible, senior management should include persons who have prior e-commerce experience.

2. Thorough Competitive Analysis: Determine Company's E-Commerce Position. In crafting an appropriate e-commerce strategy, it is vital for the company first to understand its e-commerce position relative to competitors. At this point, there are few industries where there has not been a first mover in the use of e-commerce. Even in industries where traditional companies have been laggards, pure-play companies have stepped into the void with varying levels of success. In fact, in most industries, a pure-play of some type was the first mover.

This existence of a first-mover competitor does not mean that other companies in an industry cannot gain competitive advantage over their traditional competitors by making significant e-commerce investments and efforts. CEOs who find themselves in an early-mover position should continue to invest and innovate to maintain their advantage. Charles Schwab built a significant advantage over competitor Merrill Lynch, despite having been preceded online by pure-play competitors such as E*Trade.[1]

If a company is a late mover into e-commerce, it can still desire to be the first to provide a particular service, combination of services, or other unique value proposition. Catching up, however, often requires a very high level of investment and a willingness to explore new business models and processes. Regardless of position, a CEO must adopt a broader mode of thinking about competitors because in e-commerce, industry boundaries are more blurred and competition can come from unlikely sources.

3. Significant Financial Investment: Determine Appropriate Role of E-Commerce. Once the CEO has evaluated the company's e-commerce position relative to other industry members and specific competitors, a decision must be made as to the appropriate role of e-commerce within the company. Given the increased usage of the Internet by leading companies in most industries, the senior managers will typically need to move forward with expanding or at least maintaining the company's current e-commerce position relative to its competitors.

The relevant decisions include whether the company is going to sell online and, if so, how its offerings will compare with its traditional offerings. It should also consider the geographic scope of its e-commerce sales, since the Internet permits unlimited worldwide access, which can introduce a myriad of complications and challenges. The extent to which e-commerce will be utilized in procurement and distribution must also be considered, as well as internal functions such as human resources, accounting, and marketing.

Of primary importance is that the company determine appropriate levels of IT activities and provide for appropriate levels of IT funding. This approach requires taking all necessary steps, including acquisitions or strategic alliances, to ensure that the company's IT capabilities are sufficient for a successful e-commerce venture. The CEO must then work with other executives to ascertain the amount of investment necessary to fully implement the chosen e-commerce strategy. Investment decisions should be primarily strategic, and returns should be viewed, including the measurement of both short-term and long-term value creation, with a broad view of potential impacts.

4. Cultural Transformation: Determine Implementation Needs. Since structure and systems can be used to implement strategy, most systems decisions are made after an e-commerce strategy has been formulated. But at an attitudinal level, cultural transformation will usually begin even earlier. Senior managers have a responsibility to establish a minimum level of IT acceptance and competence throughout the company by demonstrating and communicating commitment and creating appropriate training programs. Some companies will be better prepared for this transition than others; senior managers must carefully consider the required preparation and the implications for implementation speed.

To rapidly implement an e-commerce strategy, IT and e-commerce basics and the purpose of e-commerce must be understood. Communicating purpose is one of the most important actions of a CEO. Employees must realize that e-commerce represents an important challenge and opportunity rather than a threat.

Whether the e-commerce strategy is to be implemented within a month or a year, a sense of urgency is required.[2] The CEO must present e-commerce as having the power to transform the organization in a positive way. Equivocation at every level, from the CFO's hesitation to fund technology to the salesperson's fear that e-commerce will decrease personal commissions, must be avoided. That does not mean reckless risk-taking to move forward, but it does mean a committed acceptance of e-commerce throughout the organization.

STRATEGY

In designing an e-commerce strategy, it is critical to recognize what the Internet changes. Not every value proposition in traditional commerce can attract customers in e-commerce, and not every traditional strategy is a viable source of increased profitability. The best strategies do not ignore the fundamental properties of the Internet and the behavior of its users.

The organization must develop strategies for e-commerce operations that are consistent with overall corporate strategy. (Since this is a dynamic model, the order of appearance of these elements may be different. Strategy may precede leadership and resource commitments

Exhibit 1.3
Strategy

---

1. Well-positioned online brand
2. Online-friendly offerings
3. Reliable customer service
4. Cross-channel coordination

---

and structure and systems already in place may constrain the strategy decision.) The goals should include an increase in customer acquisition, enhanced channel optimization, improved customer loyalty and retention, and capturing value for the organization. Four strategic moves are displayed in Exhibit 1.3 and defined in the following discussion.

1. *Well-Positioned Online Brand: Acquiring Customers and Building Trust.* The simplest way for companies to initiate e-commerce operations is to transfer the brand name to the Internet, using the company's name as the domain name so that existing customers and potential new customers can easily find the company's Web site. The company can then advertise the Web site in various physical locations and in all print publicity materials. All letterheads, business cards, other types of business publications, and traditional advertising media should include the Web site address. In-store signage, kiosks, advertising on bags, and other materials have also been successful in drawing customers to the online channel. Large online marketing campaigns are likely to produce click-throughs and hits, but not customers, and have typically proved to have poor payoffs.

A brand name will draw customers to the company's site and can help assure customers about the quality of the offerings, the accuracy of the information, and the security of the Web transactions on that site. The brand name can also promote customer loyalty. The company must continue to provide the level of service and security that the brand name implies, or it will fail to attract repeat online customers and may even damage the traditional brand.

If the company's traditional brand is centered on price competition, it must reevaluate this strategy for e-commerce. Price competition is rarely a viable source of profitability in e-commerce. Search costs for comparing prices are negligible online, and price wars have typically led to prices decreasing to just at or above cost. The Internet also offers easy access to stores that offer price differentials, because customers do not need to travel any physical distance to get to any given store. Only in limited contexts should companies expect to achieve long-term competitive advantage based on price.

2. *Online-Friendly Offerings: Product Selection and Differentiation.* The company must decide what products to offer on the Web site. Companies such as Office Depot have found that they are able to provide more total products to customers through Web sites. Physical store space limits the number of inventory items available in stores, while the Web enables the company to provide a larger product offering. Even when integrating their offline and online brand management, a company should not feel compelled to offer precisely the same products online as in its physical stores. The ability to offer a large quantity of products,

especially in retail industries, is a major inducement to acquiring an online channel.

Further, it is fully appropriate for a company to eliminate online offerings that are simply unprofitable or otherwise inappropriate. General retailers such as Wal-Mart and grocers have used price minimums, margin requirements, and category restrictions to limit their online offerings. Some companies also require a minimum total purchase on their Web site.

Companies should also consider peripheral offerings in addition to those provided by the company's physical facilities. Such additions are especially appropriate for companies in service industries and companies with large business-to-business (B2B) components. For example, Office Depot's business services offerings are a strong complement to its office supplies business.

Another differentiator is offering customers the ability to obtain unique or uniquely tailored products or information. Customization can be a powerful differentiator because it allows customers to control the product or service choices, and loyalty can be built partly due to high switching costs. Personalization gives customers their very own version of the site that can include information and recommendations based on the customers' prior purchases and demographics.

3. *Reliable Customer Service: Inspiring Loyalty among Customers.* Building trust online requires more than a strong brand; it requires strong customer service practices that emphasize the convenience of the online channel. The customer must trust the company and its Web site. Trust can be built through assurances of privacy and transaction security and by providing accurate information. Trust in the transaction's completion is built through prompt and accurate fulfillment of orders. Many people purchase at Amazon rather than other Web sites because of its consistently highly rated fulfillment and customer service operations.

Web site design also contributes to satisfying customers. Basic characteristics of the site, such as simplicity, legibility, clarity, and a professional look, are necessities for all Web sites. Strong search engines are especially important for companies with a large number of product offerings. Information about physical stores, customer service, and delivery and return policies should be easily accessible from the home page. Technology should be a facilitator and not an end in itself, however, and the company should not invest too heavily in design features without being confident of their appeal. Neiman Marcus found that its customers were not interested in viewing luxury products on a high-technology platform. Barnes and Noble discovered that they could not create interest in online parallels to their in-store coffee bars and author visits. Functions such as discussion boards may provide information for new visitors but are unlikely to be a strong generator of new business.[3]

The site should also provide a number of services for customers who need information about the site, the offerings, or products they have purchased. These include comprehensive FAQ (frequently asked questions) sections, easily accessible information on delivery and returns, and rapid email response and technical support, where appropriate.

Numerous delivery options should be available to the customer to allow for both speed and low-cost preferences. Companies such as Nordstrom's, which offers products that need to be examined in person before the sale is complete, have provided particularly generous return policies to overcome the hesitation to purchase online inherent in their product line. Physical stores can also be used for pick-up of items that are needed immediately in industries such as pharmacies. Customers should also be offered convenient opportunities to return defective or unsatisfactory products, including returning such products to the physical stores.

4. Cross-Channel Coordination: Convenience and Revenue Stimulation. The Web site and physical stores should not be seen as two separate entities that happen to share a brand name. Cross-marketing is an important component, but ultimately, the online and traditional stores must have complementary roles in the overall corporate strategy. Exploiting the advantages of integration means more than drawing customers to the Web site through promotion in the physical store.

Allowing online customers to pick up and return orders to physical stores provides customers with choices and convenience, bringing more traffic to the physical stores. Initially many traditional companies did not allow online customers to return purchased products to their stores. Today, virtually everyone allows customers to return undesired items to physical store locations. Numerous studies have shown the propensity of customers to make additional purchases when drawn to the store by online-generated functions. Therefore, the Web site should include an easily accessible store locator function that includes a map to the location, a phone number, and store hours.

The physical store and online operations can each be used to stimulate sales in the other channel. Some products that require high levels of interaction with the product can be introduced to the online customer but sold in the physical locations. Kiosks that provide a computerized access to the online site, on the other hand, have been a successful mechanism in physical stores to stimulate online traffic. Many retailers have encouraged the use of kiosks to order online products not available in the physical store or when delivery of the products is more convenient. Kiosks are also effective in overcoming concerns about online shopping for less computer literate customers.

The Web site can also provide more convenience for customers who wish to purchase specific items immediately rather than wait for delivery. For example, Office Depot can now direct customers to local stores that currently have the product in inventory. Customers need not call all the local stores and tolerate taped messages and long waits to find a product. Even Internet pure-play companies like Amazon, through its alliance with Borders, for which it provides Web site operations, can direct customers to the nearest Borders store that has a desired product. Customers need only provide a zip code.[4]

Integration of physical stores and online operations can also lead to greater efficiencies. Supply chain advantages that lead to more effective purchasing, inventory control, and logistics management may enhance the company's overall cost structure and result in greater profitability.

STRUCTURE

After formulating an e-commerce strategy, senior managers must develop a plan for implementation. The company's organizational structure may at times conflict with the goals of e-commerce, and senior managers must anticipate these conflicts and act accordingly, whether by changing the structure of the traditional organization or by creating new structures specific to e-commerce. These considerations span the areas of financing, management teams, and operations. A final consideration is the use of strategic alliances (Exhibit 1.4).

1. Internal Investment: Maintain Full-Equity Interest in E-Commerce. The company faces a decision about equity for the e-commerce venture, whether to retain complete ownership in the e-commerce venture or to spin it off as an independent company. The lessons are clear. Many high-profile failures occurred in traditional companies that tried to imitate the pure-play model by spinning off. Investment in the venture should be made from within the firm, and reliance on outside capital typically seems like an indicator of trepidation about e-commerce on the part of senior management.

Spinning off e-commerce was popular in the early period of e-commerce, and the results have generally been disastrous. Building up large market capitalizations through IPOs was a popular trend, but

Exhibit 1.4
Structure

---

1. Internal investment
2. Integrated management teams
3. IT know-how from within
4. Strategic partnerships

---

it has become less desirable in a weaker and more skeptical stock market. The vast majority of these companies, including Wal-Mart, Kmart, Barnes and Noble, and Staples, have bought back the stock from equity partners and folded the e-commerce spin-offs back into the company.

The other main justification for spinning off was that the company lacked the experience needed to pursue e-commerce or that additional investment capital was necessary. While it may be true that stand-alone firms sometimes find it easier to quickly develop e-commerce expertise, integrated e-commerce ventures in large organizations can also do this. Since e-commerce capabilities are becoming an increasingly important core competency , companies should develop the expertise and control the e-commerce operation inside the company through a full integration into business units and functions.

2. Integrated Management Teams: Innovate without Spinning Off. From the distribution side, e-commerce should often be seen as simply another sales channel and thus changes in the management structure are kept to a minimum. In industries that already have multiple channels such as banks (i.e., physical branches, ATM) and catalog businesses (e.g., Nordstrom), an integrated structure is particularly relevant. With full integration, business functions such as marketing are easy to coordinate and organizational territorial conflicts are reduced. A less ideal but still viable alternative is to create a separate business unit for e-commerce. Many companies that began with spin-offs and then brought e-commerce back within the company chose to adopt separate strategic business units (SBUs).

Many companies have started their e-commerce operations with entirely separate management teams, often proposed to increase the focus on innovation and e-commerce, under the premise that e-commerce will not be given enough attention or independence by senior management at the parent organization. These management teams have often been established far from company headquarters, have had loose organizational cultures, and have been led by independent leadership often drawn from pure-play or other entrepreneurial companies.

Certainly innovation, flexibility, and creativity are needed to drive a successful e-commerce operation. But we have seen that this can occur successfully within traditional organizational boundaries. A formal set of management control structures and systems is necessary to balance the desired empowerment. When separate business units are established, they should function primarily to coordinate the full integration of e-commerce throughout the business units. As with other organizational functions, it is sometimes desirable initially to establish a central organization both to drive and to coordinate these new activities. But, as the function matures, it should generally be more fully integrated into the business units. The separate functional units and the integrated functions within the business units may need unique structures and systems including unique performance measures and compensation and reward systems, but this customization of the organizational structure can be accomplished within existing organizational boundaries. There is no need to spin off core capabilities and detach valuable corporate assets.

3. *IT Know-How from Within: Building Future Capabilities.* Not every company, especially those late to e-commerce, will have invested well enough in IT to develop e-commerce independently. Many e-commerce companies, even those with strong IT departments, have chosen to outsource e-commerce because of the necessity of speed. Speed is indeed a powerful motivation for outsourcing, but outsourcing should be used to catch up, not to give up. Although outsourcing may be used initially to create e-commerce solutions, the company can reassume control over e-commerce and IT and eventually can use the e-commerce systems for traditional commerce as well. Staples followed this approach in attempting to catch its IT-leader rival, Office Depot. Staples invested heavily in IT to build technology close to its core capabilities, but also created a sole-sourcing partnership to avoid delays in more peripheral areas of the business.

Another alternative is to acquire IT capabilities by purchasing a small IT firm and integrating the firm while the e-commerce solution is being implemented. UPS has followed this approach several times in its attempt to hold its IT leadership position over rival Federal Express, and UPS has been able to continually roll out new services while integrating its acquisitions.[5]

Other companies, however, have made the mistake of selling equity to venture capitalists and then relied on these partners for all of their IT needs. Barnes and Noble made this mistake and then was hamstrung further when Amazon sued them for a patent violation related to their Web platform. Borders and Toys 'R' Us have taken the dramatic approach of having a competitor, Amazon, run their Web site for them. Companies must learn from these mistakes and not place themselves in such a precarious position with respect to IT.[6]

4. *Strategic Alliances: Moving beyond Core Competencies.* Although companies are advised to maintain equity interest, management control, and IT integration, traditional businesses can benefit from alliances with online companies in other ways. These relationships are most beneficial when the arrangement gives the traditional company access to supply-chain management, peripheral offerings, and customer bases.

Supply-chain management is a particularly useful area for partnership when the company cannot simply supply online customers from the same distribution channels as physical stores. Wal-Mart, Kmart, and

Target have all made such arrangements to deal with their general merchandising businesses. CVS also simplified its procurement process for its Web site by entering into a partnership with Merck.com.

To provide peripheral offerings that will be available only online, alliances have also proven to be a successful approach. Neiman Marcus partnered with several luxury retailers to create a limited-scope "luxury portal" of high-end goods within its Web site. CVS partnered with WebMD to provide medical advice to complement pharmacy services.

Finally, traditional companies can gain access to large online customer bases by making strategic alliances with portal and ISP companies. Wal-Mart and Kmart entered agreements with AOL and Yahoo respectively to co-brand Internet service packages that would bring their customers online and to their site in particular.

Traditional companies may also profit from providing a physical presence to online companies that are realizing the inevitable trend toward integrated channels. Target has agreed to house E*Trade kiosks and customer representatives in its stores, in what has been a beneficial relationship for both parties. For E*Trade, the Target deal was just one aspect of a bricks-and-clicks strategy that culminated with the building of a New York super-center.[7]

SYSTEMS

Senior managers must finally ensure that organizational processes are capable of implementing the e-commerce strategy. Information practices, human resources, performance measures, and customer management are all areas in which traditional systems may require adaptation to implement an e-commerce strategy (Exhibit 1.5).

1. Modernized Internal Processes: Using Information Effectively. The cultural transformation described earlier may be enough to make e-commerce possible, but more must be done to maximize its benefits. Information practices must be adapted to promote transparency and availability. Changes must ensure that information flows freely throughout the company and is not hampered by artificial organizational boundaries or personal ambitions.

Exhibit 1.5
Systems

---

1. Modernized internal processes
2. Incentive-laden HR practices
3. Aligned performance measures
4. Improved customer management

In addition to information sharing, the decision-making processes of the company should be reconsidered. Cross-functional teams and remotely located teams should be assembled with greater frequency, with less emphasis on hierarchical reporting. Decision makers should also have greater self-governance and flexibility.

An important internal process is value chain management. Every company should identify ways to leverage the Internet in each part of the value chain, from procurement to distribution to delivery. In fact, failure to adopt e-commerce-specific cost savings will likely put a company at a serious competitive disadvantage. Strong supply chain management is often the basis for providing superior service. In the area of procurement, a company can reduce the cost of goods sold by obtaining products through the Internet. Distribution strategies must not only cut costs but also provide the fastest and most convenient customer service. Delivery strategies should maximize convenience and speed for customers, using both the Internet and the company's existing infrastructure to provide these benefits. The best supply-chain practices, however, depend on the type of offering.

2. Incentive-Laden HR Practices: Bringing Your People on Board. Compensation systems must be aligned with strategy and structure for the e-commerce venture to be a success. The CIO must be compensated as a member of the senior management team to signal the importance and respect shown for the IT function and the centrality and commitment to improved IT and e-commerce. At lower organizational levels, compensation systems have additional consequences on alignment. By compensating e-commerce managers the same as managers in traditional commerce, the company sometimes fails to create the necessary incentives for e-commerce success. Though parallel compensation systems can often work, both market forces and the need for speed, creativity, flexibility, innovation, and extra diligence often requires additional incentives and rewards.

Differential compensation, often through stock options, can create an incentive to cannibalize from the company's traditional channels. Such practices can cause conflicts with traditional business units but are often necessary to optimize the use of each channel, especially during the formative years of the e-commerce initiative. Typically, e-commerce compensation should be tied to the overall success of the venture rather than rewarding individual units or channels for performance. This is particularly relevant when the company is seeking full integration, because it helps ensure cooperation and seamlessness between departments.

The Internet also provides opportunities to improve the hiring process. Cisco is just one company that has found great benefits from hiring online, including lowered costs, faster filling of positions, and higher competence. Companies may also want to consider specialized HR practices for their IT departments.

3. *Aligned Performance Measures: Planning for the Long-Term.* Strong measurement practices are among the cornerstones of all good systems. Performance measures for e-commerce must overcome the uncertainty and unique dynamics associated with the Internet, and they may be more frequently adjusted in response to real-time information. With these considerations, it is clear that no company should simply extend its existing performance measures to the e-commerce venture without extensive customization. Still, long-term cost differentials, balanced with a variety of financial, nonfinancial, and leading and lagging indicators, are particularly useful for successful e-commerce implementations.

Some skeptical companies have made unreasonable demands with respect to e-commerce performance. Because they misconceived e-commerce risks and rewards, they had unrealistic expectations of immediate growth and ROI that would not be demanded of any traditional long-term investment. Worse yet, they tied further investment to achievement of these goals, dooming e-commerce before it even could get off the ground.

In most companies, new projects and ventures require short-term ROI, and revenue projections, many of which an e-commerce venture and its related projects may not meet. If the company decides to enter or expand e-commerce, it cannot hamstring the venture by insisting on such short-term requirements throughout.

E-commerce has also led many companies to create performance measures other than revenue, ROI, and traditional financial indicators. Some of the new, poorly designed performance measures have had a disastrous effect on strategy implementation. For example, indiscriminate customer acquisition and attempting to maximize revenue through online advertising often have negative implications for long-term profitability. Single-purchase customers and advertising revenue independent of the company's value proposition are not sustainable strategies. Worse still are nonfinancial measures such as Web page hits and registered users, which may not even be tied to a short-term revenue stream.

In addition to measuring the performance of the business, e-commerce brings added importance to measuring the value and functionality of operations. Most e-commerce strategies will have a strong operational component, including cost savings from value chain management and cuts in labor costs for the online channel. Operational measures should be tracked by some dedicated resource and balanced between financial and nonfinancial assessments of operational performance.

Moreover, companies must create a value capture process to evaluate the success of IT projects associated with the e-commerce venture.

Looking at nonfinancial performance measures, the value capture process can help convince skeptical employees of the importance of IT. Even with the value capture process, however, the full benefits of IT investment are often underestimated.

4. *Improved Customer Management: Better Service and Better Data.* Companies must also reconsider the internal processes required to provide the high levels of customer service necessary in e-commerce. Online customers need access to some level of customer service at all times. There is a trade-off between service that entails a high level of human input and service that is automated and more cost-efficient. Finding the proper balance is a function of the company's offerings, its customer base, and customer feedback.

Customer data is a significant benefit in e-commerce, because of the vast amount that can be learned about customers during a Web site visit in contrast to an in-store visit. Many Web sites, however, have mistakenly focused only on counting hits and visits, while ignoring the more valuable information that can be gathered. Tracking of customers' interaction with the Web site can be used to identify customers' price sensitivity and information preferences and to gauge satisfaction with the Web site design and accessibility. Gathering and using customer information is important to refine the value proposition and better allocate internal resources. Marketing strategies for the Web site can also be continually refined, using real-time information gathered from customers during their visits, a practice that Staples has used well.

CHARACTERISTICS OF E-COMMERCE SUCCESS

These guidelines provide a general outline of our prescriptions for an e-commerce venture. The following chapters provide a more in-depth discussion of the model, dedicating one chapter to each of its components. For each component, I will discuss the implications of these guidelines in retail, service, and manufacturing industries, and the relationship between these guidelines and prominent cases of e-commerce success and failure. This book summarizes what has been learned from e-commerce implementation. As with most new technologies and most new business models, the experimentation leaves some companies in strong competitive positions and others in bankruptcy. E-commerce has been no different. Only now can we try to analyze the recent attempts at success and summarize those characteristics that seem to work. Much of this is not surprising. It relies on well-accepted principles of successful business practice. But, many of the early entries in e-commerce ignored those principles. I have grounded the development of e-commerce in the traditional literature and practices of lead-

Exhibit 1.6
Characteristics of Successful E-Commerce Implementations

LEADERSHIP	STRATEGY
1. Commitment at the top	1. Well-positioned online brand
2. Thorough competitive analysis	2. Online-friendly offerings
3. Significant financial investment	3. Reliable customer service
4. Cultural transformation	4. Cross-channel coordination
STRUCTURE	SYSTEMS
1. Internal investment	1. Modernized internal processes
2. Integrated management teams	2. Incentive-laden HR practices
3. IT know-how from within	3. Aligned performance measures
4. Strategic partnerships	4. Improved customer management

ership, strategy, structure, and systems and summarized the characteristics of success (Exhibit 1.6).

I have also included a framework to analyze, identify, and measure the payoffs of e-commerce investments. In many corporate functions, and in e-commerce and IT particularly, general managers complain about the lack of rigor in investment proposals. They see these functions as cost centers and attempt to reduce expenditures. In contrast, functional managers, including e-commerce and IT, see themselves as creators of value and are frustrated that they are not able to prove the value of their services and functions. This framework and the related measures suggest an approach to better communicate with senior general managers and to better justify requests for additional resources. The approach views e-commerce as a value creation function and examines its role in increasing overall corporate profitability.

The book also includes short cases on two or three companies in each of twelve industries, summarizing their e-commerce activities and examining both successes and failures. Each case ends with a short section on the lessons learned.

I conclude with some additional thoughts on the characteristics of e-commerce success and on guidance for senior managers as to how to proceed in the formulation and implementation of an e-commerce strategy. This is an opportunity for companies to reexamine their current activities in e-commerce and further develop their capabilities utilizing the lessons learned from the successes and failures of the recent company experiences.

CHAPTER 2

Corporate and Functional E-Commerce Leadership

Success in e-commerce has become almost synonymous with the names of a few CEOs and leaders of successful companies, such as Michael Dell, Jack Welch, and Jeff Bezos. In the absence of clear guidance on e-commerce strategy and implementation, a cult of personality has developed in popular press discussions of e-commerce. Without a clearly defined approach and methodology for the formulation and implementation of an e-commerce strategy, this kind of leadership-worship[1] was the closest anyone could come to defining what actually led to e-commerce success for these companies (Exhibit 2.1).

Now, we have the opportunity to step back and appreciate the full range of critical factors that contributed to early cases of e-commerce success. Leadership is one factor, but leadership shouldn't be any more or less important in e-commerce than in any other aspect of business strategy. Still, it makes sense to discuss leadership as a precursor to formulating strategy and designing structure and systems.

The special conditions associated with e-commerce make the discussion of leadership excellence especially critical. The individual roles of the CEO, CIO, and CFO concern more than an organization chart or delegation of responsibilities. In e-commerce, the coordination between these leaders becomes as important as their actions. Failure to achieve this coordination will undermine any hope for corporate e-commerce integration.

Exhibit 2.1
Exemplars of E-Commerce Leadership

Company	Leader	Important Contributions
Dell	Michael Dell, CEO	Pioneer of e-commerce thinking and hands-on leader in IT planning
GE	Jack Welch, CEO	Created company-wide e-commerce initiative, Destroy Your Business
Tesco	John Browett, CEO	Vision of Internet's potential use for delivery; patience in implementation
Merrill Lynch	John McKinley, CIO	Convinced reluctant CEO of Internet's importance
Office Depot	Patricia Morrison, CIO, and Charles Brown, CFO	Cooperative working relationship on IT to be central to integration strategy
Staples	Paul Gaffney, CIO	Led efforts to integrate operations and advocated kiosks to bridge channels
Charles Schwab	Christopher Dodds, CFO	Advocated integrated financial measures that explained benefits of e-commerce to investors.

We can identify the aspects of leadership that are applicable to all businesses wishing to implement an e-commerce strategy. Leadership occupies the first link between the inputs of the traditional business and the subsequent process elements of e-commerce strategy, structure, and systems (Exhibit 2.2). Placing it here emphasizes the role that leadership plays in moving from traditional strategy, structure, and systems to those in e-commerce.

Leadership is about both people and actions. Each of the major leadership roles in a company—including the CEO, the CIO, and the CFO—requires a person with a positive, reasoned approach toward e-commerce. Just as the CFO should not trivialize the importance of IT, neither should the CIO exaggerate the role of technology over strategy. These leadership roles require technical competence related to the business operations, IT, and e-commerce, as well as a positive attitude. Knowledge and experience in the uses of technologies and an understanding of the implications of the use of technology in specific business operations are necessary for e-commerce leadership positions.

Exhibit 2.2
Antecedents and Consequences of E-Commerce Success

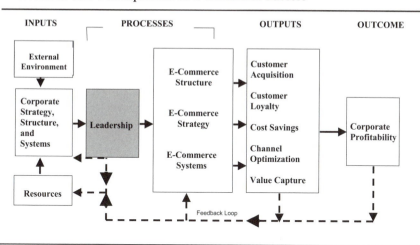

Some major assessments must be made by the company's leaders before they can consider the formulation and implementation of an e-commerce strategy. An assessment of competitive position is often particularly challenging in a dynamic e-commerce environment. Strong traditional competitors may be currently irrelevant if their e-commerce strategy is undeveloped, but that can change quickly. Weaker traditional competitors may be able to use e-commerce as a catalyst to make the gains they couldn't make in traditional brick-and-mortar business. Pure-play Internet companies may already have established themselves in the industry or may be in the process of moving into the industry. Disruptions in the marketplace can cause additional challenges.

Thus, to assess the proper role for e-commerce, leaders must evaluate the nature of the company's offerings, traditional strategy and business models, and the geographic scope of the company. Though current capabilities may be limited, opportunities for growth in revenue and reductions in cost must be assessed. With the data, leaders can then properly evaluate the appropriate levels of investment and potential returns.

Leadership requires some initial steps to prepare the organization for a transition to e-commerce. Some changes are of such importance that they must be addressed early in the evaluation of e-commerce strategy formulation and execution, especially discussing basic e-commerce functionality and communicating the potential impact of e-commerce on company operations.

FIRST STAGE E-COMMERCE
LEADERSHIP REQUIREMENTS

Senior corporate leaders must complete the following first stage e-commerce leadership requirements:

- Assessment of the company's e-commerce competitive position
- Assessment and communication of the value of e-commerce to corporate, business unit, and functional operations and necessary technical and integration issues
- Creation of a company culture conducive to the introduction of e-commerce

The following sections highlight each of these aspects of e-commerce leadership with stories of companies that took the first step toward success or failure before the first strategy was ever formulated. Other discussions and company cases illustrate how leadership impacted the e-commerce successes and features.

LEADERSHIP ROLES

The CEO

In the late 1990s, spin-offs were a popular strategy for e-commerce ventures. Leadership consisted of finding someone, often from outside the company, who would lead the e-commerce venture. Leaders for these ventures were frequently selected because their resumes included technology experience, often without considering their understanding of the business or its environment. The CEO of the brick-and-mortar company, on the other hand, was regarded only as a sponsor, with little involvement expected.

We now know that the appropriate role for the CEO undertaking an e-commerce venture is a highly proactive one with a strong level of commitment and a vision of e-commerce within the company. Instead of delegating the responsibilities of e-commerce to an outside "expert," leaders must take the steps to transform the company into one that can utilize and profit from e-commerce. These e-commerce transformations are part of an ongoing process that is certainly not complete when a company successfully establishes an e-commerce foothold.

Cisco CEO John Chambers has kept Cisco at or near the top of the market through considerable market fluctuations and changes in the nature of e-commerce, through his willingness to change Cisco according to the demands of the market.[2] Similarly, Amazon CEO Jeff Bezos has consistently altered prices on books and other products to meet competitive challenges. He also began strategic alliances with other merchants such as Target and Toys 'R' Us to better serve Amazon customers and improve profitability.[3] This flexibility is one important key to success in the ever-changing world of e-commerce. Monitoring company and industry changes, along with the constant technological improvements in e-commerce, are critical leadership issues.

CEOs do not need to become technology experts. Instead, CEOs need a basic understanding of how e-commerce works and, more important, how it affects current and potential business models and processes. This knowledge can be easily obtained through interaction with the CIO and senior IT personnel or by interaction with e-commerce savvy leaders at other companies. At Merrill Lynch, the impetus for e-commerce came from the CIO, who convinced a skeptical CEO of the merits of an e-commerce venture through persistent discussions of technology and strategy.[4]

The CEO must also be convinced of the specific potential benefits of e-commerce to the company and begin to take action for the implementation, demonstrating commitment in both communications and actions. For a successful transformation, the CEO must express the appropriate attitude, personal commitment to e-commerce, and understanding of the technical issues to make it clear that the CEO is not ceding leadership to the IT specialists.[5] E-Bay CEO Meg Whitman is credited with transforming e-Bay from an "online flea market" to a "virtual, self-regulating global economy."[6]

Leadership is also demonstrated through the commitment of financial resources, including adequate funding for the IT department and the modernization of the company's information systems. E-commerce and IT should be seen as value creators rather than cost centers. The CEO must be also committed to a leadership role in IT planning, facilitating communication between IT and business units and challenging the IT department to maximize business functionality.

The CEO must also emphasize a long-term commitment and ensure that the other senior corporate and business unit leaders are also fully committed to e-commerce. The role requires collaboration of the CIO, CFO, and business unit leaders and a vision for the entire organization. The role of coordination, communication, and motivation with business unit leaders is critical. The business units ultimately have the major responsibility for execution, as it is the business unit leaders who find opportunities for e-commerce value creation. The CEO must take the lead in driving the integration process.

The CIO

The rise of e-commerce has brought far more attention to the role of the CIO as an integral part of the senior management team. Companies that have previously treated their CIO as a technologist face the largest changes as they prepare for e-commerce. For e-commerce to be fully integrated, the CIO's place in the organizational structure must report directly to the CEO or COO. Without direct access to the CEO, the CIO plays a lesser role in influencing strategy, which may push IT and e-commerce into the position of a cost center. Such factors contribute to the finding that CIO tenure is quite short, compared to that of CFOs.[7]

Even in companies whose CIOs already play an important role in senior management, CEOs should continuously work to increase coordination and interaction between the CIO and other key members of senior management, to increase the visibility of e-commerce initiatives. The CIO should provide both information and analysis and should have a relationship with the CEO that empowers the CIO to challenge both strategic direction and technology usage. Merrill Lynch faced a severe loss in margins as Schwab began to pass Merrill in market value in late 1998 and 1999. It wasn't until then-CIO John McKinley convinced his CEO to fully embrace online trading while using the company's IT budget to develop its Web site that the company was able to reestablish itself after being a late mover in e-commerce.[8] When Mattel Inc.'s Joe Eckroth took over as CIO, he immediately transferred toy design online to allow virtual models to be zipped electronically to all of the company's factories, cutting development time by 20 percent. In addition, Eckroth installed Mattel's $2 billion licensing program online to automate and expedite the licensing approval process and significantly increase profitability.[9]

To improve the decision-making process in organizations as well as to obtain increased resources for e-commerce, the CIO needs to provide more complete measurements and analysis of the benefits and costs of the business impacts of IT and e-commerce investments. It is important that potential projects are analyzed in a strategic context, and the financial payoffs are clear. More generally, the CIO has a large stake not only in directing business change but also in taking on the role of educator for the CEO and CFO. While senior business leadership should still undergo specialized training to gain a basic understanding of the technologies associated with e-commerce and IT, the CIO should be capable of explaining the business implications of technology to internal and external partners so that the company makes sound business decisions based upon adequate knowledge.[10]

As with the CEO, it is not necessary that the CIO have a specific resume or previous experience in e-commerce. Certainly an understanding of the technology side of e-commerce is necessary. The most important skills for a CIO include the ability to complete an accurate technology risk assessment, to objectively gauge strategic benefits of technology, and to manage the complications of both the technical and the human sides of an e-commerce implementation. As we will revisit later, the nontechnical components of an e-commerce implementation are far more challenging than the technical ones. The CIO must have an integrated view of the business and be able to communicate that view to the senior corporate managers, the business unit leaders, functional staff, and many others both inside and outside the company.

The CFO

Many studies have shown high levels of conflict between CFOs and CIOs, and e-commerce is purported only to increase that conflict. The long-term and nonspecific benefits of IT projects, especially those relating to e-commerce, are often seen as anathema to the strict measurement standards of the archetypal CFO. That conflict, however, arises from a misunderstanding of the proper roles of each position and often from a lack of rigorous analysis. For e-commerce to be successful, the CFO must be more sensitive to the challenges of IT and e-commerce, and the CIO must complete more comprehensive financial analysis of e-commerce projects to better articulate the likely costs and benefits. A formalized approach to understanding and measuring the payoffs of e-commerce activities is the focus of chapter 6. The analysis of the causal relationships between e-commerce investments and financial payoffs provides a new basis for discussion between CIOs, CFOs, and CEOs. It also permits e-commerce to fit more effectively into the traditional resource allocation decisions made in the CFO's office.

When the CIO's reporting responsibility is to the CFO, the wrong message is communicated to every aspect of the business, from investors, to employees, to customers, especially in an e-commerce context. The CFO must recognize IT's strategic role and its vital role in bringing about business process changes. The CFO must also take the lead in helping the CIO with the methodology, as discussed in chapter 6, of measuring the payoffs of e-commerce investments. It is only in this way that IT and e-commerce are seen as value creators and can compete effectively for resources within the company.

The CFO need not have the same content knowledge of IT as the CIO, or even the CEO. A modicum of technology understanding, however, is likely to strengthen the CFO's relationship with the CIO and can lead to better-coordinated analysis of project benefits. Alignment is likely to be strongest when the two leaders can move beyond their specific domains and focus on the strategic context. This united front usually also improves the coordination with business unit leaders and improves decision making.

For e-commerce to be successful, business leadership must be able and willing to expand their essential functions within the company.

While old responsibilities are not to be neglected because of the addition of e-commerce, the new demands of e-commerce are of such importance that senior leaders must assume additional expertise and responsibilities.

DETERMINING COMPETITIVE POSITION

There is little consensus on the importance of timing in e-commerce. Traditional perspectives on first-mover advantage were popular at first, but proved to be an unreliable predictor of success.[11] Companies that consciously employed a "follower" strategy had equally mixed results. Few companies have, at this point, a legitimate opportunity to be the first mover in any broad sector. If a company is not yet online, it is a near certainty that some competitor, broadly defined, is.

This fact makes it critically important that a company complete a rigorous analysis of its competitive position before designing an e-commerce strategy. The first consideration is whether any significant pure-play Internet company is an established leader or strong presence in the industry, or in related industries. Pure-play competitors may be more vulnerable to a strategy that exploits the company's physical, intellectual, or financial resources. In that sense, being the first mover among traditional companies can still provide an advantage, even if a company is not the first overall mover (Exhibit 2.3).

However, it is important to note that many pure-plays have realized the advantages of traditional business and have acted to preempt that advantage among their more traditional competitors. The two main ways of doing that have been to build a physical presence or to partner with a company that can provide one. E*Trade has simultaneously

Exhibit 2.3
Determining Competitive Position in E-Commerce

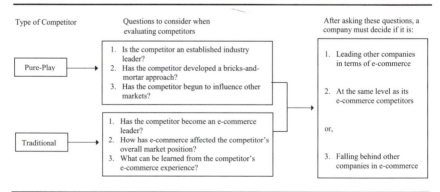

pursued both strategies, building a giant E*Trade center in New York and introducing kiosks in Target stores. Of course, any pure-play capable of this type of investment is likely to be a difficult adversary anyway.

If the company also lags behind its traditional peers in e-commerce, the situation is somewhat more difficult. While being second, or even later, gives a company the opportunity to learn from competitors' mistakes, the disadvantages are far greater. In the early days of e-commerce, mistakes were rampant enough to neutralize the disadvantage of not being first. Now, companies who are laggards must be especially creative with their business models to overcome this disadvantage.

Perhaps the most understated consideration is the fluidity of the term "competitor" in e-commerce. To make a thorough analysis of one's competitive position, one must examine companies from many other industries, both pure-play and traditional, that have used e-commerce as a way to expand into one's own industry. A CEO must recognize both general and industry-specific trends in e-commerce well enough to predict potential competitors.

The need for cross-industry information regarding e-commerce is due largely to the blurring of industry lines that is facilitated by e-commerce and is evidenced by companies such as Amazon. The list of businesses that can consider Amazon a competitor is now almost endless. Not only does Amazon now have partnerships with many specialty retailers, but its range of offerings is so wide that many have referred to it as the "Wal-Mart of e-commerce." Any company in a retailing business would be compelled to consider Amazon a potential competitor.

This blurring of industry lines should be expected. E-commerce encourages such expansion because of the potential for supply chain improvements and the economies of scale associated with product heterogeneity. In particular, the phenomenon of offering related business services is an avenue for cross-industry expansion. Office Depot's foray into small business services and Bank of America's home financing and improvement services are just two examples.[12] Expansions into e-commerce come from many directions. Sometimes initially motivated by cost reductions and sometimes by revenue imperatives, the cost of entry into broader e-commerce utilization is often small and brings new challenges to both traditional and pure-play Internet companies.

For some local companies or certain industries, competition may not be a traditional primary concern. Although such instances are rare and confined mostly to small businesses, some businesses have geographic restrictions that limit the customer base. The grocery business has been a prime example. Nearly every company that has experimented in grocery delivery online has initially restricted delivery to a small radius, from either the physical store or the warehouse.

The reasons are numerous. Perishable items obviously require short delivery times and distances, and low-margin items cannot justify large shipping costs. The small delivery radius has shifted from an experimental position to an industry standard. Even companies such as Tesco, which have greatly expanded their online operations, have done so by increasing the number of physical stores from which to make deliveries. As a result, competition has been somewhat minimal among grocers. Grocery chains, especially in the United States, vary greatly by region. Very few chains are national enough even to justify the strategy followed by Tesco.

For most companies, however, competitor analysis is an essential input for determining the appropriate e-commerce strategy. Such analysis, along with the CEO's leadership in forecasting e-commerce trends and technology and changes in business opportunities, is vital to properly gauging that position.

COMPETITIVE CONSIDERATIONS FOR TRADITIONAL FIRMS BEGINNING AN E-COMMERCE VENTURE

Among the competitive concerns that brick-and-mortar companies must consider are:

- Pure-play e-commerce competitors
- Traditional competitors that have already moved into e-commerce
- Outside companies using e-commerce to establish a foothold in a new industry
- The limitations, geographic and otherwise, of these competitors

These factors are all part of a broad, comprehensive analysis of both competitive positioning and customer needs. The list of potential competitors is endless. They include both the traditional brick-and-mortar companies and the new pure-play Internet companies. The analysis requires an evaluation of both the current landscape and the future customer needs and how they are likely to be served. Cannibalization and disruptions in the marketplace are likely to continue. It is critical that leaders continually monitor developments within and outside their industry for these developments.

DETERMINING E-COMMERCE ROLE AND INVESTMENT

Understanding competitive position is necessary but not sufficient to formulate the e-commerce strategy. Companies must also determine the appropriate role for e-commerce inside the company and the level of investment to be made. Thus, the external positioning must be supplemented with an internal analysis of company fit. The fit may be related to items such as organization structure, product type and mix, customer type and mix, channels, geographical breadth, and financial resources. Thus, every company utilizes e-commerce by directly selling goods or services on the Internet. Some find profitability in supply-chain management, procurement, marketing, and providing general information online. That decision may become obvious before any significant strategic planning or may be determined after a fuller examination of the facts. But, a full examination of the broad opportunities must be completed and becomes an important input to the investment decision.

Among the most important issues is the amount of resources to be committed to e-commerce. As companies examine reports of competitor investments, companies often question whether the size of their commitment is adequate. Though the late 1990s saw some reckless spending on e-commerce without any justification of an ultimate payoff, current approaches to e-commerce require a carefully determined return on investment, as determined by a methodology as discussed in chapter 6. But, the investment must follow a serious commitment to an e-commerce strategy and should not waver with modest changes in either the technology or the business environment.

For companies selling online, the geographic scope of sales efforts is also a consideration. Selling overseas creates numerous challenges, many of which are known to traditional business but are complicated further by e-commerce. Demographics of Internet users, online payment mechanisms, online marketing, and patterns of online buyer behavior all vary greatly by country[13] and may present too many permutations for a nascent Internet venture to handle.

A company may be understandably hesitant to begin global e-commerce immediately, even if its traditional business contains a global component.[14] Some companies have chosen to limit the geographic scope of the venture until it has proven feasible and profitable on a domestic scale. The wisdom of such a limitation has been shown clearly in the case of grocery stores such as Tesco.

Among the geographic considerations for an e-commerce venture are:

- A Web site can be viewed from anywhere around the world. Companies should be equipped to handle such a change in market size, or be prepared to explain the reasons for necessary geographic limitations.
- Product type is a key factor in any geographic consideration. Customers have far different expectations when using the Internet to order computers than when ordering groceries.

PREPARING IMPLEMENTATION AND
ALIGNING COMPANY CULTURE

Most laggard companies do not have the luxury of delaying the implementation of e-commerce until the company culture is sufficiently prepared. Instead, company leaders must constantly reinforce the importance of IT in order to build the appropriate culture for e-commerce. As their personal behavior and attitudes often send the strongest messages, private behavior must not undermine or contradict public statements about company commitment to e-commerce ventures.[15] Senior managers must reinforce the message that while technology itself is not a strategy, it remains a tool with strategic implications, and that the introduction of technology does not change the role of every contributor to the success of the company. Leadership must also choose the proper motivational tools, including incentives, coaching, and creating stretch targets.

For an e-commerce venture to be successful in a traditional company, senior managers must also impart a number of clear messages on company strategy and its value proposition. Instead of trying to create a unique culture for units handling the e-commerce venture, the company must create a culture conducive to integrating e-commerce throughout the company. Attitudes of either "the Internet changes everything" or "the Internet changes nothing" should be avoided, and a much more moderate position endorsed. Employees should not feel threatened or overwhelmed by the introduction of e-commerce.

The purpose of the e-commerce venture must also be carefully outlined to all employees, with a focus on the benefits of integration and the notion that e-commerce is typically a new channel for business, not a new business. People in each business unit must be apprised of the way e-commerce interacts with their current work and how best to develop that relationship to maximize integration benefits. At GE, this was achieved in the form of a company-wide initiative called Destroy Your Business, which required business units to analyze the impact and potential pitfalls of e-commerce on their business. Its associated program, Grow Your Business, required units to formulate solutions to each of these problems.

Belief in the value of IT must be instilled throughout the organization, and resistance to IT generally, and to e-commerce specifically, must be handled through education that emphasizes the functionality of these endeavors and their importance to long-term corporate success. Training programs must ensure that everyone, especially those employees who directly interact with customers, understands basic e-commerce concepts. Senior management is not immune to these requirements and must lead by example in this area with both public statements and behavior.

Finally, a sense of urgency must be created throughout the organization, and business decisions should reflect that urgency. The pace of e-commerce is faster than that of traditional commerce, and easing into an e-commerce venture is not a promising strategy. In all areas that impact e-commerce, aggressiveness should be rewarded, and the value of speed should often supplant cost considerations.

Many of these considerations must be addressed by specific changes in the company's systems and business processes, but the CEO should be prepared to create this orientation long before strategy implementation begins. Without strong leadership in the early stages, the changes in systems will be too drastic to implement the e-commerce strategy in a timely manner. Thus, to create a proper culture for e-commerce, companies must recognize that:

- Attitudes are as important as company policies regarding e-commerce. Company leaders must not only work to make an e-commerce venture a success, but show that they actually believe in the venture.
- E-commerce should be treated as a new channel for business, not as a revolution for the company. Employees need to be encouraged to embrace e-commerce instead of fearing it.
- The goals of the e-commerce venture need to be clearly outlined for everyone in the company.
- Aggressiveness in e-commerce should be rewarded.

E-commerce represents a major transformation, and the general principles of organizational change management are as applicable as advice specific to e-commerce. John Kotter's organizational change model[16] provided a general framework for the consideration of how to approach significant change in business (Exhibit 2.4). As one can see, it can be easily adapted to the challenge of the changes necessary in the implementation of an e-commerce strategy.

CONCLUSION

To improve the prospects for success of an e-commerce implementation, dynamic and strong leadership is required. The coordination, preparation, and attitude that are necessary for both the formulation and execution of a successful strategy are important characteristics of successful e-commerce leaders.

The CEO cannot transform an organization until there is a strong commitment to the importance of e-commerce. Not every CEO must be

Exhibit 2.4
E-Commerce Change Management

Kotter's Guideline	Applicability to E-Commerce
1 Establish Sense of Urgency	Speed and commitment are needed both to get ahead and to stay ahead in e-commerce
2 Form Powerful Guiding Coalition	CFO and CIO must join CEO in formulating technology's role in strategy
3 Create a Vision	CEO must have clear ideas for gaining competitive advantage from e-commerce
4 Communicate the Vision	CEO must take lead in explaining purpose of e-commerce, dispelling myths
5 Empower Others to Act on the Vision	Traditional practices should be altered if adverse to e-commerce
6 Plan and Create Short-Term Wins	Create an e-commerce friendly organization even before strategy is fully implemented
7 Consolidate Improvements	Continue investing to maintain both strategic advantages and IT strengths
8 Institutionalize New Approaches	Find new ways in which e-commerce promotes organizational improvement

Source: Adapted from John Kotter. "Leading Change: Why Transformation Efforts Fail." *Harvard Business Review*, March-April 1995, pp. 59–67.

an e-commerce pioneer, or even a technology expert, but the CEO does have to share, and understand, the perspective of the most successful e-commerce leaders. Leaders need to be believers in the benefits of e-commerce and surround themselves with other senior executives who share this vision and can coordinate their efforts successfully, despite their differing roles. With this leadership team in place, the CEO must immediately begin taking steps to assure that e-commerce isn't undermined. Company resources must be available, the company culture must adapt, and initial evaluations of the company's position must be developed. Only then is the company prepared to begin looking at developing and implementing an e-commerce strategy.

In summary, the leadership team must:

1. coordinate among the CEO, CFO, CIO, and business unit leaders

2. have a strong commitment at the top that is also communicated and demonstrated through action
3. complete a thorough competitive analysis, examining both competitors' and customers' needs currently and prospectively
4. complete rigorous financial analysis of the payoffs of e-commerce investments
5. lead the major cultural and organizational change effort related to e-commerce implementations

CHAPTER 3

Formulating an E-Commerce Strategy

E-commerce strategy, more than any other aspect of e-commerce, has been broadly addressed throughout the past few years. Yet these discussions have often been narrowly tailored and have failed to put strategic ideas into a context that includes both traditional commerce and e-commerce. The approach here articulates e-commerce strategy within the context of traditional business strategy and links it to implementation through structures and systems (Exhibit 3.1).

Many analysts have identified the tactics that led to the demise of the high-profile e-commerce failures filling the news pages. Methods such as seeking revenues through online banner ads, indiscriminate customer acquisition and partnerships, and deep discount pricing models have all been exposed as doomed substitutes for sensible business models.[1] Some mistakes of the Internet boom were to be expected of experimentation in the development of any new business model. Others were due to a lack of attention to basic business principles. Discussions of e-commerce strategy have yet to identify the elements of successful e-commerce strategy and put those practices within the framework of traditional business strategy.

Certainly appropriate strategy must reflect a company's customer type, product type, geographic scope, procurement and distribution channels, and so forth. Timing and speed of entry into the e-commerce environment must also be considered. How to provide differentiation in the marketplace is important, since strategy is about being different—in

Exhibit 3.1
Antecedents and Consequences of E-Commerce Success

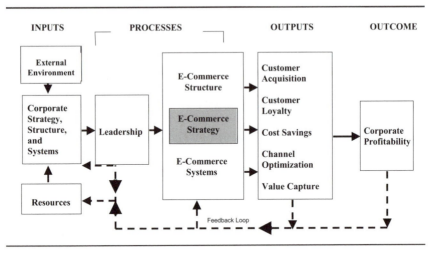

contrast to operational effectiveness, which is primarily about being faster.[2]

Discussions of strategy also must focus on an identification and articulation of the company's value proposition. What unique products and services does the company provide? In this context, companies can determine how much e-commerce is core to company success and position e-commerce and IT strategies within overall company strategy. They then can determine how to proceed toward converting their traditional brick and mortar company to one with a significant e-commerce component. The e-commerce strategy must fit within the overall company strategy and is an integral part of the entire e-commerce integration process, including e-commerce structure and systems. Though one e-commerce strategy does not fit all companies, examining recent successes and failures provides substantial guidance to companies as they formulate or revise e-commerce strategies.

Though with a variety of terminology, e-commerce integration strategy has often been grouped into three categories: full integration, partial corporate integration, and business unit integration (Exhibit 3.2). This categorization relates to the strategic decision of how e-commerce will fit into the company and how fast to proceed with the integration, rather than how to execute it (the focus of subsequent chapters).

The *full integration* strategy focuses on folding e-commerce into the traditional business structure. Here e-commerce activities are encouraged to cannibalize existing business operations, and multi-channel coordination is pursued. These activities can cause challenges through-

Exhibit 3.2
Three Models of E-Commerce Strategy

	Full Integration	Partial Corporate Integration	Business Unit Integration
Description	Complete integration of e-commerce throughout all company operations and activities	Promotes the use of e-commerce throughout a company but without full dedication or implementation	Fully implements an e-commerce venture but only for select business units or functions
Benefits	Unified strategy for both e-commerce and traditional business, with e-commerce being given full support	Significant cost savings and reduced risk	Companies are able to modify the characteristics of e-commerce to fit particular business needs
Shortcomings	Does not always adequately consider the potentially broad corporate impacts of cross-channel conflict and cannibalization	Innovation, technological advantages, and potential benefits over competitors are underemphasized	Benefits of integration are not realized throughout company

out the organizational systems and structures, and their implementation can cause cross-channel conflicts. Some analysts have even criticized the use of terms such as "e-commerce" for contributing to a division between traditional business and Internet-related business activities.[3] Eventually e-commerce need not be separated from traditional business strategic considerations. However, during early stages of e-commerce implementation and for strategies that do not fully integrate e-commerce immediately, such separations may be necessary. Further, the terms e-commerce and e-business are used interchangeably here to denote broad considerations and aspects, including all uses that lead to either increases in revenue or decreases in cost—thus including sales, supply chain, functional integration, logistics, cost control, and so forth. When managing an e-commerce integration strategy, careful planning is necessary to overcome the obstacles that occur from cannibalization and cross-channel conflict. Full integration is certainly desirable when the trends are clear and when the benefit cost analysis yields a significant payoff from the e-commerce investment. It is also certainly a challenge to achieve, and there are many legitimate reasons for companies to choose another strategy.

Partial corporate integration takes a slower approach to the implementation of an e-commerce strategy, while recognizing that full integration between the systems of e-commerce and the traditional business is ultimately desirable. The decision to integrate slowly and follow market leaders can be due to resource constraints or to a desire to limit the business disruption. Though the resource constraints can be significant company-wide, often they are imposed on the e-commerce function because the payoffs of the potential ecommerce investments and the ROI are not effectively calculated. Partial corporate integration, a more cautious strategy, certainly involves all the limitations of follower strategies. Innovation is often limited, as is growth. The CEO makes these strategic choices, often to avoid diverting employee attention and focus from even more compelling initiatives.

Companies adopting this strategy are often encouraged to spend less on IT and to wait for a technology to become mainstream and the trends to become clearer before implementing it. They also view IT as a commodity available to the entire market, similar to the availability of electricity and other technologies that companies use on a daily basis.[4] While there is some historical merit to this argument, a significant problem is the danger of not doing enough to compete with the IT solutions of other companies. A slower strategy might work for an industry leader, yet enough innovation remains to be accomplished in IT and e-commerce that the companies able to identify unique opportunities in e-commerce are going to benefit the most from the nearly ubiquitous presence of the Internet and its related technologies in the marketplace. A partial corporate integration provides support and direction for e-commerce throughout the organization, monitoring of external customer and competitor e-commerce activities and needs, without making the major financial or organizational commitment of full integration. Of course, in many cases industry leaders have wasted assets on e-commerce investments, with no payoff.

Business unit integration uses a building-block approach to determine how e-commerce can fit within a company's larger business strategy, choosing to fully integrate e-commerce into one or more business units or functions, rather than throughout the company. E-commerce may be integrated by business unit, functions, product lines, customers, or suppliers. Essentially, companies look at their business and decide where e-commerce could fit within different parts of their pre-existing model.[5] An analysis of e-commerce success stories shows that companies can use a similar model, but often only temporarily, as a way to move toward a fully integrated e-commerce solution. Many companies just do not have the resources to fully implement an e-commerce solution. One challenge for companies adopting this strategy is that some of their competitors may have significant revenue and cost advantages with a more complete e-commerce integration throughout all of their business units, functions, and operations.

Some companies choose to introduce e-commerce into their strategy slowly, creating stepping-stones that can eventually result in a full implementation of the e-commerce strategy. They may include an evaluation of the elements of strategy that can be implemented at any given time. The implementation can be accomplished through a number of different methods, such as the creation of a temporary separate business unit with the sole purpose of developing a company-wide e-commerce solution as efficiently as possible before being folded back into the larger business structure. Of course, some companies do not desire, or require, that e-commerce permeate all aspects of their business structure. Limiting e-commerce to certain company functions such as HR, payroll, marketing, or customer service may be optimal, but only when these limitations are dictated by the needs of the company rather than by the fears of a company's leadership. In these implementations the process can permit e-commerce to take hold in particular units or functions that require it while not interfering with others. Such an approach allows for the creativity of a separate unit model to find the best ways to incorporate e-commerce in its limited role, while still keeping the project close enough to the core of the company to ensure that the e-commerce initiative maintains a certain company focus.

There are two critical success factors to formulating a coherent e-commerce strategy: multi-channel coordination and effectiveness.

- Multi-channel coordination encompasses the wide variety of aspects of traditional business that must be modified to fully utilize the advantages made available by the opportunities of e-commerce. This includes a focus on creating value primarily through revenue increases, though cost savings also can be significant.
- Effectiveness deals not only with the financial characteristics of e-commerce, but also with the effective use of e-commerce–related technologies and functions to take advantage of company capabilities. The focus tends to be more on creating value through cost control and operational effectiveness.

MULTI-CHANNEL COORDINATION

Although many large brick-and-mortar companies are attempting to integrate and transform into "clicks-and-mortar" organizations, many of their strategies are poor, and the implementations are often worse. The short-term question may indeed be how to enter e-business. The longer-term issue will likely be how to do business. The "e" will probably disappear as the Internet dominates much of business activities. Complete integration will be key to traditional companies' success.

Those who don't build on their existing competitive advantages may find that they've missed out on the greatest change in global business in a century.[6]

While a traditional business strategy is optimally a well-coordinated effort, the conventional aspects of business not only need to change to accommodate an e-commerce strategy, but are likely to be enhanced in ways that were not possible before e-commerce implementation. E-commerce becomes an important new channel of procurement and distribution and causes many challenges to optimize all of the channels and minimize cross-channel conflict. The following drivers of success of e-commerce are not only new ways to think about business, but ways in which traditional business structures will sometimes need to adapt to take advantage of the benefits of e-commerce (Exhibit 3.3).

Brand Management

Brand management is a strategic element that is not unique to e-commerce. The use of brand management to build customer trust and loyalty is similar in both traditional commerce and e-commerce. In both, the brand name is used to attract customers to visit new physical or online locations, try new products, or use new services. The naming, e-commerce awareness and association, and bricks and clicks are important factors to manage.

Naming

Customers who are skeptical about the security and reliability of e-commerce purchases can be influenced in many ways, including customer communities and various guarantees. But none of these can

Exhibit 3.3
Multi-Channel Coordination

Individual Key Success Factors	Sub-Factors
Brand Management	Naming
	E-commerce Awareness and Association
	Bricks and Clicks
Offerings Strategy	Product Selection
	Pricing
	Customization and Personalization
Customer Service	Personal or Automated Interaction
	Specific Support Mechanisms

match the importance of brand name in winning customer trust. A brand name can facilitate the transfer of corporate values into the realm of e-commerce. Customers may associate the brand with friendly, helpful people, and a helpful Web site has the potential to mirror this expectation even without the personal contact. Whether a company is well known for exceptional customer service, low prices, or any other exceptional characteristic, brand name has the potential of transferring those elements of the traditional business into an e-commerce venture. Such branding can provide significant advantage over competitors, where either a lack of brand recognition or poor brand association make e-commerce more difficult.

Utilizing the brand online has many challenges. The Web site's name is an important aspect of maintaining or building a strong brand online. Customers must be able to find the site easily, whether by trial and error or by using a search engine. Companies with names that are long or difficult to spell may find that their original brand name is inconvenient for an online brand. Barnes and Noble attempted to operate under barnesandnoble.com but later switched to bn.com after determining that the first name was unwieldy. Ideally, typing in any brand name associated with the company should lead the customer to the correct site, but promotions should emphasize the most succinct or common name.

For some, purchasing unclaimed Web site names has become a profitable business, and companies that have failed to reserve their names may need to buy the rights to them at a high cost. E-companies became the archetype of the business willing to pay anything for the perfect Web site name, paying $7.5 million for the rights to "business.com" in 1999,[7] though the cost of naming rights has since declined. (In late 2003, the Web site name "men.com" was sold for $1.3 million by someone who had paid $15,000 for the name in 1997.) Presently, though many are obtaining domain extensions such as ".org" and ".net," it is the ".com" domain extension address that is clearly most important. It is useful, however, to obtain the others that could be interchanged with the company's .com moniker and might confuse customers or damage the brand.

To protect and build the brand, excellent online service is necessary. A well-known brand can easily raise the expectations of customers beyond a company's e-commerce capabilities, especially when a company first moves into using the Internet.[8] This problem occurred in many early e-commerce ventures, including Wal-Mart, which needed to implement a well-documented e-commerce shutdown to resolve its Internet difficulties.

Awareness and Association

Building awareness of the Web site has also seen dramatic failures in the short history of e-commerce. Many companies began with marketing campaigns that relied on banner ads on other Web sites, which proved to bring many viewers to the site, but produced few sales. Another approach consistent with an overall integration strategy is to include the name of the Web site in all aspects of the business: in-store signage, bags and boxes, business publications, and so forth. Some companies go beyond these in-house solutions and choose to use other media to promote e-commerce, such as radio or television.

A more complicated issue regarding brand management is whether the expectations associated with the brand translate well into the online medium. For example, can a company deliver the same or comparable information and experience online, and if so, is that desirable? Second, is the brand at hand associated with technology and innovation? Some companies are so closely tied to human interaction that automation would have the potential to change the company's relationship with its customers. Though the e-commerce services may be beneficial to both the company and its customers, the new association, and the possible perception of a decrease in customer focus and service, must be managed carefully.

Companies with strong brand awareness, where appropriate, typically transfer their brands online. Where brands are weak, other approaches are desirable. Rite Aid chose not to transfer its brand online, instead entering into a partnership with Drugstore.com, in which the latter's name was retained.[9] Kmart and Bank One, however, introduced their online brands, Bluelight and Wingspan respectively, and expended large marketing budgets with little apparent value creation.

Bricks and Clicks

Often, e-commerce strategy is described in terms of drawing customers, either from the traditional business or entirely new customers, to the Web site. But a well-coordinated strategy uses each channel to generate further sales in the other. The company should concentrate on highlighting the benefits of each channel while emphasizing multichannel coordination to drive higher revenues.

Traditional retailers have significant advantages over e-retailers, since storefronts attract customers and provide a place where they can view, return, and exchange merchandise. Physical stores also remind customers that there's a branch of the Web site down the street that they can visit. Traditional retailers that are already established names can also capitalize on their competitive edge by quickly establishing a Web-based operation that's as nimble and customer-focused as Internet companies. Their experience and the brick-and-mortar operation can complement the e-commerce activities, but only if they build on their superior market positions and design and implement strategies that capitalize on that positioning.[10]

Using the physical locations to stimulate online sales can be easily accomplished. The most obvious is to market the Web site by including its name throughout the store and on bags, receipts, signs, and anywhere else appropriate. An increasingly popular approach has been to include online kiosks in-store. This is an especially strong tactic for attracting new customers. The kiosks allow instant ordering of products that are not available or out of stock in the physical location. Store employees are available to assist in kiosk use. While kiosks ought to have the full capabilities of the company's Web site, content specifically tailored to in-store customers, such as in-store inventories, is also helpful. Many companies have found ways for e-commerce and traditional business to complement one another. Charles Schwab found that opening local offices has the effect of greatly increasing online sales, because it gives customers a physical branch with a human touch to fall back on when problems occur with the online channel.

The Web site can be used equally well to stimulate sales in the physical stores. An essential feature of the Web site is an accurate and easily accessible store locator function. Customers should be able to locate the nearest store and get directions and hours of operation in a matter of seconds. This also provides an opportunity to forge relationships with other companies with a strong online presence, in this case, mapping technologies such as those provided by MapQuest or Yahoo Maps.

In-store pick-up and returns are two other ways in which the Web site can draw customers into physical stores. Many Web sites allow customers to order online and then pick up or return the items at the closest physical store These policies provide convenience for the customer and create a second opportunity for a customer purchase. Thus, store employees must be well-trained to handle situations resulting from the online channel, and companies must efficiently manage the multi-channel coordination.

Since Web sites often have far greater product selection than physical stores because of shelf and floor space limitations, many customers may make their first stop online. If the customer needs the item faster than it can be shipped, the Web site should aid the customer in finding the closest physical location that carries the item. Customers who lack confidence in the availability of a desired product in a particular store are then able to get valuable product availability information.

In addition to physical stores and the Web site, many businesses have catalog sales, which represent a third major channel. Catalog sales in many ways represent a less efficient form of the Web site, with higher labor costs, printing costs, and less convenience for customers. Catalogs also have a much less accurate representation of available inventory, in that the Internet can be updated in real time to reflect changes in offerings, while catalogs are printed infrequently. Though eliminating catalog sales may not be desirable, companies might offer incentives to gradually transfer catalog sales customers to the Internet. Companies with strong personalization features on their Web site can make this transition especially attractive. For customers who still prefer to use the catalog, the company should at least integrate its internal practices so that call services can take full advantage of e-commerce technology.

Successful e-commerce brand management requires taking advantage of the innovation and flexibility made possible by e-commerce, while at the same time meeting the expectations traditionally associated with a brand name. Limiting the offerings and policies to those traditionally associated with brands greatly limits the success of the e-commerce venture; but moving too far beyond traditional methods of business in an e-commerce venture can create risk to the brick-and-mortar operation. Companies must permit the brand to adjust adequately to develop creativity in an e-commerce venture, while at the same time maintaining the traditional credibility of the existing business.[11]

Offerings Strategy

When companies decide to sell directly online, a major strategic element is to decide which specific goods and services to offer. For most companies, setting up an e-commerce Web site that mimics the offerings at physical locations is not a logical or profitable choice. In traditional retailing, holding physical inventory and dedicating shelf and floor space in a store are both impediments to offering extremely high product variety. Scarce shelf space is dedicated to items with high sales volumes. In e-commerce, neither of these issues is as critical. Companies can often offer a much greater variety online without high incremental costs. While product variety is clearly a differentiator between traditional commerce and e-commerce, it is unlikely to be a source of long-term competitive advantage between e-commerce competitors.

A company can expand its offerings to attract customers through the convenience of "one-stop shopping," but this type of reach has its challenges. If the company's offerings remain within its traditional domain, its competitors can easily imitate the expansion of offerings. If the company moves beyond its traditional domain, it may attract new customers, but it risks damaging the strategic fit of the e-commerce venture in the overall company. When products are hard to differentiate, customers who originally frequent the first mover are unlikely to switch on the basis of offerings alone.[12] A brand strategy can help attract traditional customers to frequent the e-commerce site, but for some products brands provide less advantage over Internet-only companies.[13]

Other products require more information than a simple description for most customers. The offerings themselves require stronger tools for conveying information to customers, which means investments in technology, including interaction, are important. Companies with a strong, traditional brand have an advantage over Internet-only companies because customers who trust the brand will be more willing to overlook the difficulty in assessing the offerings online. Once trust is established through a satisfactory transaction, repeat purchases are more likely.[14]

Product Selection

An important element of the offerings strategy is the type and range of products to be offered online. Just as companies should not waste shelf space on slow-selling products, similar considerations affect online offerings even though space is unlimited. Scarcity of space is not the problem online, but rather the profitability of selling the product with the Internet medium. Some products have such small margins that they may not be profitable for online sales, while they also clutter the Web site. Wal-Mart and Kmart both discovered that low-priced products were unprofitable and began introducing various restrictions such as price minimums at checkout, margin requirements, and category restrictions. These and other items also suffer from a small value-to-weight ratio,[15] referring to the challenge of shipping online products. Companies are forced either to charge shipping rates that make the products undesirable or to subsidize the shipping costs. Neither is a profitable option.

Product variety has numerous potential benefits in e-commerce. In addition to the vast number of products that can be offered, organization and information control is much easier to maintain and modify online than through traditional business channels. Further, the company has a greater opportunity to promote products not associated with the traditional business brand.

Although it might sound impressive for a Web site to claim the widest variety of selection, a customer who must sort through thousands of offerings without adequate information control is likely to move on to another online retailer. Although it may be desirable to include higher-margin offerings not available in physical stores, either because of lack of demand or because of inconsistency with brand image, care must be taken to protect the brand image.

Online offerings need not be based on physically tangible offerings. Even when company offerings are primarily based on information or services, the careful analysis and evaluation of product selection alternatives is critical. Charles Schwab established an online presence by competing with others not on the basis of cost, but instead on the amount of information available to the consumer.[16] Such a strategy not only avoided price competition, but set Schwab apart from its competitors because of its unique value proposition.

A company also must consider including offerings in e-commerce that would be peripheral to the traditional business, such as consulting or other services. Office Depot and UPS have both used e-commerce to become total service providers to their clients. Office Depot, in an effort to push more traditional customers online, expanded its Web site into services like accounting and payroll, while UPS began to offer full logistics services instead of simply contracting to ship goods.[17] These offerings illustrate the blurred industry lines in e-commerce. Just as UPS seeks to provide logistics support for its shipping customers, so too can logistics providers expand online offerings to include courier services.

A somewhat nascent element of offerings strategy is to use Web site layout to entice manufacturers to bid for prime Web site real estate, similar to magazines and newspapers. Thus, every Web site has the potential to become a small, privately held, advertising venture. EBay was perhaps the pioneer of this concept, in that sellers could highlight their sales with front-page placement, bold lettering, and other attention-drawing techniques.

Certainly, the offerings element of strategy has a major impact on brand management. Consistency of product offerings is important to translate an existing brand image into e-commerce. When companies expand e-commerce offerings beyond their brick-and-mortar offerings, they must be cognizant of the potential danger of blurring the meaning of the brand.

Pricing

One of the most difficult aspects of e-commerce strategy is online pricing. Buy.com learned the hard way that by attracting customers through deep discount offerings, neither loyalty nor profitability is achieved. Even companies whose traditional brands are based on low prices have found limited advantage in extending those images online. To offer lower prices than competitors, a company must have stable supply chain superiority, similar to that of Dell or Wal-Mart. Even then, one's prices can be undercut, at least temporarily, by new online competitors operating with a deep discount model.

Certainly, one of the major differences with online selling is that search costs for discounted prices are so much lower than in traditional commerce. Stores with lower prices can be accessed with the click of a mouse without any travel requirements. With continually improving technology available to find the lowest prices automatically, the prospects for strategies based solely on price competition are dim. However, these same mechanisms can be utilized by any company to continually evaluate market position and identify strengths of competitors that can either be counteracted or emulated.

Pricing can be an integral part of e-commerce strategy when cannibalization of a company's traditional business is critical. Even when companies cannot use e-commerce to acquire new customers or provide superior convenience for existing ones, the online channel may still be a source of improved efficiency for the customer. In industries where obvious labor, marketing, and facilities costs exist, enticing customers to do business online may be worth the use of differentially lower online prices. In this way a company can cannibalize its business before an online competitor gains the advantage.

Pricing, like other tools, has the capacity to increase value in both online and traditional commerce. However, pricing plans, whether differential or universal, must be carefully developed and integrated into an overall offerings strategy. Because of the increased information available to consumers, e-commerce pricing is particularly critical.

Customized, Personalized, and Standardized Internet Capabilities

Choices related to customized, personalized, and standardized offerings are an essential part of e-commerce strategy (Exhibit 3.4). Whereas standardized offerings provide one uniform Web site and array of product offerings, customization refers to offerings that can be tailored, reconfigured, or designed to fit the specific needs of individual custom-

Exhibit 3.4
Extent of Web Site Personalization

	Customizing	Personalizing	Standardizing
Description	Tailoring, reconfiguration, and design of offerings to meet customer needs	Adjusting the format and content of a Web site to cater to individual customers	Providing uniform products and Web site design options for all customers
Advantages	• Customers better satisfied with self-tailored goods	• Efficient shopping experience for customers	• Efficient front-end process for the company
	• Customization through e-commerce is more efficient than customization through traditional channels	• Marketing advantage for the company and company's partners	• Less intrusive and potentially easier format for customers

ers. In contrast, personalization involves adjusting the format and content of a Web site both to meet the needs of the customer and to allow the business to present narrowly tailored information, such as suggested sales, to appeal to individual customers.

Standardization is particularly relevant for companies whose products are not especially well suited for e-commerce or when personalized solutions are too expensive to justify. Standardized solutions are far easier to implement, but companies must determine whether payoffs might accrue from additional expenditures to focus more on customers' individual needs.

The concept of *customization* is neither new nor unique to e-commerce; in traditional commerce, too, certain retailers have been known to customize. In e-commerce, companies can now introduce a customization element at a smaller additional cost than in traditional commerce. Customization both gives customers a compelling reason to shop online and adds a differentiation from competitors, and possibly even the company's own brick-and-mortar offerings.

For physical products, customization requires adjustments to a company's entire supply chain, particularly when the customization occurs in manufacturing. Certainly, higher costs will occur, but if the changes needed for customization can be made concurrently with other e-commerce-related upgrades, the incremental costs may be less intimidating. Strong candidates for customization are higher-priced goods, products with simple shapes, and products whose uniqueness comes from combining a variety of existing products in different combinations.[18]

Easily customizable types of products are information products, such as music or proprietary databases. Not only can these products be customized, but e-commerce strategy can push to deliver these products digitally. For this to be effective, the products must lend themselves to nonphysical form. Thus, the company can provide added speed and convenience to the customer and reduce delivery cost. In addition to customized physical or information products, service packages can also be customized. For those that make repeat purchases or have frequent service needs, such packages allow customers to specify the level of advice, technical support, or special preparation associated with their orders. For example, BMW now provides customers the opportunity to design their own car. Up to 30 percent in the United States and 80 percent of cars in Europe are now built to order. To provide this customization, BMW overhauled its Web site and network, providing more options to customers, cutting overstock, and slashing the time it takes to deliver cars by one-third.[19]

In contrast, *personalization* does not entail creating new products of any kind, but simply adjusting the format or content of the Web site for specific customers. Personalization is well suited to many companies when customization is not, including retailers of standardized goods and information-based Web sites, such as those for news providers and education-oriented business. While designing such programming may entail some expense, the incremental cost for each customer is minimal. Typically, personalization will not be a direct source of additional short-term revenue in e-commerce. For most companies, these features are intended solely to help customers, increase the level of trust, build brand loyalty, and provide information to the company for future marketing.

Personalization can, however, provide an indirect source of revenue. Suggested sales, based on purchase patterns of other customers, were one of the first uses of personalization. Many e-commerce leaders, such as Dell and Amazon, have successfully embraced that strategy. Companies can suggest products and offer custom-made deals, all using the same databases. Corporate and frequent customers can also use personalization to make automatic reorders. In fact, personalization alone has been credited for Amazon's repeat customer rate of 70 percent.[20] Meanwhile, the company benefits further by gathering information to make the entire system still smarter and more sensitive to customers' desires.[21] These choices of standardization, customization, and personalization are critical elements of e-commerce strategies.

Customer Service

The importance of customer service practices in e-commerce strategy cannot be overstated. For some companies, this might require a departure from their traditional business, in which they have built a brand that emphasizes low prices or the uniqueness of their offerings. In e-commerce, every company must seek to be an industry leader in customer service practices, even if that area is not a part of their explicitly stated appeal to customers or the value proposition. Further, the impact of e-commerce operations and the Web site on the traditional brand can be significant. Poor customer service practices online will not only dissuade customers from shopping at a particular Web site, but they may also cause declines at physical locations.

Personal or Automated Interaction

Companies must determine the amount of human interaction to be built into the Web site's customer service practices. E-commerce provides a great opportunity to automate some practices and significantly reduce labor costs. Automation can also provide customers greater speed and convenience. It also increases the risk that customers needs will not be met, causing serious potential damage to future revenue. Thus, the evaluation of how much human interaction to include is important.[22]

For example, in the FAQ (frequently asked questions) section available on most Web sites, customers can, to some extent, help themselves. But, since no company can anticipate every question, the company must decide on a level of service. It can provide an email response service, a forum for unanswered questions, a customer assistance phone line, or some combination of these services.

Ultimately, automation made possible by e-commerce must be dictated by the relationship that the company desires with its customers. Cisco's customers have traditionally been tech-savvy, so the use of e-commerce to assist in customer service was a boon for the company's efficiency, while at the same time meeting the expectations of its particular customer base.[23] High-end retailers may benefit from instant messaging or voice-enabled customer service, while some companies might not find such solutions cost-effective.

Specific Support Mechanisms

To effectively provide high levels of customer service, specific support mechanisms are needed. Customer service practices are typically oriented toward either customer acquisition or customer retention. Customer acquisition requires a customer-friendly Web site design with full and accurate information. Customer retention requires a smooth and accurate fulfillment process with satisfactory solutions to problems with products or services.

Many purchases in e-commerce are initiated but never completed, and confusing Web site design and lack of trust are two primary causes. The Web site should be designed to permit easy use by customers and a high level of confidence. The layout should make important features easy to locate, and the site should load quickly for customers on slower connections. Products should be described accurately to compensate for the customer's inability to examine the product physically. Colors and other physical attributes should match the attributes of the actual products. The price listed should reflect what the customer will actually pay, without any hidden costs at the end, aside from shipping. If a product is temporarily unavailable, the Web site should reflect this fact and provide information, if possible, on when the item will next be available. Some companies choose to temporarily remove unavailable items from the site.

Proper Web site design characteristics include:

- A design based on the needs of the customer first and the needs of the company second

- Quick loading times for customers on high-speed and low-speed connections
- As much descriptive information on products as possible
- Images of products that are true to reality when possible
- Full pricing and shipping information
- Product availability

New and returning customers should not be immediately accosted by registration or log in requirements. The site should allow customers to shop until they are ready to check out, without intervening steps that might discourage the purchase. And while credit cards are the currency for most transactions, service companies with frequent payments should consider other payment options, such as automatic bank withdrawals.

Customers should also be apprised of the company's geographic limitations, if any. Some companies do not ship or sell overseas; and in certain industries, such as grocery stores, the local delivery area may be as small as a single zip code. Customers should not have to wait until the final step of the purchase process to discover this. Shipping policies should also be clearly outlined both in the FAQ section and explicitly to the customer during the purchase process. Customers should have multiple shipping options, including both high-speed and low-cost alternatives or possible pick-up at physical stores where appropriate. Providing such information also provides an opportunity for businesses to partner with other categories of Internet services from reputable providers, such as mapping technologies, directory listings, and shipping industries, to increase customer confidence in the e-commerce capabilities of the Web site that they are accessing.

Companies should also try to ensure satisfied customers through an emphasis on prompt and accurate fulfillment. During the holiday season this is typically difficult, given the often significantly increased volume of sales. For businesses in which delivery must be scheduled and met by the customer, care must be taken to avoid the need for redelivery. Grocery Web sites have experimented with various windows of time within which to make deliveries. The window must be small enough to be convenient for the customer, but large enough to guarantee making all deliveries within the constraints of traffic and other impediments.

In addition to delivery, returns and support are important aspects of e-commerce customer service. Return policies should be clearly stated at an early step of the purchasing process, and should also be extensively covered in the FAQ section. In many cases, retailers should encourage the return of items to physical store locations. Companies whose products are better judged by physical examination should consider particularly generous return policies. Nordstrom, whose traditional brand is built on both top-notch service and experimentation with products, includes full return shipping papers with all purchases, to encourage online customers to do as they would in the store: to try on numerous pairs of shoes and keep the ones they like.

Technical support should also be a priority of the service function, especially for companies that offer technology or information products. Here, offering technical support 24/7 may be worth the added labor costs for many companies. These various support mechanisms are important for high-quality customer service. Brand management, product offerings, and customer service are among the most important individual key success factors in e-commerce and are critical complements of a successful e-commerce strategy.

EFFECTIVENESS

Success in multi-channel coordination through the use of brand management, product offerings, and customer service is necessary if one is to achieve e-commerce success. But, the recognition of the most cost-effective uses of e-commerce and where competitive advantage can be achieved is also critical. How should companies approach the use of e-commerce in their business?

Two basic principles of effectiveness are necessary to guide the creation of an appropriate e-commerce strategy:

- Principle #1: Take advantage of e-commerce solutions that have been *commoditized.*
- Principle #2: Find unique *uses* of e-commerce in order to gain competitive advantage.

These principles do not fully encompass a successful e-commerce strategy, but they do assist in the creation of appropriate boundaries for most ambitions in e-commerce. Here, companies recognize that they are often simultaneously attempting to create a truly unique and profitable Internet experience and seeking out available opportunities tied to outsourcing and commoditized solutions.[24]

Commoditized Solutions

Principle #1: Take advantage of e-commerce solutions that have been commoditized. Some have argued that e-commerce, along with all other forms of IT, has become a commodity and typically has few or no unique attributes. However, companies can determine which elements of e-commerce are core to their business strategy and often keep these elements from becoming commoditized. Most companies may find some low-value processes to be potential candidates for commoditized e-commerce solutions. Many hardware and software packages have come into the market recently to help with the transition and maintenance of e-commerce. To ignore the cost savings afforded through such mass production only puts a company at a disadvantage in the market.[25]

However, companies should not rely on these purchases for their e-commerce solution. Businesses with significant e-commerce aspirations must continually reevaluate the efficacy even of previously implemented e-commerce solutions. They must determine whether or not newer e-commerce solutions might better fit the firm's e-commerce strategy and whether or not the company might be better served by an in-house replacement for the commoditized solution. Without such considerations, companies run the risk that commoditized solutions will dictate their business structure, by limitations in design.

The advantage of commoditization is not simply saving money in every case. Much as other innovations serve a company by finding areas in which challengers are lagging behind, commoditization allows a company to gain an advantage by identifying cost-saving opportunities that may have gone unnoticed by competitors. While stagnation can sometimes be viewed as a side-effect of the use of commodity-based solutions, the choice to commoditize certain aspects of an e-commerce model is a strategy innovation choice. However, the fear of stagnation should also encourage companies to continually reevaluate commoditized solutions to determine whether another commoditized solution might be available, or if a particular aspect of an e-commerce model has become a candidate for an in-house solution. Where commoditized solutions are available and effective, they should be adapted, as they are often useful approaches to e-commerce implementation.

Unique Solutions

Principle #2: Find unique uses of e-commerce to gain competitive advantage. When companies are attempting to provide differentiation in the marketplace, relying only on commoditized solutions is seldom enough. It is essential that companies developing e-commerce solutions evaluate existing technology with which to uniquely and creatively implement an e-commerce strategy. This selective experimentation has the goal of refining traditional business rules while creating new rules for the e-commerce venture.[26] At the core of such a strategy is the ability of a company not only to *formulate*, but also successfully to *implement* creative applications of e-commerce.

Such uses of technology can provide both short-term and long-term advantages for an e-commerce venture. Some have argued that the short-term advantages afforded by technological advances and unique uses of technology are not worthwhile, as they can easily be copied at a lower cost at a later time. However, such short-term advantages are often important for market positioning. Although other companies may be able to mimic such advantages, waiting for the technology to reach an acceptable price level permits the first mover the opportunity to further establish itself with its customers, thereby turning a short-term advantage into a longer-term customer base. Wells Fargo tracks and analyzes every transaction made by its millions of retail customers, whether at ATMs, bank branches, or online through its in-house net technology. The company can now better target its products, whether mortgages or credit lines, and it now sells twice the industry average per customer.[27]

The long-term advantages afforded by unique uses of e-commerce are less dependent on finding uses of technology that could potentially benefit any similar company in the market. Rather, long-term advantages are derived from finding unique applications of e-commerce to the company's specific business strategies. The e-commerce strategies of companies such as Dell, Cisco, and Wal-Mart are known to the business community. However, their long-term success has not relied solely upon e-commerce. Rather, their previous business strategies were already uniquely suited to the advantages they were able to derive from e-commerce.

In the end, commoditized e-commerce solutions can greatly improve the effectiveness of a company's e-commerce venture. However, not many e-commerce success stories have relied entirely upon commoditized solutions. It is the ability to recognize the complexities of the opportunities, and the threats, afforded by e-commerce for their business that has enabled some companies to excel at e-commerce. E-commerce opportunities, while numerous, need to be tailored to the strengths and weaknesses of particular company characteristics.

CONCLUSION

Many choices are possible in the formulation and implementation of an e-commerce strategy, including choices of integration strategy and the key success factors (Exhibit 3.5). From formulation to implementation, companies should strive to make e-commerce a core part of company strategy not only to create a new realm of business opportunity but also to augment the company's traditional business operations. The alternatives presented here can serve as a guide to finding a proper role

Exhibit 3.5
Key Success Factors of E-Commerce Strategy

for e-commerce within a specific corporate strategy and structure. Among the critical elements are the following.

- Successful e-commerce strategy must include considerations of a company's traditional business strategy.
- Full integration, partial corporate integration, and business unit integration all have positive aspects as strategies for e-commerce and are viable choices.
- Multi-channel coordination is a key success factor not only in formulating and implementing an e-commerce strategy, but in integrating it throughout company operations.
- Companies must carefully coordinate new online services to enhance and protect their brands.
- The number and variety of products that companies can make available is far greater through e-commerce than through a purely traditional offerings strategy. At the same time they can meet particular needs of customers through customization and personalization.
- A successful e-commerce strategy must include special attention to customer service, even if it is not a core component of a company's overall strategy.
- A proper balance of the use of commoditized solutions and unique uses of e-commerce can help a company utilize effectiveness to gain a competitive advantage.

CHAPTER 4

Organizational Structure and Design for E-Commerce

Once a company has established an e-commerce strategy, organizational structure becomes a primary concern in the process of implementing that strategy. In many cases, e-commerce will not initially fit neatly into the existing organizational structure of a traditional company. E-commerce, even to the most technologically savvy company, represents a new channel for procurement, distribution, and sales. E-commerce ventures also put new demands on individuals and business units at every level of the company.

The previous chapters outline a dynamic model in which strong and supportive leadership and a well-formulated strategy provide the basis for transforming a company through e-commerce. To implement that strategy, structure and systems must be adapted for e-commerce (Exhibit 4.1).

Corporate strategy, structure, systems, resources and the external environment are all both inputs and constraints to the determination of e-commerce strategy, structure, and systems. Planning for an e-commerce venture should use the existing structure to determine what existing company strengths can be utilized or enhanced with e-commerce.[1] Implicitly, even some companies that have been unsuccessful in e-commerce have grasped this fact. But instead of treating existing structure as an input, companies have often treated it as an impediment to e-commerce, deciding to create an entirely new structure outside the organization. They believed that they could not create a new e-com-

Exhibit 4.1
Antecedents and Consequences of E-Commerce Success

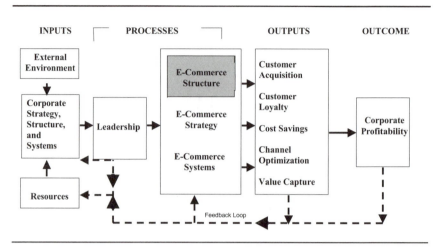

merce structure inside the organization that could effectively implement the e-commerce strategy. They also did not believe they could
integrate an e-commerce operation into the corporate strategy, structures, or systems. Sometimes e-commerce was split off as a separate
company, sometimes it was separated as a separate functional or business unit, and in a few cases it was fully integrated.

These concerns have been at the core in the debate over structure
in e-commerce. Through the late 1990s, companies feared the disruptive nature of e-commerce and were unwilling to make changes in
existing company structures and systems. Many companies chose to
separate e-commerce from the main company structure. These separate-
structure decisions included establishing separate business units far
from company headquarters, creating separate management teams,
outsourcing of the entire e-commerce platform, and selling large
equity ownership of the e-commerce business to venture capitalists
and other outside interests.[2]

Many of these companies have belatedly realized the value of an
integrated structure for e-commerce. High-profile failures may have
served to convince uncommitted leaders, but the rationale for integration runs much deeper than an analysis of past outcomes. The application of fundamental business principles should also make the benefits
of an integrated organizational structure abundantly clear.

Some previous discussions on e-commerce have divided the debate
of e-commerce structure into a number of separate decision dimensions.
Some have encouraged executives to consider integration or separation

of equity, brand, management, and operations,[3] while others focused on leveraging two dimensions, the financial and the operational.[4] Although these dimensions are relevant in terms of developing an e-commerce structure, careful choices must be made. Companies must rely on a well-developed and coordinated implementation of an e-commerce strategy, with aligned e-commerce structure and systems. It would have made little sense, for example, if Wells Fargo had integrated its management structure and operations and then followed in the footsteps of competitors, such as Bank One, by creating a new brand for e-commerce. Likewise, Office Depot would likely have destroyed most of the benefits of its operational integration if it had sold equity in OfficeDepot.com to a venture capitalist.

In the final analysis, the most fundamental analysis is whether or not to integrate e-commerce, and this choice should direct all the subsequent financial, management, and operational decisions. The implementation of an e-commerce strategy can take different forms, and the structure and speed of implementation are part of the strategic choices, as discussed in the previous chapter. However, companies should make a commitment to long-term full integration. It is the path to that full corporate integration that is an issue. A lack of commitment to e-commerce integration can cause wavering dedication on the part of the company. While Bank of America is currently a leader in online banking, it faced early obstacles because it initially pursued an integrated e-commerce approach. It later moved on to a separate strategic business unit to foster creativity, and then had to switch back to an integrated approach.[5]

Throughout this chapter, the benefits of integration in different facets of e-commerce and in a variety of industries are presented. Solutions are also described for problems faced when companies lack the internal capabily to fully implement the e-commerce strategies presented in the previous chapter. Finally, the contexts in which external strategic alliances can be a desirable solution are presented.

MOVING TOWARD AN INTEGRATED COMPANY

It's clear that, while looking at integration as the ideal solution is a useful mantra, implementing a full integration strategy is challenging. Systems and strategy must be aligned to both the corporate and the e-commerce structures for success. There should be a commitment to stay within the organization for the financing, management, and operational capabilities that e-commerce requires, where possible (Exhibit 4.2).

At times, this commitment is difficult. Challenging financial decisions may make venture capital and the prospect of an initial public

Exhibit 4.2
Using E-Commerce Structure to Drive Success

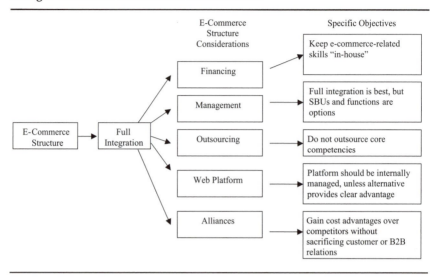

offering of a separate e-commerce entity look desirable, as it did to many in the late 1990s. In addition, managers may need to take on new responsibilities, implement new policies, and deal with conflicts that could be more easily handled by a separate management team. Systems will likely need to change. Speed may be sacrificed to develop a Web platform internally, when outsourcing could put the platform online weeks or months earlier. None of this, however, justifies the inconsistency that occurs between a viable internally constructed e-commerce strategy and a separated e-commerce structure.

At its most basic level, integration means viewing e-commerce as an integral part of an existing business. Many companies have demonstrated a commitment to integration by refusing to break out e-commerce profit, revenue, or other financial figures to the public. Rather, it is an additional important channel for procurement and distribution in addition to other important uses.

Financing E-Commerce and E-Commerce Structure

An integrated company should not spin off its e-commerce operation, because this new aspect of a company's business is essential to the future of the organization and creates significant future corporate value. Unfortunately, this lesson has been a painful experience for many companies in e-commerce's brief history.

Companies have turned to venture capitalists to sell stock in their e-commerce venture for several reasons, which have not always been about money. E-commerce expertise was one of the main capabilities sought by companies such as Wal-Mart, Staples, and Nordstrom. Other reasons for turning to venture capitalists have included access to managerial talent, back-end technological capabilities, speed of implementation, and fulfillment services (Exhibit 4.3). Unfortunately, a major contributing factor to the decision of many companies to spin off their e-commerce venture has been the need to respond to a perceived competitive threat.[6]

But the venture capital model of e-commerce has been exposed as doing significant damage to integration strategies. In most cases, selling equity to venture capitalists was followed by setting up a new management structure with reduced input from the parent company and more input from those interested in bidding up the stock price of the dot.com. At the same time, the technical side was almost entirely outsourced, often to the consulting arm of the venture capitalist, with little or no input from IT professionals who knew the industry. Under these conditions, nearly every benefit of e-commerce, including cross-promotion, economies of scale, and supply-chain efficiencies, was wasted or rendered impossible. This system also created a cycle of dependency, wherein companies were rendered incapable of further advances in e-commerce without the support of this new management structure or a second outside source of e-commerce experience.

The examples are numerous, and the experiences of companies across industries have been remarkably similar:

Exhibit 4.3
Why Companies Spin Off E-Commerce

Reasons for turning to venture capitalists and IPOs to raise funds for e-commerce ventures	Problems associated with these methods of funding for e-commerce ventures
1. Desire for separate management with e-commerce experience.	1. Parent company has less input than is desirable in an integration strategy.
2. During the e-commerce boom, such funds were easy to acquire.	2. Artificially high values for e-commerce initiatives have since collapsed.
3. These methods were seen as faster than using in-house funds and solutions for e-commerce.	3. Speed does not compensate for poor strategy and poor integration of e-commerce within the parent company.
4. Other companies were doing it.	4. Looking to outside solutions contributed to company's becoming dependent on outside assistance for all aspects of e-commerce.

- Barnes and Noble sold a 50 percent interest in barnesandnoble.com to Bertelsmann in 1998, hoping to imitate rival Amazon with an innovation-friendly organization, while improving weaknesses such as service and fulfillment. In 1999 it went public, raising nearly a half billion dollars. By 2000, when its competitive fortunes failed to improve, it had replaced its CEO, and slowly an integration strategy began to take shape. It started with more consistent pricing, cross-promotion, and putting Web site kiosks into stores. The integration process eventually led to a stock buyback from the public.
- Wal-Mart partnered with Accel Partners in 2000, seeking to quickly redesign a struggling Wal-Mart.com with an infusion of e-commerce expertise. After numerous redesigns, an industry-shocking shutdown of the site, and a sequence of changes in selling strategies, Wal-Mart found little growth in revenue. It decided that integrating physical stores and the Web site presented the best avenue for growth and folded the Web site back into the company in August 2002.

Further examples of failures of such e-commerce spin-offs are available throughout the individual case studies at the end of this book.

What we see is that these spin-offs have been consistently unsuccessful across industry lines regardless of what motivated the spin-off, how much equity in the venture was sold, or whether an IPO occurred. The importance of the details paled in comparison to the deadly conflict between strategy and structure. These examples make it abundantly clear that e-commerce should be funded internally, both to reap the benefits of integration and to ensure the parent company has control of the long-term financial future of the e-commerce channel.

E-Commerce Management and Separate E-Commerce Business Units

While the spin-offs were failing, companies looked for other creative ways of achieving "separation" without spinning the e-commerce venture off entirely. One method has been to create a separate business unit so divorced from company headquarters as to seem to be its own organization. This separation may be achieved by physical distance, radically different business unit structure, systems, rewards, and culture, or the selection of leadership to run the unit. Some companies have elected to have entirely separate management structures. One concern is whether these structures can aid in the implementation of an effective e-commerce strategy that is focused on ultimate company-wide integration of e-commerce.[7]

For many companies, the preferred approach is to establish an e-commerce unit flexible enough to foster innovation but integrated enough to be consistent with a well-formulated e-commerce strategy. This type of unit should largely resemble the company's other business units, serving as a profit center and reporting through normal channels and the existing hierarchy on issues ranging from the effectiveness of e-commerce initiatives to the integration of those initiatives within the overall structure of the company. It may, however, have different management control systems from the rest of the company, especially in the areas of performance measures and incentive systems.[8] It is these differences, not pretenses of geographic distance or office design, that can truly foster innovation.

A successful separate business unit for e-commerce displays numerous attributes.

- The SBU should be well integrated into the traditional business management structure so that the goals of the SBU are aligned with those of the company.
- A primary function of the SBU should be to lead the company's integration effort to the point where the e-commerce initiative becomes a part of every level of the company, not just the original SBU, to both increase revenues and decrease costs.
- The SBU should be given enough freedom to utilize e-commerce in ways that were not possible for the traditional business of the company.
- The SBU should be charged with specific goals regarding the company's e-commerce strategy and integration efforts.

The e-commerce unit, however, may also take on some characteristics of a traditional functional unit. Depending on their breadth, these units are sometimes treated instead as cost centers to serve the business units rather than external customers. In addition to integrating the Web channel with other channels and business units, the unit (whether functional or business unit) may also provide e-commerce solutions to other parts of the company and integrate the company's back-end systems. Some examples of separate business units and the forms they have taken include the following.

- UPS formed a wholly-owned subsidiary, e-Ventures, in 2000 to provide services for small and medium e-commerce companies. The unit operated semi-autonomously but used the same trucks and warehouses as the rest of the company. The unit boosted its capabilities by acquiring a number of smaller logistics firms.
- Tesco built its grocery internet unit out of Tesco Direct, a small unit that began direct retailing in the mid 1990s, and opened a Web site

in 1996. Tesco.com was also a 100 percent–owned subsidiary, although at one point there was discussion of a possible spin-off. Internal investment in the unit was cautious, with an eye on gradual geographical expansion. The unit chose not to build in-house warehouses, instead supplying customer orders directly from the physical stores' shelves. The Web site did, however, offer more heterogeneous product offerings, including music, small electronics, and dishware.

- Wells Fargo runs e-commerce from a very tightly integrated "total business unit" that treats the Internet as another delivery channel. There is strong integration on both the front end and back end, with offline customers automatically signed up for an online account, and aggressive cross-promotion. The unit does not separately track profitability for e-commerce, but it points to lower attrition rates and higher purchase rates as measures of success.

Some successful companies have chosen not to create a separate business unit for e-commerce, instead treating the Web as a co-equal with other sales channels and integrating it throughout the organization. Still others have created a hybrid business unit that combines e-commerce and other parts of the business, such as catalog sales, in a much more limited fashion than full integration. The rationale is that catalog sales and Web sales have much in common, especially in contrast with a physical store channel. Moreover, because of the expenses associated with mailing catalogs and maintaining catalog call centers, an effort to shift catalog customers to the Internet is highly cost-effective. Nordstrom Direct, which evolved after Nordstrom.com was folded back into the parent company, is an example of this structure.[9]

Keeping e-commerce management internal is vital to implementing e-commerce strategy, but the successful implementation of e-commerce must also allow for flexibility in the management structure. The IT backbone that implements back-end systems for e-commerce should also provide the basis for a highly networked organizational structure. As such, the company can reap the benefits of decentralization without incurring the high costs or loss of the advantages of a more centralized and integrated structure.

Outsourcing

Though typically not desirable, outsourcing of IT as a part of e-commerce is not always a harmful decision. In limited contexts, the benefits of outsourcing can outweigh the costs of contradicting the integration paradigm. Back-end capabilities should, however, be developed internally in cases where they are related to a core competence, represent a source of competitive advantage, or involve unique or idiosyncratic activities. To understand those proper contexts, one must examine the range of IT capabilities relevant to e-commerce.

- IT infrastructure is a first priority for a company seeking an integrated e-commerce effort, and speed is a strong consideration. Although a company's legacy systems may have their unique characteristics, the software and hardware in this area is highly imitable and does not represent a likely source of competitive advantage. Therefore, a company should feel equally comfortable outsourcing this task or acquiring the capabilities and handling it internally.[10]
- In functional areas such as payroll and human resources, e-commerce can also provide ample opportunities for cost savings. Software packages in these areas are also commodities and an unlikely source of competitive advantage. If upgrading capabilities in these areas is a part of the overall integration of e-commerce and it is not a core organizational competency, outsourcing may be an acceptable approach. For smaller firms, these commoditized solutions can provide relatively similar, if not superior, capabilities in areas such as payroll and human resources at a fraction of the cost of an in-house approach.[11]
- Logistics is a third area in which a company has a reasonable choice between internal fulfillment and outsourcing. If logistics has been a core competency in traditional commerce, such as was the case with Wal-Mart, it should continue to be handled internally for e-commerce. If, however, fulfillment capabilities cannot be quickly and cost-effectively developed from within, outsourcing may be an acceptable alternative, in that it is unlikely to matter to customers by whom the order is fulfilled.[12]

Despite its spin-off model of e-commerce, Staples showed an understanding of this contrast through its model of IT development. Its IT department focused on solutions that directly impacted the customer, while it outsourced back-end operations to a single vendor. This single-vendor form of outsourcing sometimes increases costs in the short term, but it often saves costs related to future vendor competition and is a good alternative to internal development because of uniformity and clear lines of responsibility. It also facilitates a much easier integration if the company decides to bring the capabilities inside at a later date.[13]

When operational capabilities involve direct interaction with the customer, outsourcing becomes a generally undesirable choice. Web site design and customer service related to the Web site must be core competencies for any large company seeking success in e-commerce.

Failure to develop core competencies in these areas is an indication that a company has not made enough of a commitment or investment in e-commerce. Proceeding without developing these competencies is likely to do considerable damage to the brand name and future customer acquisition and retention efforts.

Web Site Design and Internet Platform

Building a Web platform is an activity that should typically be handled internally. Web site design expertise is widely available and may be acquired if necessary. Though utilizing consultants and Web site design firms can provide some valuable needed guidance and experience, handing the task off completely to a consulting firm often prevents the company from imparting vital business-specific knowledge into building the site. It also lengthens the learning period for employees who will need to understand the site's design, while at the same time handicapping the company's future e-commerce development by not cultivating this knowledge internally.

The design of the site is closely tied to the customer service and support capabilities of the site, which are among the most vital capabilities to develop from within.[14] Many companies that have gone outside the company for Web site design have done so because of the service capabilities provided by their partner. The highest profile examples have been alliances between Amazon and Toys'R'Us, Borders, and Target, among others. No one story describes the relationships with the companies that have partnered with Amazon.

- Toys 'R' Us partnered with Amazon because of its failure to develop internal e-commerce capabilities, especially in the area of fulfillment. Even as a venture capital–funded spinoff, the e-commerce venture of Toys 'R' Us was running out of money and had created too much damage to the company's reputation to grow revenue.
- Borders joined Amazon because they realized that Amazon's first-mover advantage within the bookstore industry prevented Borders from becoming an industry leader in e-commerce capabilities. This union permitted Borders to have a relatively easy-to-maintain digital "storefront" for its traditional brick-and-mortar operations, without competing against Amazon on the electronic front.
- Target's agreement sought to capitalize on Amazon's unique customer-care capabilities while eliminating the need for separate fulfillment partners. Target had rejected the spin-off model of e-commerce initially attempted by competitors Wal-Mart and Kmart but determined that its brand-driven integration strategy would not work without stronger fulfillment capabilities.

These alliances notwithstanding, a company often sacrifices a substantial amount by turning its customer service capabilities over to a third party. Amazon's reputation and capabilities are unique online, and since not every company can hope to strike a similar alliance with Amazon, its example should not be viewed as a generalizable model for e-commerce success. The more reliable approach is to build and acquire the necessary resources to handle customer service from within and integrate both online and physical channels for maximum customer convenience.

PARTICULARS OF E-COMMERCE ALLIANCES

In the previous sections, we have provided a strong rationale for funding, managing, and providing IT solutions for e-commerce from within the organization. Selling part of the e-commerce venture or outsourcing operations to IT firms simply does not usually permit a company to reap the maximum benefits of e-commerce. At times, however, it may be in a company's interest to go outside the firm and form strategic alliances with companies in the same or complementary industries.

As is the case with outsourcing operations, such as the relationships with Amazon, alliances should not generally relate to the company's core competencies.[15] They also should not typically relate to customer interaction activities such as customer service and fulfillment, unless there are clear advantages related to a company's capabilities. In two areas, however, alliances have been very successful in e-commerce: procurement and customer acquisition.

For procurement, alliances can help overcome some of the unresolved issues on the B2B side of e-commerce.[16] Although e-commerce clearly provides a potential for vast savings in purchasing, not all industries have been able to realize these savings. Industry leaders such as Dell, GE, and Wal-Mart have been able to realize these savings, while at the same time sending their competitors scrambling to catch up, as detailed in the following.

- The union of HP and Compaq has provided many challenges and opportunities. However, a major obstacle in the company's competition with Dell has been its attempt to meet Dell's level of productivity by cultivating the type of supplier alliances that have given Dell such an advantage over others. The merged company is hoping that the union of the two companies will allow it to overcome its entrenched supplier methods and improve performance.
- Omnexus is an alliance of many of GE's competitors in the plastics industry. Facing competition from both GE's well-established

Polymerland and pure-play public market PlasticsNet, the founders of Omnexus tried to carve out a position by offering scale (founders included BASF, DuPont, Bayer, and Celanese) while maintaining GE's more private format and hosting value-added services. Omnexus' alliance partners, many of whom have their core competencies in chemicals rather than plastics, maintain some internal control over the venture while having the advantages of a collaboration that may lead to a less costly and more successful strategy.

- The Worldwide Retail Exchange (WWRE) is a large partnership that includes discount retailers Kmart and Target, pharmacies, and a host of specialty retailers. The WWRE allowed Kmart and Target to compete with Wal-Mart on the procurement side because of the sheer scale of the WWRE's buyers. Because the WWRE is integrated with each company's systems, these benefits are achieved without damaging the overall integration for the company, which is especially relevant for Target, which was one of the earliest advocates of full e-commerce integration.

Alliances have also been used to gain access to new customer bases through some of the sites that serve as portals for the Internet. Viewed broadly, this category includes Internet service providers such as AOL, portals such as Yahoo, browser operators like Microsoft, and the increasingly ubiquitous Amazon.com and eBay. Companies in a variety of industries have attempted to draw customers from these central locations to their businesses.

- Office Depot struck a deal with Amazon that allowed it access to the bookstore giant's huge customer base. Unlike deals with Toys 'R' Us and Borders, this deal did not entail Amazon taking over operations for Office Depot. Rather, it is only a complement to the originally successful OfficeDepot.com. The Amazon component of Office Depot is more targeted to the individual consumer than the B2B-friendly OfficeDepot.com.
- Bank One was the first company to partner with Microsoft and its new line of .NET services in 2002. The partnership allows BankOne's online customers easier access to a variety of online services, but it also calls for Microsoft to sell BankOne products through the widely used MSN.com and Hotmail.
- UPS entered a partnership with eBay to allow customers in the consumer to consumer (C2C) transactions easier access to shipping options. The deal was more than simply a link to UPS.com; a special shipping function was integrated directly into eBay's site. UPS was able to access a new customer base in an industry that does not typically lend itself to online marketing.

In each of these deals, the company was able to benefit from an outside alliance without threatening an overall integration strategy. Some of the characteristics of successful e-commerce alliances are:

- Alliances should not be used to substitute for deficiencies in aspects of a company that are core competencies.
- Typically, alliances should not be used in ways directly related to customer interaction.
- Alliances can be used to reinforce B2B relationships for needs such as procurement and support systems.
- Sharing of information, ranging from customer information to production data, is essential in successful alliances.

CONCLUSION

To choose separate equity, management, and IT functions is to choose shortcuts to e-commerce development; they have poor track records. They avoid the challenges an e-commerce strategy must address, and their success in integration and profitability are generally suboptimal. Integration forces companies to address the core strategy, structure, and systems issues and to develop needed core capabilities, which provides a more solid foundation on which to implement an e-commerce strategy. Thus, though separate e-commerce units may be useful for the initial development of an e-commerce operation, they are generally undesirable for the long term. The decision to fully integrate generally has benefits that far outweigh any potential benefits of separation (Exhibit 4.4).

The role of leadership in establishing an integrated structure should not be overlooked. The CEO must be willing to invest resources in e-commerce instead of looking to venture capital or other forms of financing. Managers must commit to innovation and flexibility by allowing traditional systems to be adjusted for e-commerce and must overcome status quo resistance through strong communication. Finally, senior managers must recognize the centrality of IT to both e-commerce and traditional commerce and let this guide the decision to integrate the e-commerce function, rather than blindly outsourcing without maintaining internal control.

This guidance as to e-commerce structure is ultimately just a starting point. Most of the specifics with regard to structure must be decided in the context of the industry, the company's position, and the company's existing structure. The single overriding principle, however, is that structural integration has proven to be the most likely path to e-commerce success. Obtaining these benefits must be at the

Exhibit 4.4
Benefits of E-commerce Integration

Management Concern	Rationale for Separation	Integration Alternative	Benefits from Integration
Financing e-commerce	Company feels it can't raise investment capital fast enough and turns to IPO.	Raise funding from within or from banks.	Maintains control over long-term financial future of e-commerce.
Overseeing e-commerce	Company fears effects of traditional business practices on e-commerce venture.	Create specially designed management structures and systems for e-commerce venture.	Transfer of traditional company's competitive advantages to e-commerce.
Hiring for e-commerce	Senior management lacks experience and wants to attract talent.	Hire experienced managers to join traditional management team.	Knowledge sharing between traditional business and e-commerce benefits both.
Managing e-commerce	Company wants to encourage focus and innovation with separate management structure.	Encourage innovation from within through structures and systems including rewards.	Coordinated strategies benefit both traditional and e-commerce.
Obtaining IT capabilities for e-commerce	Company believes that traditional systems are antiquated and incompatible with e-commerce.	Acquire small IT firm or engage consultants to help build new systems.	Traditional business will benefit from e-commerce information systems, and control over core competencies is retained.

heart of all decisions related to organizational structure and design for e-commerce.

In the end, the elements of structure to be considered by any firm implementing an e-commerce strategy include:

- A company's traditional business structure is an important consideration when implementing an e-commerce initiative. It should be viewed as an input to a new company structure that is more supportive of e-commerce.
- Commitment and consistency are important to achieving an integrated e-commerce solution throughout the company.
- Financing should be kept internal, avoiding IPOs and venture capitalists, in order to avoid problems related to integration and dependency.
- Separate business units are an acceptable short-term solution to implementing an e-commerce strategy. However, an integrated

and internalized e-commerce structure should be the primary goal of such a strategy.

- Outsourcing, externally designed Web platforms, and other alliances can help resolve deficient aspects of a company's e-commerce initiative. However, these tools should typically not be used to implement elements of an e-commerce strategy that are core company competencies.

CHAPTER 5

Management Systems for E-Commerce Success

Over the past five years, e-commerce has rapidly evolved from an experiment for trend-conscious businesses to a vital channel in the business world that no company can afford to ignore. In response to this change, there has been a plethora of studies on the subject of e-commerce, most of which have focused on the formulation of e-commerce strategies. More recently, the importance of structure has come to the forefront, as the dot.com bust caused a reexamination of failed e-commerce structures and as a trend toward integration has spread throughout business.

The importance of management control systems in e-commerce, however, has often been overlooked by both managers and observers of managerial practices. Although studies of traditional business readily acknowledge the importance of various systems, studies of e-commerce have given rather scant attention to systems, in part because the early e-commerce environment embraced two opposing positions on systems.

One view was that e-commerce changes everything and that traditional systems were obsolete. Many e-commerce startups reveled in their rejection of traditional business systems, embraced creativity as the ultimate virtue, and ran companies that barely resembled traditional businesses. At the most trivial level, this meant behavioral changes, such as the rejection of dress codes and cubicles in the work environment. More important, it comprised the rejection of traditional business models and operating procedures and traditional measures of success. In the stock market, these changes were reflected in huge market capitalizations that had no relation to company profitability. Many traditional companies strived to imitate the startup model and gave their spin-offs similar operating rules.

The second position, held by many traditional companies less convinced of the validity of the e-commerce model, was that e-commerce changed nothing. To many corporate boards, e-commerce was derided as "just technology," and this condescension was reflected in the type of systems that were set up for e-commerce ventures. Spending was tightly controlled from above, budgeting had to conform to outdated corporate standards, innovation was discouraged, and few incentives were created for employees working in e-commerce. Often, e-commerce would be a part-time project or diversion for both employees and the executives charged with overseeing it.

We now know that neither of these visions is appropriate for the creation of an e-commerce business or for e-commerce systems. The values that underlie those two visions are certain to doom any e-commerce venture, regardless of the specific strategy or structure. With our new understanding of the proper role of e-commerce, it is necessary to articulate how proper management control systems are critical for a successful e-commerce venture.

As with strategy and structure, the relationship between e-commerce systems and the traditional business is dynamic. There is an ever-changing dynamic relationship between corporate strategy, structure, and systems and e-commerce strategy, structure, and systems. The systems used to implement an e-commerce strategy will have implications throughout the company and its traditional business, and the effects of changed policies and regulations will not be limited to e-commerce. Our general e-commerce business model highlights the importance of e-commerce systems and the relation of these systems to corporate and e-commerce strategy and structure and to organizational systems (Exhibit 5.1).

Owing to this dynamism, commenting on e-commerce systems requires two separate but equally important perspectives. One is the extent to which traditional systems must be altered, augmented, or eliminated to create a business environment in which e-commerce success is possible. The second perspective examines how a focus on the success of e-commerce can bring greater effectiveness to the governance of the traditional business.

These e-commerce systems decisions fall into four broad areas: information practices, human resources, measurement processes, and customer service. First, a company's information practices can become the bridge from appropriate corporate culture to successful individual and organizational behavior. Though strong leadership and resource com-

Exhibit 5.1
Antecedents and Consequences of E-Commerce Success

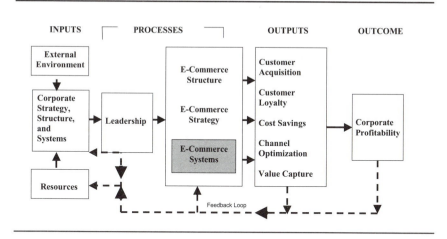

mitment can help to create a culture in which IT knowledge and stature are sufficient for starting e-commerce, long-term e-commerce success requires more. The company must categorically promote information sharing and information transparency, instill a sense of urgency, and enable real-time and flexible decision-making processes. The company can also benefit from e-commerce by putting these information practices to use throughout the value chain. E-commerce provides opportunities for cost savings and speed improvements at every stage of the value chain.

Human resources policy and practices is the second area of systems that needs to be carefully managed for e-commerce success. Because e-commerce is characterized by speed, risk-taking, and new business models, a company must create the proper incentives for those overseeing e-commerce. For the CIO and for all IT and e-commerce personnel, employees must sometimes be rewarded outside the traditional compensation structure. Managing incentives and rewards to give organizations equity and the appropriate incentives for creativity, flexibility, and innovation is often a significant challenge. E-commerce can benefit the traditional business in the hiring practices of HR. Using the Internet to stimulate job applications can bring both efficiency and a more IT-knowledgeable applicant base.

Measurement is another area in which the nature of e-commerce demands rethinking traditional systems. E-commerce facilitates improvement in measurement systems throughout the organization, allowing a better flow of timely information to decision makers and an aggregation and disaggregation of data never before possible. It permits an analysis of causal relationships and the business model to better understand the payoffs of various corporate actions.

Finally, the systems that govern customer relationships must adjust to implement the important customer service aspects of an e-commerce strategy. Providing service at all times and across channels makes unique demands on the parts of the company closest to the customer. But e-commerce also provides unprecedented capabilities to learn about customers, their behavior, and their interaction with offerings. Mining this customer data is an area that is still maturing and offers new competitive advantages.

INFORMATION PRACTICES

For e-commerce to be successful, it is necessary but not sufficient that members of the organization are competent and confident in their use of IT. Strong leadership and investment can bring an organization to that stage, but systems must be created to harness the power of IT for organizational integration. It has recently been emphasized that interactive control systems in traditional business must focus on constantly changing information. These systems provide the sensing and monitoring that is necessary whenever strategic uncertainties are high. In most businesses today, more interactive control systems are needed as strategic uncertainties have been increasing.[1] In e-commerce, these systems become increasingly central to the successful implementation of strategy.

A new policy on information practices must become a central component of the company's systems. Information should be transparent and the sharing of information facilitated. Organizational boundaries must not impede the flow of information. An integration strategy cannot be properly implemented if information about e-commerce stalls within the e-commerce unit and is not disseminated widely. Ideally, internal processes are developed in-house with substantial consultation and communication; obstacles are easily recognized, understood, and dealt with, internally and quickly. Companies such as Amazon and Office Depot not only have garnered more efficient business practices because of their internal development, but also have been able to expand into other markets such as technology consulting and Web design because of their in-house expertise.[2]

Companies can also use the implementation of an e-commerce strategy as a starting point for proper information practices. Prior to moving online, 3M had a fragmented information system that made it difficult to cross-sell to existing customers. Even having the same customer listed in different systems had additional costs. After moving online, the company created a $20 million data warehouse to store all information, as part of a larger restructuring of information systems.[3]

Senior management must set the example of open information practices and transparency, even when the information is bad news for the company or reflects negatively on an individual or business unit. Problems should be discussed openly, without fear of repercussions. As appropriate, information on the company's goals, measures, and progress should be made available to all employees and the public through the company's Web site. This information is increasingly available to interested parties, and by making it transparent, a company may build trust with its constituent groups. In addition, it is often beneficial to increase the information flow to the public to ensure that accurate information is communicated, rather than to risk inaccurate information being made public by a third party.

Further, many organizational processes should be restructured to fully take advantage of e-commerce. In particular, e-commerce should encourage and facilitate companies to move away from strict hierarchical reporting in some areas and move toward the use of cross-functional remote teams. By collaborating with other business functions and units, the e-commerce initiative is likely to encounter less resistance in the traditional business.

Processes should also be adaptable and flexible enough to respond to changes in real-time information. Numerous virtual organization techniques serve these purposes, including:

- cross-functional teams that form themselves
- teams that may go into and out of existence regularly
- use of both in-person and remote meetings
- teams that span organizational boundaries
- encouragement of innovation through mutual trust
- self-governance
- harnessing global resources to solve local problems[4]

An organization that utilizes these processes should then be able to assemble teams to innovate or to resolve challenges associated with e-commerce. Most important, all these techniques should be fully consistent with an integration strategy, eliminating any need for moving e-commerce outside the organization.

By upgrading these information practices, a company positions itself to make significant improvements throughout the value chain. For many companies, value chain management is an integral part of the e-commerce strategy. But even for those companies that focus primarily on selling online, subtle improvements can be made with minimal extra cost and effort. Thus, improving information practices can create significant benefits for sales, distribution, and procurement, along with various other processes throughout the organization.

Cisco has used its real-time capabilities to create supplier-side processes that vastly improve its supply-chain management. Cisco and its suppliers and manufacturers share extensive information on product quality. This allows Cisco to measure the number of defective products while they are still in the supplier's possession, rather than after they have been delivered. In turn, the supplier can make faster adjustments in its manufacturing process to minimize future quality problems.[5]

Dell has mastered the use of e-commerce in limiting the amount of inventory kept on hand. Many component parts such as monitors and peripherals are never kept in inventory by Dell, and their movement and distribution is entirely handled by email communication. But even for parts retained by Dell, real-time ordering forecasts are sent to suppliers to minimize the inventory and buffer stocks on a cycle as short as two hours. This relationship with suppliers, coupled with its information practices, also permits a *negative* cash conversion cycle.[6]

At the delivery end of the supply chain, Tesco spanned traditional organizational boundaries to create the most efficient delivery process. While many in the grocery industry mimicked the Amazon model by attempting to deliver from large, high-tech warehouses, Tesco chose to deliver directly from stock at local physical locations. While this limited the potential delivery zone, it also saved Tesco the effort and resources of building expensive warehouses with uncertain profitability. Delivering from the store meant no separate inventories and no need for entirely new processes.[7]

Nike, Inc. recently implemented a supply-chain system linking the company with its manufacturing partners. Before these system changes, 30 percent of Nike's total volume of shoe orders were based on estimates; now, only 3 percent of the orders are guesswork, because of better forecasting and planning.[8]

Whirlpool Corporation has linked every Whirlpool factory and sales site worldwide through e-business software, allowing factories and sales sites to coordinate with suppliers and key retail partners. This has reduced inventories and increased vital communication.[9]

Krispy Kreme Doughnut is another company that has used e-commerce to its advantage by devising an intranet network linking its stores. The Web system tracks doughnut mix, doles out the right colors of sprinkles, monitors managers' decisions, and permits users to fix errors such as damaged goods, by allowing replacements to be sent. The system allows employees to focus more on customer service, reduce problem orders, and increase productivity.[10]

For proper information practices to improve the success of e-commerce implementations:

- Organizational boundaries should not represent an impediment to the free flow of information in a company.
- Company leadership must set the example of open information practices.
- Companies must be willing to move away from strict hierarchical reporting systems.

HUMAN RESOURCES

Management of personnel is also central to the implementation of e-commerce strategy. Even in the aftermath of the fallout of the dot.com bust in the stock market, e-commerce is still inexorably linked to the notions of large performance bonuses, stock options, Silicon Valley whiz kids, and new-wave office environments. It is still necessary to find ways to develop and retain employees who are creative, flexible, and innovative—in addition to competent and diligent. In this light, a company must endeavor to put systems in place that retain key personnel and make strategic new hires throughout the course of an e-commerce venture.

Designing appropriate compensation systems is instrumental both in attaining initial e-commerce success and in retaining the leaders and employees who made that success possible. Above all, compensation systems must be properly aligned with strategy and structure. Symbolically, the CIO's compensation is one of the more important decisions a company dedicated to implementing e-commerce will encounter. CIO compensation should be in line with that of other members of senior management to signal respect for the IT function as a creator of value. Failure to fully and explicitly acknowledge the value of IT and e-commerce contradicts the other messages that must be communicated for e-commerce to succeed.

At lower levels of the company, compensation systems have more practical consequences for alignment. Some companies believe that compensating e-commerce managers the same as managers in traditional commerce fails to create proper incentives for e-commerce and value creation. Differential compensation sometimes creates an incentive to cannibalize from the company's traditional channels as well as more effectively and more quickly to execute an e-commerce strategy.

But, e-commerce compensation should be tied to the overall success of the venture company-wide, rather than rewarding performance within an individual unit. This is particularly true when the company is seeking full integration, because it helps ensure cooperation between departments.

Companies must be prepared to manage the channel conflict that often arises when e-commerce begins to cannibalize the traditional business. Cannibalization is necessary to optimize the use of each channel, and an integration strategy cannot succeed if traditional business units do not accept it. Companies must design compensation systems that gradually shift compensation toward the creation of value, particularly in businesses heavily dependent on salespersons who work on a commission basis. Traditional business units must be placated not by compensating inefficiencies, but by carving out new roles that optimize the use of each channel and produce a successfully integrated and profitable multi-channel coordinated effort.

At aviation parts distributor Aviall Inc., a few weeks after an upper-management shakeup brought in a new CEO in 1996, a new Web-based order-entry system was introduced. In response, Aviall's 300 sales reps feared their jobs were at stake and told customers not to use it. Despite the benefits to the consumer that were realized through the Web-based system, the role of the sales reps had not been modified to permit them to survive such a drastic change in company strategy. As companies develop and implement e-commerce strategies, the Internet must be examined and the pre-existing channels must be modified in a way that complements the e-commerce initiative.[11]

While compensation systems must often be reevaluated and reconstructed in e-commerce implementations, hiring practices can be improved simply by using the same Web site that showcases other e-commerce activities. Hiring online can significantly reduce advertising costs associated with print and other listings. It can also ensure that potential applicants possess at least some skills in using the Internet and implies a confidence and understanding of the importance of e-commerce. Cisco is one company that greatly improved its hiring process by advertising openings online. Further, special attention should be paid to HR policies covering to those who work in e-commerce and IT. Companies should recognize the fluidity of the IT labor market and must often create more flexible labor policies than for other employees.[12]

To ensure that proper human resources practices are employed in an e-commerce implementation;

- Compensation systems for traditional and e-commerce personnel should be properly aligned with the company's new e-commerce strategy.
- Companies must be prepared for channel conflict due to cannibalization of traditional company segments into an e-commerce venture.
- Hiring practices must fully take advantage of the exposure opportunity and cost savings made available by Internet hiring.

MEASUREMENT

Strong measurement practices form one of the cornerstones of good systems, particularly in e-commerce. Performance measures for e-commerce must overcome the uncertainty and unique dynamics associated with the Internet and must be more frequently adjusted in response to real-time information. With these considerations, no company should simply extend its existing performance measures to an e-commerce venture. Still, long-term cost differentials must be balanced with other financial and nonfinancial measures and leading and lagging indicators that are particularly useful for successful e-commerce implementations.

The information systems of the 1990s gave CEOs a new method of accessing, analyzing, and reporting on the accountability of their organization. The systems developed during this time of advancement in information technology helped to create a more streamlined capability for centralized accountability. The variety of data made available to a company at that time ranged from corporate-level results to the small-scale measurements of performance that enabled management to recognize advantages and potential problems in real-time.

E-Commerce transforms these capabilities. Like the root system of a massive tree, IT accountability systems helped management reach and observe every aspect of their business. With the addition of e-commerce to a pre-existing IT accountability system, companies can simplify access to previously collected information for those within the company and for external stakeholders, including partners, customers, and investors. New information could be created and both financial and nonfinancial measures could be integrated into the decision-making process. The information could also be easily and quickly aggregated and disaggregated to facilitate various decisions. Managers could now measure inputs, processes, outputs, and outcomes in ways never before possible.

Cisco's new systems permit outsiders to view on its Web site not only its general business plan but also the company's performance statistics at any given moment. Seamlessness between internal IT systems and e-commerce gives Cisco the ability to provide such information with relatively little effort. This transparency between internal and external systems also helped Cisco endure many of the pitfalls associated with the technology bust by expanding the role of e-commerce to replace human positions throughout the company.

But e-commerce can be used for more than simply replacing employees. Instead, the information made available through a well-developed e-commerce initiative can empower employees at every level of business. Improved measurement is a key component. Management receives information in a timely manner, which lets it act on up-to-date measures of performance, while lower-level employees can access information at any time and take the initiative based on that information, with or without direct managerial direction.

Among the most important aspects of e-commerce as it applies to system management and measurement is maintaining consistency across all company lines. A company implementing a new e-commerce solution should ensure consistency among accounting systems, information technology systems, and e-commerce systems and related measures. However, the implementation of an e-commerce solution also necessitates working to ensure compatibility between the systems of business partners using unified e-commerce solutions. The uniquely advantageous relationship between Dell and its suppliers would not be possible without seamless internal and external systems that enable a free flow of information and measures between companies. E-commerce can facilitate consistency of information and measurements by cascading information throughout the organization and then externally to other stakeholders.

In addition to measuring the performance of the business, e-commerce brings added importance to measuring the value and functionality of operations. Most e-commerce strategies will have a strong operational component, including cost savings from value chain management and cuts in labor costs for the online channel. Operational measures should be tracked by some dedicated resource and balanced between financial and nonfinancial assessments of operational performance.[13] This analysis can lead to a better understanding of the payoffs of investment in e-commerce initiatives.

CUSTOMER RELATIONSHIPS

Under traditional business models, it may be sufficient to offer customer service during normal business hours, either at physical locations or over the phone. E-commerce dramatically changes those expectations both in terms of company strategy and the customer's perspective. Near-universal and constant customer service availability is expected for almost any viable e-commerce strategy. Companies must re-examine their customer service practices and make numerous key decisions in moving toward universal availability. Two of the main considerations are the distribution of response tasks between human and automated systems and the operating hours for human responses. Each of these include trade-offs among speed, cost, convenience, and efficiency.

Most e-commerce ventures have developed some FAQ (frequently asked questions) function on their Web sites. This function may consist of rudimentary inquiries only or a highly sophisticated taxonomy of nearly every conceivable question. The nature of the offering and the Web site dictates how sophisticated the FAQs should be, but no company can exhaust the list of possible questions.

The challenge then becomes how to provide service to customers who are dissatisfied with the FAQs. A company may choose to provide immediate or delayed email support to customers or may offer a phone line for further inquiries. The company must weigh the value of instant response and satisfaction to the customer against the added costs associated with phone banks or with rapid and 24/7 email response. Some pure-play companies like Half.com chose to keep the process entirely online and not offer phone service. For traditional companies, however, this strategy is more difficult, as it can inundate the traditional business phone lines with Internet inquiries.

Delta Airlines, on the other hand, was able to reduce its phone volume and increase its status among elite customers by moving reservation information online while simultaneously implementing a wireless initiative. Delta first identified such a program as "nice to have" but not a necessity, but the company quickly recognized the appeal of wireless capabilities to its elite customers by providing quick access to vast amounts of information. Implementing this program was not only a cost-saving move, but also a successful effort to appeal to customers who desired this level of functionality.[14]

For companies that do provide phone service in addition to their FAQs and Internet support, a decision must be made on availability. Limiting phone support to normal business hours reduces some of the value added associated with the Web site. On the other hand, labor costs may not justify 24/7 phone service for industries that offer commodity goods. More technical industries, B2B companies, and companies with customized and personalized Internet-related offerings should carefully consider offering a 24/7 service.

Another aspect of customer service practices is the development and implementation of policies on shipping, delivery, and returns. In particular, companies that use physical branches as part of a bricks-and-clicks strategy must not neglect proper training on the traditional commerce side necessary to facilitate e-commerce developments and service. Customer service representatives in physical branches must be thoroughly familiar with the Web site, its function, and its policies.

While e-commerce requires changes and enhancement to customer service policies, it also affords most companies excellent opportunities to refine marketing strategies, selling practices, pricing, and Web site design by observing customer behavior. Physical branches have more limited opportunities to collect customer data, particularly data from sites where customers can impart complaints or grievances. When customers shop online, however, their every mouse click is potentially revealing and useful for future improvements in e-commerce service.

Although these methods require substantial analysis, companies can draw strong implications and direction about customer behavior from this data. Unused search results may indicate a problem with the search engine. Aborted purchases may indicate that the checkout procedure is unclear or too time-consuming. Consistent nonpurchase of a product may indicate that more precise information is needed to inspire consumer confidence.

Corporations must be willing and able to redesign their Web sites and refine customer processes based on the gathered information as well as direct feedback from the customers. Since convenience is a prime source of competitive advantage, problems with customer service systems must be addressed immediately. Although shutting down the Web site is undesirable, important changes should be made by closing the site for a few hours in nonpeak time and by warning the customers in advance of this downtime.

Thus, to effectively manage and enhance customer service attributes,

- Companies with an Internet presence should provide any information that a customer might need while online.
- Corporate Web sites should incorporate some form of direct contact mechanism, whether it is as simple as a service phone number or as advanced as online chat capabilities.
- Companies should ensure that the Web site easily connects to any other aspect of the company service that a customer might need information about, ranging from traditional brick-and-mortar locations to shipping policies.

CONCLUSION

Implementing an e-commerce strategy, especially one focused on full corporate integration, is a challenging task, owing in part to the entrenchment of many behaviors, systems, and processes within traditional units. Attempting to impose an entirely new set of systems in companies can often promote e-commerce and jump-start integration efforts. It also risks destroying value in the company by altering many of the fundamental ways people work. Yet, attempting to begin an e-commerce venture under the same systems as used in traditional commerce is a dubious idea. E-commerce is not compatible with many existing systems, as many of these systems were developed for an industrial age before e-commerce was conceived.

Exhibit 5.2
Organizational Changes Needed for and Enabled by E-Commerce Systems

Systems Focus	Changes Needed for E-Commerce	Improvements Enabled by E-Commerce
Information Practices	Processes that promote networking and information sharing	Demand and supply chain management
Human Resources	Incentives built into compensation systems	Online hiring
Measurement Practices	Adjustments made to performance measures throughout organization	Operational measures aid focus and improvement in organizational decision making
Customer Relationships	Improved service practices	Customer data applications

Companies must find a proper balance between change and continuity, knowing when the traditional business impedes e-commerce and when e-commerce can improve the traditional business. Implementing these systems well can create substantial corporate value through both the e-commerce and traditional commerce environments. Exhibit 5.2 summarizes the dual effects of e-commerce in these systems.

As more and more companies recognize the full range of potential e-commerce strategies and their benefits, the battle for success is increasingly being fought on the implementation side. And while prescriptions for structure can be concisely subsumed under the label of "integration," the systems needed to implement an integration strategy are spread throughout all functions of an organization.

Information practices, human resource management, measurement, and customer relationships are all part of the equation. By transforming its systems in these areas, a company can maximize the benefits of e-commerce, minimize the associated risks, and put itself on the path to a fully integrated organization. A summary of the elements of the systems, the impacts in the implementation process, and the outcomes in overall company performance can be seen in Exhibit 5.3.

Exhibit 5.3
Management Systems for E-Commerce Success

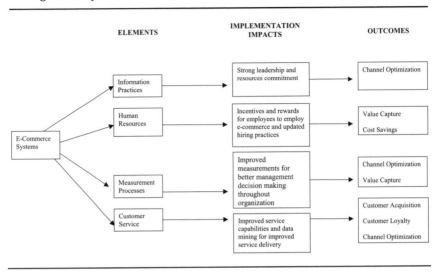

CHAPTER 6

Measuring the Payoffs of E-Commerce Investments

We have examined how various organizational inputs and processes can impact the outputs of e-commerce. We have examined leadership, strategy, structure, and systems both in the corporation generally and related specifically to e-commerce. We have also seen how these key factors of success can be successfully managed in a formal process to improve customer acquisitions, customer loyalty, cost savings, channel optimization, and value creation. Although these outputs are important, the resource allocation decision should rely on understanding the impact of e-commerce decisions and actions on the outcome of improved corporate profitability (Exhibit 6.1).

Many researchers and managers have recognized the need to identify and measure the impacts of corporate actions and to provide a better analysis of the return on investment (ROI) of e-commerce expenditures.[1] However, the appropriate metrics have not been well developed. The framework presented here provides the necessary specificity to identify both the causal relationships that lead to e-commerce success, and related measures. In this way, both general managers and IT and e-commerce professionals can more effectively evaluate the success of e-commerce and the potential and actual payoffs of e-commerce investments.

Managers now can also examine the interrelationships among the characteristics of e-commerce success discussed here. The causal linkage analysis illustrates the importance of leadership, strategy, structure,

Exhibit 6.1
Antecedents and Consequences of E-Commerce Success

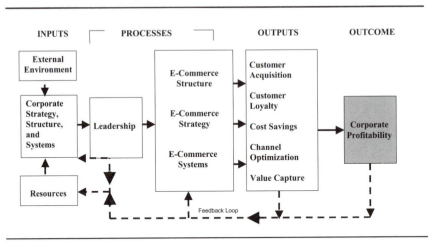

and systems and highlights the specific managerial actions that lead to success.

Some writers have suggested the need for more measurements of the effectiveness of IT. They note that corporations have overlooked economic rationality in justifying IT expenditures and instead have leaned toward a strategy that resembled an arms race, where firms acquire the best and most recent technologies to outpace others, regardless of the results.[2] To assess the payoffs of e-commerce investments, companies must implement systems that evaluate the impact of e-commerce initiatives on financial performance and the trade-offs that must be made among competing organizational constraints and barriers to implementation. These systems assist senior executives as they develop an e-commerce strategy and allocate corporate resources to support that strategy. The systems also assist e-commerce managers to evaluate the trade-offs and decide which projects provide the largest net benefit to both short-term financial performance and the long-term success of the firm. The careful identification and measurement of the payoffs also permits e-commerce and IT managers to demonstrate the impact on corporate profitability and value creation. It also provides information for better corporate resource allocation decisions in the CEO's and CFO's offices, based on a better understanding of the ROI—including a fuller understanding of the benefits and costs of e-commerce. Hence, to implement their e-commerce strategy, companies are faced with a significant challenge: to quantify the link between corporate actions in e-commerce and corporate financial performance.

Indeed, only by making the "business case" for e-commerce expenditures can managers truly integrate potential e-commerce impacts into their business strategies. Yet, many companies have failed to make a case for e-commerce initiatives. Instead, they have often acted because they had a feeling that it was the right thing to do or because their competitors were making the leap into e-commerce ventures. However, projects put into place for these reasons alone are vulnerable to cost overruns and poor ROI, changes in senior management, or shifting corporate or consumer priorities.

To present a clear business case for e-commerce initiatives, senior managers need to identify the metrics of e-commerce performance and how that performance impacts overall long-term corporate profitability. This increased attention to the thorough identification and measurement of the metrics of e-commerce is echoed in popular measurement frameworks such as the popular strategic management system "balanced scorecard."[3] Frameworks such as balanced scorecard and shareholder value analysis focus on the causal relationships and linkages within organizations and the actions managers can implement to improve both customer and corporate profitability and drive increased value.[4] However, substantial work is required to establish the relationships that relate specifically to e-commerce strategies. Undeniably, the identification and measurement of the impact of e-commerce strategies is particularly difficult as they are usually linked to long time horizons, a high level of uncertainty, and impacts that are often difficult to quantify. But this analysis is important to improve resource allocation, decision making, and profitability.

In recent years, companies have placed increasing importance on the development of performance metrics to better measure and manage e-commerce performance. Software programs and information systems have been developed to provide a broader set of measurement tools to incorporate into new strategic management systems. Although the need for performance measures for e-commerce has been identified, a large number of specific metrics have not been proposed. E-commerce analysis has typically been operating without measures that permit an effective evaluation of e-commerce benefits, success, or value. This lack of performance metrics has meant a lack of both actual and perceived accountability for firm e-commerce operations to various stakeholders.[5]

This chapter examines how companies can properly measure the benefits and value resulting from e-commerce-based initiatives. It also examines how companies can make a compelling business case for e-commerce programs. This chapter can help senior managers understand how to measure the value of e-commerce and understand the payoffs of e-commerce investments. Its purpose is to answer the question, "Is it worth it?" for companies deciding to start or expand e-commerce projects.

This quandary is compounded as senior managers consider the high costs typically associated with e-commerce and the seemingly small percentage of e-commerce or IT projects that succeed. Sometimes the projects are flawed, but often the measures of success are flawed.

Examples abound where companies have attempted e-commerce initiatives and have either failed dramatically or have incurred costs that far outweighed the gains. The case examples in this book illustrate this point. Though some would suggest that those failures occurred when companies were not so well centered on ensuring that IT-related funds were well spent, companies today face similar questions about the value of their e-commerce initiatives.

For most companies, it is not a question of whether or not to invest in e-commerce, but when and how: Should it be a large amount up front, or perhaps a smaller expenditure at a later date? Such decisions are critical and difficult. Key to making these decisions is understanding the causal relationships and identifying and measuring the success of the specific actions that managers can take to drive e-commerce success.

ENSURING E-COMMERCE SUCCESS: IDENTIFYING KEY INPUTS AND PROCESSES

Many decisions related to the operations of the company significantly affect the success of all e-commerce initiatives, including decisions related to leadership, strategy, structure, and systems. In this section, determinants of e-commerce success are identified. As they are essential to superior e-commerce performance, these success factors become the foundation for rigorous performance evaluation systems for e-commerce.

The main model describes the inputs, processes, outputs, and outcomes of e-commerce activities (Exhibit 6.2). These are further articulated as e-commerce objectives within the e-commerce causal model of performance. Corporations must make important choices regarding the formulation and implementation of e-commerce strategies in relation to the overall external environment and corporate resources, strategy, structure, and systems (inputs). Other factors, such as leadership and e-commerce strategy, e-commerce structure, and e-commerce systems (processes) also significantly affect the performance and success of e-commerce initiatives. The consequences and success of the company's actions on these inputs and processes impact

Exhibit 6.2

E-Commerce Causal Model of Performance: E-Commerce Objectives

Outcomes	Long-term Corporate Profitability
Outputs	Customer Acquisition Customer Loyalty and Retention Cost Savings: Related to customer and supplier interactions Channel Optimization: Increased site traffic and sales Value Capture: Increased e-commerce profits
Processes	Leadership: Commitment and focus on e-commerce initiatives E-Commerce Structure: Integration into business unit structure E-Commerce Strategy: Coherent and aligned strategy E-Commerce Systems: Appropriate processes for effective implementation
Inputs	Resources: Adequate capital and people Corporate Structure: Appropriate organizational structure Corporate Strategy: Alignment with type of products offered, customers served, and competitive positioning Corporate Systems: Suitable training, information, and processes External Environment: Adapted to external forces

various outputs, including improvement in customer acquisition and loyalty, in cost reduction, in channel optimization, and in overall value capture. If the strategy formulation and implementation is successful, these outputs should ultimately be seen in improved overall corporate profitability (outcome).

After carefully identifying the specific e-commerce objectives, the drivers of success must be defined. These help specify more precisely the keys to e-commerce success and the actions that managers must take to improve corporate profitability.

Managers must make many choices. The uses of management control levers and performance measurement and management systems typically affect the implementation of e-commerce strategies. The objectives, the drivers, and the metrics related to e-commerce success should be part of a clear articulation of the causal relationships leading from the inputs to the processes and then flowing to the desired outputs and outcomes. It is important to identify and communicate these causal links throughout the organization to guide the formulation and implementation of e-commerce strategies. The causal linkage map of drivers (Exhibit 6.3) is useful to ensure that all necessary actions are taken to achieve success, that unnecessary actions are not taken, and that all employees understand their critical roles.

Exhibit 6.3
E-Commerce Causal Model of Performance: E-Commerce Drivers

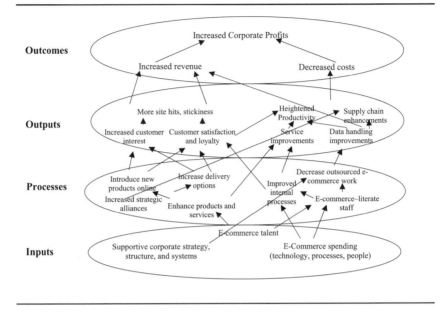

INPUTS: EXTERNAL ENVIRONMENT, CORPORATE RESOURCES, STRATEGIES, STRUCTURES, AND SYSTEMS

As discussed earlier, in the past many companies made decisions related to e-commerce with an arms-race mentality, where the focus was on the competition rather than the potential benefits of the new technology. In the current business climate, with increased focus on corporate accountability and efficiency, it has become increasingly important to estimate and monitor the costs of an e-commerce project in comparison to the benefits likely to accrue. When considering e-commerce ventures, it is crucial that senior managers fully evaluate the external environment and the resources, strategies, structures, and systems already present in the company to determine an initiative's fit and its likelihood of success.

External Environment

Though many inputs to e-commerce success are controllable by corporate managers, some inputs constrain many corporate activities, require significant corporate adaptation, and influence success. The external environment may include changes in the business environment, the economy, technological developments, competitors, suppliers, and customer needs. Even though companies may have coherent strategies, structures, and systems and adequate corporate capital and labor resources for e-commerce success, changes in the external environment can be an important input that will significantly impact corporate decisions.

Corporate Resources

The most important corporate resources within an organization are its people and its capital. In determining whether a corporation has the capabilities and resources to support new or expanded e-commerce operations, it is necessary to look at the people and capital that currently exist in the corporation. Are the company's employees highly motivated and trained? Do they have the skills necessary for success? Such questions convey the conduciveness of a company's employees and organization to the changes and challenges that accompany an escalation in focus on e-commerce. From a capital perspective, if a firm is already overextended and short on funding, it may have trouble allocating sufficient funds for a major e-commerce initiative. The availability of financial resources is also dependent on the commitment of the senior management to new or expanded e-commerce initiatives. Without adequate financial resources, these ventures cannot succeed. Thus, corporate resources are a critical input for e-commerce success.

Corporate Strategies

The development of e-commerce strategies must fit within an overall corporate strategy. Thus, though the model is dynamic and corporate strategy may be altered by the development of e-commerce, the corporate strategy remains an important input to the formulation and implementation of an e-commerce strategy. Companies make very different choices as to geographical diversity, product type, product mix, customer type, level of service, and pricing. These choices not only impact corporate strategy but also, as discussed earlier, significantly affect e-commerce strategy.

Corporate Structures

An organization's corporate structure plays a big part in determining the organization of e-commerce operations within it. Whether a company has a large number of strategic business units or networks across a wide geographical area with many different languages will influence many e-commerce decisions. Whether the company is more or less decentralized with independent business units and whether the organizational structure is arranged by geography, by product type, by customer type, by channel, or with a matrix will influence the choice of e-commerce strategy and implementation. These structures become inputs to the e-commerce strategy, structure, systems, and leadership necessary for e-commerce success.

Corporate Systems

A company's corporate systems are highly relevant in weighing the appropriateness of a new or expanded e-commerce venture. The corporate systems related to information flow, human resources, compensation, management control, measurement, and others will affect the choice of e-commerce strategy, structure, and systems.

PROCESSES: LEADERSHIP, E-COMMERCE STRATEGIES, STRUCTURES, AND SYSTEMS

Once the viability of e-commerce initiatives is determined, by evaluating the inputs available in an organization, senior managers who are planning and developing e-commerce programs can focus on the processes that drive superior e-commerce performance and connect the inputs to e-commerce success. Four main processes are critical for e-commerce success: leadership, e-commerce strategy, e-commerce structure, and e-commerce systems. The managers' effective use of these processes will determine the outputs and outcomes.

Leadership

A company's leadership must be both knowledgeable about e-commerce and committed to the e-commerce venture for it to succeed. Senior managers must provide full support to all e-commerce initiatives and communicate that support throughout the company. If a company cannot secure strong public support of e-commerce programs at the senior management level, then even though an e-commerce program may be installed effectively by technical staff or consultants, it is unlikely to reach its potential.

E-Commerce Strategy

E-commerce success is dependent on a well-formulated and well-executed e-commerce strategy. The strategy must be consistent with both corporate strategy, structure, and systems, and e-commerce structure and systems. Its alignment with these other inputs and processes is critical to success. The company's choice of the number of products and services that it wants to provide online, the costs and prices related to its online offerings, the customer profile, and the product and service capabilities the firm already has are just some of the factors that will affect the e-commerce strategy. These and the other strategic choices described in chapter 3 will then impact the company's success in customer acquisition, retention, and loyalty, channel optimization, and overall value creation.

E-Commerce Structure

Choices about how a company decides to design and implement its e-commerce structure are key process issues that companies must address in relation to their e-commerce initiatives. Factors critical for this decision, such as the level of outsourcing appropriate for the company, the relationships the company wants to develop with partners, the existing organizational structure, and the level of desired e-commerce integration, affect the ultimate outcome of the e-commerce initiative on overall corporate profitability.

E-Commerce Systems

To ensure that highly qualified employees and proper processes are in place to meet a company's stakeholders' needs, senior managers must develop and implement appropriate systems for e-commerce. E-commerce system issues such as employee e-commerce literacy, measurement, and data collection are part of the processes pertinent to e-commerce. The effects of senior managers putting systems in place to best meet their employee, customer, partner, and other stakeholders' needs extend far beyond items such as lower costs and more timely customer service systems, to heightened productivity and greater sales. The systems move the company toward decreasing overall organizational costs and increasing company revenues, with an ultimate goal of increased corporate profitability.

MEASURING E-COMMERCE SUCCESS

CIOs often suggest that better measures of the payoffs of e-commerce operational and capital investments are necessary to demonstrate the value creation of e-commerce initiatives and to obtain additional resources for critical e-commerce projects. The measures are essential to monitor the key performance drivers (inputs and processes) and assess whether the e-commerce initiative is achieving its stated objectives (outputs) and thus contributing to the long-term success of the corporation (outcomes). Companies often waste resources on e-commerce initiatives or do not invest when they should because they cannot effectively evaluate the potential payoffs of e-commerce investments.

Measuring returns on e-commerce projects can be a daunting challenge. Predicting customer behavior is difficult, because using the Web to do business is still relatively new to many businesses and thus forecasting sales and profits is typically imprecise. There is not much historical data and experience for managers to draw upon when developing or applying metrics, and many economic benefits of e-commerce projects are seen as difficult to measure. Further, the pace of change in e-business and Web-based technologies has been so rapid that precise measurements are often difficult.

Many senior managers have come to believe that further investment in new technology and e-commerce is an imperative that is required to maintain or develop a competitive position. They often make expenditures without completing a rigorous analysis. However, today's more stringent economic environment and the widely publicized negative impacts of many e-commerce initiatives has caused many senior managers to question the payoffs of e-commerce investments.[6]

As companies assess the choice of appropriate measures to evaluate e-commerce initiatives, numerous potential issues arise. Since the choices are different for each company, because the strategies, structures, and systems are different, substantial customization is necessary. Senior managers should consider six initial questions that can lead to the development of appropriate measures for e-commerce operations:

- What measurement systems are currently in place and being utilized within the organization?
- What are the important criteria to the company and its constituencies and stakeholders?
- What does the company desire to accomplish with the e-commerce initiative?
- What is the anticipated time frame associated with the e-commerce program?
- Who are the parties involved in implementing the e-commerce project, and who will be affected by the results?
- What critical processes are associated with the successful execution of the e-commerce project?

To address these questions, it is imperative that companies not only specifically tailor their e-commerce measurement approach but also utilize multiple measures to fully analyze their situations. Different measurement criteria are important for companies that have different strategies or may be in a different stage of their life cycle or their e-commerce development. The multiple measures will typically include both financial and nonfinancial measures that are leading and lagging indicators of performance. They may be used in a balanced-scorecard, shareholder-value-added, or other approach and can be developed specifically for IT or e-commerce or as a part of an overall corporate performance measurement system. Companies can also use a weighted scoring system to evaluate investments related to overall IT, e-commerce, or business strategy.[7]

There are many obstacles to implementing a successful measurement system, whether a lack of focus, a low priority, or just difficulty. It is the responsibility of senior managers to evaluate the e-commerce initiatives and decide on the right measures for their organization and ensure that the measures are captured and responded to properly. To obtain adequate resources for e-commerce and to effectively manage e-commerce initiatives, the payoffs of e-commerce investments must be calculated and integrated into management decision-making systems.

DEVELOPING APPROPRIATE METRICS

To closely monitor the cause and effect relationships evidenced in the e-commerce causal linkage model, appropriate metrics must be developed. These metrics must be consistent with and support the objectives and drivers and key success factors already defined. The selected metrics will likely include a combination of input, processes, output, and outcome metrics to effectively measure performance (Exhibit 6.4). Senior managers involved in the e-commerce decision-making process should develop metrics appropriate to the strategy and objectives of the e-commerce initiative, the company, and its stakeholders. During the measure selection process, it is useful for the involved individuals to choose just a few measures, to focus those senior managers involved in the e-commerce initiative on the critical performance indicators.

The list of metrics presented here is not meant to be a comprehensive set of e-commerce performance measures. Rather, it is a selection and example of some metrics that may be appropriate. Managers must select those that most closely fit their strategy and adapt or develop others. There is no rule for the right number of metrics to include in a measurement system; however, including too many tends to distract managers from pursuing a focused strategy. Generally, a complete measurement system includes perhaps three to six measures for each element being evaluated and no more than twenty measures in total.

Exhibit 6.4
Metrics for E-Commerce System: Inputs, Processes, Outputs, and Outcomes

Processes	*Metrics*
Corporate Strategy	• Competitive position within industry
	• Cost, development time, delivery time, quantity, price, and channels of products offered
	• Number, complexity and size of competitors, customers, partners, and suppliers
	• Dollars of resources available
Corporate Structure	• umber of Strategic Business Units (SBUs)
	• Geographic diversity of production and sales
	• Level of empowerment to SBU and functional managers
Corporate Systems	• Customer and employee satisfaction and retention rate
	• Product and process quality scores
	• Investment in training
Resources	• Dollars available for e-commerce investment
	• Skills assessment of existing employees
	• Quality assessment of current technology and processes
Processes	*Metrics*
External Environment	• Assessment of competitor e-commerce investments
	• Assessment of customer needs
	• Assessment of supplier needs and capabilities
Leadership	• Time dedicated to e-commerce
	• Budget percent allocated to e-commerce initiatives
	• Performance percentage linked to e-commerce success
	• Objectives for e-commerce initiatives clearly communicated to senior managers and employees
	• Percent of senior managers who are "e-commerce literate"
Create & Execute Appropriate E-Commerce Strategies	• Number, cost, price, and perception of products and services offered online
	• Availability and planning for e-commerce security features
	• Perception of online brand
	• Amount and quality of information available on the site
	• Quality levels, delivery options, fulfillment rates, and customer satisfaction of orders placed online
	• Profitability of e-commerce operations
	• Quality of e-commerce Web site
Design & Institute Proper E-Commerce Structure	• Amount of e-commerce that is outsourced
	• Quality of strategic partnerships formed
	• Change in cost and quality of procurements from suppliers
	• E-commerce integration across business units and functions
	• Number of channel-specific products and services

Exhibit 6.4 (continued)

Processes (cont'd)	Metrics
Develop & Implement Appropriate E-Commerce Systems	• Number and quality of employee e-commerce skills and knowledge • Amount and quality of e-commerce training • Percentage of performance measures and rewards aligned and linked to e-commerce activities • Amount and quality of customer data acquired through e-commerce systems • Time required to fill customer orders and service requests made through e-commerce • Level of intradepartmental integration by electronic means • Quality of e-commerce sales and delivery performance

Ouputs	Metrics
Channel Optimization	• Dollar value of activities completed through e-commerce sites • Site traffic (number of visits) and functionality of Web site (click-through rate, stickiness) • Amount of Web site downtime • Partner and supplier satisfaction levels • Improvement in cross-selling
Cost Savings	• Dollars saved in employee expenses, product and material acquisition, data storage, processing, and communication • Dollars saved in new product development and introduction • Spending saved on customer acquisition and service (online and non-online) • Labor costs per unit sold
Customer Acquisition	• New customers gained through e-commerce • Percentage of customers using e-commerce exclusively • Percentage of visitors to e-commerce Web site who are visitors versus those who are buyers (reach) • Number of new customers in other channels informed through Web site • New unique visitors who convert into customers (conversion rate)
Customer Loyalty and Retention	• Frequency of customer return visits to the e-commerce Web site • Average yearly sales per e-commerce customer • Customer satisfaction with e-commerce activities • Customer shopping cart abandonment rates • Percentage of customer attrition • Ratio of new visitors to repeat visitors

Exhibit 6.4   (continued)

Outputs (cont'd)	Metrics
Value	• Cost and price of products and services offered to customers
Capture	• Average of prices paid by customers
	• Number of new products and service lines introduced
	• Profitability of e-commerce operations
	• Revenues generated through the initiative (total revenue, e-commerce revenue, revenue per e-commerce customer) customer)
	• Customer profitability

Outcome	Metrics
Long-term	• Stock price
Corporate	• Income growth
Profitability	• Sales growth

For each key success factor, a specific target should be identified and results should be measured against these targets. These results should be widely communicated among not only those senior managers directly involved in the e-commerce initiative, but also other individuals within the organization upon whom the initiative will have an impact. One of the important contributions that e-commerce can make to an organization is an expanded communication and informational capability. Any e-commerce measurement system will have little impact if the results are not fully discussed. Results should be monitored regularly and used to identify areas of weakness, address the plans and systems in place, and establish new initiatives to improve deficiencies.

The measures chosen should be quantifiable, in either absolute or percentage terms, as well as complete and controllable. They should be complete in that the measure sums up in one number the contribution of all elements of performance that matter; for example, profitability is a summary measure of revenue generation and cost control. They should be controllable in that employees in the organization can actually influence improvement in the factor measured.[8]

Some of the metrics shown here are evaluations of overall firm performance. Others are indicators of e-commerce performance that are derived through an aggregation of measures of individual business units and functions. It is important to evaluate the performance of both overall e-commerce performance and the specific aspects of e-commerce that lead to revenue enhancement or cost savings to determine the success of various operations and corrective action that can be taken to make improvements.

The measures should be of use to both senior and middle managers in the business units and functions. Thus, they must be disaggregated so each unit can examine its contribution to the achievement of the company's e-commerce strategy. These analyses ensure that each unit is making a contribution to the e-commerce initiative and improving corporate profitability. Additionally, these metrics can be used to provide a gap analysis that permits managers to determine what other inputs or processes are required to meet the company's e-commerce project objectives.

Different tools and techniques are available to measure the different aspects of e-commerce performance. For example, online surveys and polls are powerful tools to help e-commerce enabled companies to better understand the benefit of Internet usage for increasing revenue or decreasing costs related to their customers, thus providing valuable information regarding opportunities to improve overall profitability. Internally, surveys, focus groups, and other techniques are increasingly being used to measure and monitor employee, personnel, and stakeholder reactions and provide valuable feedback.

Once metrics have been developed, data on these indicators must be collected and statistical analysis, such as multiple regression, should be performed to analyze and test the validity of the customized e-commerce measurement system and causal relationships hypothesized by the company. As companies evaluate the initial measurement system's performance, they will typically add some metrics and drop others because of a lack of evidence of a strong relationship. It is here that a final measurement system emerges, and the focus then shifts to applying the model to support improved decision making.

OUTPUTS AND OUTCOMES: OVERALL-FIRM AND E-COMMERCE-SPECIFIC PERFORMANCE

If the e-commerce initiatives are well designed and executed and the model of causal relationships properly specified, the identified inputs and processes should lead to improved performance. This should include increasing the success of the e-commerce initiative (outputs) and ultimately to improve corporate performance either through increased revenues or decreased costs (outcomes). To properly evaluate e-commerce performance, input, process, output, and outcome measures are all necessary and should be clearly linked in a causal relationship.

These performance indicators empower senior managers with the information to evaluate whether the e-commerce program is achieving its stated objectives and contributing to overall corporate profitability. For example, metrics such as the percentage of customer attrition are indicators of the e-commerce customer service provided by the company and the related level of customer satisfaction. Since the goals relate to increasing corporate profits, not just improving customer satisfaction, both output and outcome measures are necessary.

A weak performance on the output metrics should signal a need to examine the inputs and processes and determine whether they have been misspecified or just poorly executed. It also can provide an opportunity to identify potential benefits to organizational effectiveness and profitability from e-commerce that may have been overlooked. This is an opportunity to examine how well e-commerce programs are contributing to corporate profits and should unveil specific opportunities, directions for improvements, and standards of performance. The e-commerce measurement system should highlight the specific contributions of the e-commerce activities, in addition to providing valuable feedback that can lead to future e-commerce program and corporate improvements.

Results from the e-commerce evaluation and measurement process should be widely communicated throughout the organization. In a well-executed e-commerce venture, all units of the company will have some involvement in the e-commerce initiative. The evaluation and measurement of the e-commerce program will have little impact if the results are not disseminated throughout the organization to the many disparate areas that both affect and are affected by it. Results should be monitored regularly and used to identify areas of weakness, challenge the plans and systems in place, and present new initiatives to improve deficiencies.

OUTPUTS: CHANNEL OPTIMIZATION, COST SAVINGS, CUSTOMER ACQUISITION, CUSTOMER LOYALTY, AND VALUE CAPTURE

Channel Optimization

Achievement of channel optimization is accomplished and exhibited through an array of items that vary from increased site traffic to informational gains and improvements in demand and supply chain relationships. As consumers become more aware and partial to a company's Web site, traffic typically increases. Managers are able to evaluate increases in metrics such as site hits, page views, and stickiness. While additional analysis is necessary to properly assess the impact of these gains, some of the frequent outputs of these items are greater sales and an expanded market base. It also encourages cannibalization and provides opportunities to increase revenues through the use of an additional or alternate channel and reduce costs through the use of this lower-cost channel of distribution. By encouraging customers and suppliers to use the channels that provide the highest revenues and lowest costs, the e-commerce initiative's outputs are evident and the impact on the ultimate outcome of corporate profitable becomes achievable.

E-commerce also permits the gathering of increased information on customers, partners, and competitors to improve the accuracy of business forecasting techniques and improve relationships in both the acquisition and distribution of goods. Information can be more widely disseminated in a more timely and consistent manner. This permits companies to communicate with remote, mobile, and distant parties in a way never before possible. The electronic information also tends to be more accurate due to fewer transcription errors and lower costs related to printing, distribution, and updates.

It is through improvements in data handling that e-commerce endows the greatest gains to demand and supply chain relationships. Studies have shown that when companies establish demand and supply chain relationships that are facilitated by online means, they can markedly decrease their costs of doing business. The benefits to doing business in this way can be shared among customers, suppliers, and others. These benefits can take many forms, including increased partner collaboration on products and services, reduction in time and cost associated with product acquisition, delivery, and development, freeing up employees to complete other tasks, as well as reducing inventory shortages and costs of procurement.[9]

Cost Savings

Though much of the early focus of e-commerce initiatives was on increasing revenue, the potential for cost savings is at least as large. This could include savings in administrative, customer service, material acquisition, distribution, and sales costs. E-commerce can support improvements through online processes that assist in activities such as ordering, invoicing, tracking, payment, and delivery. Superior cash flow can be accomplished with e-commerce–facilitated better management of inventory levels. Also, critical business processes such as procurement, sales, and customer relationship management can be increasingly automated. These create cost savings through reduced paper handling and requirements for human intervention in administration.[10] IBM recently realized significant cost savings by creating an online intranet for employees to Web conference, collaborate on ideas, and improve skills. In the process, IBM realized $375 million in annual savings from the training budget and another $20 million from reduced travel expenses due to the high-volume use of Web conferencing. General Motors Corporation now uses online auctions to sell used cars to auto dealers at the end of the cars' leases, saving about $180 million yearly.[11]

Customer Acquisition

Providing company products and services over the Internet creates a new channel for a company's existing and potential customers. Further, though many potential customers were previously able to access a company's products or services through other channels before e-commerce was available, providing a business channel on the Web allows customers to reach companies beyond their local areas in a manner never previously available at the same scale. Companies that move more commerce to the Web can accomplish significantly expanded global coverage and exposure with a relatively minimal investment. This wider coverage encompasses new products, new markets, new distribution channels, new partners, and so forth. Through online activities, companies can offer products or services directly to their consumers. The e-commerce initiatives and the e-commerce leadership, strategy, structure, and system should permit an increase in new customer acquisition as a powerful potential output.

Customer Loyalty

Customer loyalty can be seen through both repeat customers and increased overall customer satisfaction levels. The common business truism that it is less costly to make additional sales to existing customers than to develop sales through new customers is certainly applicable in an e-commerce environment. The Internet permits companies to connect with their customers, partners, and suppliers in a virtual environment. This permits increased communication and a greater ability to intertwine the company's operations with the external stakeholders' needs and requirements. The intertwining of interests not only allows the company to provide better customer service to these external stakeholders, but also links the two groups in a manner that facilitates recurring purchases. E-commerce activities can provide an important opportunity to improve customer service levels and relationships leading to increased customer loyalty and repeat purchases.

Value Capture

Capturing additional value is at the core of company objectives. As customers are better able to compare the products and services offered to them through e-commerce, they can more easily compare alternatives and competitor offerings in an expedient manner. Thus, it is critical for each company to be able to differentiate itself from its competitors, for the benefit of its customers as well as itself. Companies also capture additional value through improvements in both costs and prices. As the cost of sales is reduced, the opportunity to offer lower prices to the customer is greatly increased, leading to the ability to be more competitive and drive increased revenues. Companies can also create and capture additional value by providing additional services to their customers such as customization and personalization. These services are far reaching, and the opportunities for the creation and capturing of value for the company and its various stakeholders are significant.

OUTCOMES: INCREASED REVENUES AND DECREASED COSTS LEAD TO IMPROVED PROFITABILITY

One important lesson from the development of e-commerce is that improving customer traffic and other outputs of e-commerce activity is not enough. For e-commerce initiatives to be of value, the intermediate outputs must eventually pay off in increased corporate profits. Viewed simply, increased profitability can only be achieved through improving revenue or decreasing costs. To evaluate the payoffs of e-commerce investments and better allocate corporate resources, senior managers must be clear about the ultimate goal and develop ways to measure success. Further, if IT and e-commerce managers want to obtain additional resources for e-commerce investments, the ultimate effect on corporate profitability must be measured and the payoffs and ROI be clearly calculated.

CONCLUSION

The bursting of the dot.com bubble and increased scrutiny of corporate spending have spurred far-reaching changes in business, and companies are now being required to take a more measured approach to introducing e-commerce into their organizations. Gone are the days when companies would blindly make expenditures on e-commerce initiatives for reasons only related to keeping up with competitors.

Companies are being asked to focus on evaluating the costs, payoffs, and performance affiliated with e-commerce initiatives.

Numerous perspectives on the measurement of e-commerce performance have been developed in both the academic and business press. Yet, while these articles are quick to highlight the need for e-commerce measurement within organizations, few have provided measurement systems, strategies, and specific metrics to evaluate the performance of e-commerce initiatives. Firms can significantly improve the evaluation, management, and performance of e-commerce programs through improved measurement systems.

Potential e-commerce investments should be evaluated in the same way as all other corporate investments. Return on investment or other commonly used metrics should also be applied to e-commerce. This requires a careful identification, analysis, and measurement of the likely payoffs on some intermediate inputs, processes, and outputs and on the ultimate outcome of improving overall corporate profits. This analysis should improve both the corporate resource allocation decision and the ability of e-commerce managers to obtain funding for proposed investments with a positive net payoff. By carefully analyzing, articulating, and measuring the inputs, processes, outputs, and outcomes associated with e-commerce investments, corporations can dramatically improve both individual e-commerce program performance and overall corporate performance.

Part II

Company Cases

Prior company experiences in e-commerce have resulted in dramatic successes and failures. Their performance differed substantially on leadership and the formulation of strategy, along with execution through structure and systems. Earlier chapters present frameworks by which to identify key success factors for the development and execution of a successful e-commerce strategy. The next three chapters provide short case descriptions of the experiences of thirty-two companies in twelve industries. Though some of these examples are cited briefly in the text, providing a more in-depth discussion of these experiences allows us more readily to identify the causes of success and failure. By aggregating these cases by industry and by sector, comparisons between the companies can be made more easily. These achievements and failures vary from company to company, industry to industry, and sector to sector, providing insight on how e-commerce can be uniquely tailored to meet the needs of any company.

While it is important to look at the stories behind these cases of success and failure, case studies also provide an opportunity to initially examine the characteristics presented throughout this book, which are in fact the common characteristics of successful e-commerce companies. These characteristics are not always present in the same form, or emphasized in the same manner, by the companies described in these chapters, but one can observe a complementary nature to these attributes. Some characteristics are illustrated in Exhibit II.1. One message is that seldom do a company's attributes preclude it from succeess in an e-commerce venture. Whether a company is looking to become an e-commerce leader or simply to expand into new markets, e-commerce can be utilized by nearly any company, however late it begins its e-commerce initiatives.

The company cases include both successes and failures. They include challenges to e-commerce implementation, and how these were successfully (or unsuccessfully) addressed, and an evaluation of the implementations. These cases do not simply show what did not work for companies attempting early e-commerce initiatives, but also demonstrate how in some cases companies were able to overcome early e-commerce adversity and establish a viable Internet presence. Some of these success stories clearly demonstrate that companies can recover from early e-commerce mistakes. But, they also show that such a recovery requires a considerable commitment from corporate leadership.

The company cases include traditional companies that have pursued e-commerce solutions for their business, along with the pure-play Internet competition that these companies faced. Ten years ago, companies such as Amazon and E*Trade were but specks on the horizon for industry leaders. Today, they are often significant competitive threats to traditional companies expanding into the realm of e-commerce. In other cases, they are formidable allies for companies that have taken advantage of the pure-play's e-commerce expertise to begin an e-commerce venture. In either case, today's senior managers cannot adequately analyze the state of e-commerce within an industry without considering the impact that these pure-play e-commerce companies have had over time and continue to have.

WHAT TO EXPECT FROM THE CASE STUDIES

These case studies have been organized into three chapters, according to the characteristics of the industries examined. Chapter 7 comprises companies that are primarily in retail businesses, selling products to the ultimate consumer. Chapter 8 focuses on companies that primarily provide services. Chapter 9 contains cases of companies that primarily sell business to business. These groupings are not discrete, and there is considerable overlapping of their attributes among all three classifications. However, the focus is on the attributes of their e-commerce initiatives. For example, while the operations of Dell include a retail component both offline and online, we focus on the B2B components—the e-commerce initiative that has been central to its e-commerce strategy.

Each chapter begins with a brief introduction to the topics addressed in each industry and some unique company and industry characteristics. Each industry case begins with an industry overview. I then examine two or three companies within each industry to show a range of e-commerce initiatives, including both traditional industry leaders and pure-play Internet companies. In each case the focus is on the charac-

Exhibit II.1
Company Cases and Characteristics

SECTOR	INDUSTRY	COMPANY	Industry Leader?	E-commerce Leader?	Bricks and Clicks (BC) or Pure-Play (PP)?	Early Mover?	Used E-commerce to expand into new Business Opportunities?
Retail	BOOKSTORES	Amazon	Yes	Yes	PP	Yes	Yes
		Barnes and Noble	No	No	BC	No	Yes
		Borders	No	No	BC	No	No
	DISCOUNT RETAIL	Wal-Mart	Yes	Yes	BC	No	No
		Kmart	No	No	BC	No	No
		Target	No	No	BC	No	No
	LUXURY RETAIL	Nordstrom	Yes	Yes	BC	Yes	No
		Neiman Marcus	No	No	BC	No	No
		Ashford.com	No	No	PP	Yes	No
	GROCERS	Tesco	Yes	Yes	BC	Yes	Yes
		Webvan and Homegrocer	No	No	PP	No	No
		D'Agostino's-MWG	No	No	BC	No	No
	OFFICE SUPPLIES	Office Depot	Yes	Yes	BC	Yes	Yes
		Staples	No	No	BC	No	Yes
Services	STOCKBROKERS	Charles Schwab	Yes	No	BC	Yes	No
		Merrill Lynch	No	No	BC	No	No
		E*Trade	No	Yes	PP	Yes	Yes
	CONSUMER BANKS	Wells Fargo	No	Yes	BC	Yes	Yes
		Bank of America	Yes	Yes	BC	No	Yes
		Bank One-Wingspan	No	No	BC	No	No
	PHARMACIES	CVS	No	Yes	BC	Yes	No
		Walgreens	Yes	Yes	BC	No	No
		Rite Aid-Drugstore.com	No	No	BC	No	No
	POSTAL SERVICES	UPS	Yes	Yes	BC	Yes	Yes
		Federal Express	No	No	BC	Yes	Yes
B2B	COMPUTERS	Dell	Yes	Yes	BC	Yes	Yes
		Compaq/HP	No	No	BC	No	No
		Cisco	Yes	Yes	BC	Yes	Yes
		Lucent	No	No	BC	No	No
		GE Plastics	Yes	Yes	BC	Yes	No
		Omnexus	No	No	BC	No	No
		PlasticsNet.com	No	No	PP	No	No

teristics that today's senior managers must consider when evaluating or implementing a new e-commerce initiative. The cases are historical, over a particular period of time, and there is no attempt to provide current company data. Rather, the focus is on the chronology of the development and implementation of e-commerce strategies and an understanding and critical evaluation of those initiatives.

Each case concludes with a set of lessons that can be drawn from these company experiences. No one company tells a complete story of how *all* other companies can achieve e-commerce success. However, these "lessons learned" contribute to a greater understanding, so that companies can increase the likelihood of success for their own e-commerce ventures.

We encourage senior corporate, IT, and e-commerce managers to examine the e-commerce elements of these companies to find the aspects of e-commerce best suited for their own company. However, some general lessons can be learned from these companies that should be considered while examining the state of e-commerce in any industry.

The implementation of an e-commerce venture is not a complete method to achieve company goals. E-commerce potentially can provide a new distribution channel and perform a number of new functions that a company may lack the resources to accomplish otherwise. However, this new channel typically does not replace existing elements of company structure and systems. E-commerce should be used to augment, not to replace critical elements such as customer service, B2B relations, or a company's sales force. Most companies with successful e-commerce ventures have discovered ways to pair the advantages of e-commerce with the aspects of their traditional business that made them successful in the first place. The goal is to find ways that e-commerce can enhance already existing competitive advantages.

E-commerce requires a significant commitment on the part of both senior managers and staff to ensure that the venture is initially designed properly to achieve particular goals and ensure that the role of e-commerce within the company is continually reevaluated and improved. E-commerce cannot be of interest to only a small group of IT personnel within a company. It must be an integrated and focused endeavor with ample leadership, funding, and expertise to ensure its success.

E-commerce ventures often become balancing acts between two factors: commitment to traditionally successful aspects of a company and commitment to a new e-commerce strategy. Companies that are able to achieve this balance can maintain previously successful aspects of business while simultaneously using e-commerce to find new sources of both cost reduction and revenue enhancement.

CHAPTER 7

Company Cases: B2C—Retail

INTRODUCTION

The e-commerce activities of retail companies have been the subject of substantial examination, certainly more than other e-commerce sectors. Observers have been able to gain an especially clear perspective of the successes and failures associated with retail-focused e-commerce. This perspective reveals that customer service, a willingness to change a failing e-commerce strategy, and measures to determine what specific products are most appropriate for e-commerce are keys to retail e-commerce success.

Online price wars do not typically lead to profitability. Repeat customers do. Companies wishing to establish a credible online presence should not typically focus on using temporarily low prices to attract customers without loyalty or a likelihood of repeat business. Rather, companies should to use e-commerce to acquire and retain customers who are likely to maintain long-term relationships with the company. Elements that have proved successful in promoting such customer retention include well-developed Web site design, liberal return policies, and targeted customer incentives based on records of customer activity.

Companies must also be willing to revamp an unsuccessful e-commerce strategy when necessary. Not only has the realization that an early e-commerce strategy was not performing up to expectations saved some e-commerce ventures from demise, but some redesigned e-commerce ventures have enabled companies to emerge as industry leaders. Wal-Mart's temporary termination of online operations, Barnes and Noble's stock buy-back, and Office Depot's partnership with Amazon were all efforts to dramatically change the direction of e-commerce strategy and resulted in improved e-commerce success.

Retail companies must also ensure that they market appropriate products on their Web sites. Achieving profitability while selling low-margin goods can prove difficult. For luxury retailers, shoppers often are reluctant to make high-end purchases while online, partly because it is often a challenge to appreciate the value of an item from a Web site photo alone. Price is only one of many variables that a company must consider when evaluating goods for potential Web exposure. In the end, companies cannot simply toss together a listing of available products for the customer to choose. Careful thought is necessary regarding what products will be not only included, but emphasized through this new channel.

The companies discussed in this chapter encountered a wide array of issues related to their e-commerce activities. Senior managers may benefit from examining lessons that these companies have learned from their e-commerce ventures. Companies in the early stages of e-commerce can improve the formulation and execution of their own e-commerce strategy. The industries and companies examined in this chapter are the following, by industry.

Bookstores
  Amazon
  Barnes and Noble
  Borders

Discount Retail
  Wal-Mart
  Kmart
  Target

Luxury Retail
  Nordstrom
  Neiman Marcus
  Ashford.com

Grocers
  Tesco
  Webvan/HomeGrocer
  D'Agostino's-MWG

Office Supplies
Office Depot
Staples

BOOKSTORES

The online bookstore industry has had a lower sense of fragmentation from its inception. By 2001, the industry had effectively been pared down to two major competitors, Amazon and Barnes and Noble. Borders ran a distant third, until it ceded operations to Amazon in 2001, and other competitors have been insignificant in the industry.

The three companies followed clearly divergent strategies. Amazon is a pure-play retailer that originally eschewed any physical retail presence, but later built high-cost, high-technology warehouses to control distribution. Barnes and Noble's early strategy was to operate the site as a spinoff, without relying on the strengths of the physical stores, although it later moved toward a more integrated strategy. Borders pursued more integration than Barnes and Noble, hoping to leverage its customer-focus strategy to get its in-store customers to shop online.

First-mover advantage was clearly a strong basis for Amazon's domination of the industry. Amazon launched an aggressive marketing campaign before it began taking orders,[1] and has succeeded in creating a strong association between its brand name and Internet book sales. Barnes and Noble was able to survive because of its strong brand. But Borders' demise as a separate online retailer[2] and the lack of other pure-play competitors can be strongly attributed to Amazon's first-mover advantage.

Amazon

Amazon was established in Seattle as a micro-enterprise in 1994. In 1995, Amazon opened its Web site, as a site with a modest discount for books, and quickly established a reputation for offering a larger selection of books than any bookstore, with a selection of 1.1 million titles. In 1998, it diversified into music and quickly became a leader in that category. It has since expanded into thirteen primary categories and an offering of 18 million items.

Amazon also recognized quickly that simply being a distributor would subject it to online price wars and reduced margins. Its first expansion into other roles came in 1996, when it began the Amazon Associates program, which linked customers to Amazon through other content sites. Affiliates received commissions of 5 to 15 percent.[3]

Another program is the Advantage program, which allows independent publishers to sell books on Amazon's site; Amazon pays the publisher 45 percent of list price.[4] Another development was the zShops program, in which Amazon hosts small providers on its site, providing its distribution technology in exchange for a commission. Amazon also receives benefits from the additional traffic and the ability to cross-sell.

Finally, Amazon developed larger distribution partnerships. In August 2000, it created a strategic alliance with Toys 'R' Us to provide logistical support for a co-branded Web site. Amazon received a small percentage of revenue, per-unit payments, and fixed payments. Amazon handled site development, order fulfillment, and customer service, while Toys 'R' Us handled inventory.[5] The deal boosted sales for both companies and forced a pure-play competitor, rival eToys, to fold.

In August 2001, Amazon took over operations for Borders.com, providing inventory, fulfillment, site content, and customer service. The Borders site adopted Amazon's one-click ordering and personalization.[6] In teaming up with Borders, Amazon gained both customers and an offline presence. In 2002, the deal was enhanced to include the ability to check physical stores' inventory online and for Borders stores to accept returns from Amazon. It also took over operations for CDNow, a leader in online music sales owned by Bertelsmann, a major stakeholder in barnesandnoble.com.[7]

Amazon has designed most of its own functions, including the search system, customer accounts system, and IT infrastructure. The design of Amazon's site contributes heavily to its high repeat customer rate. A key aspect of Amazon's site design is its personalization technology, which tracks customer preferences and informs customers, both on the site and through email, of products that might appeal to them. Amazon content is provided both by Amazon's staff and by users, who may submit reviews and other forms of feedback on products.

For customer service, Amazon offers dedicated email addresses that deal with specific customer topics, areas, and other functions. It also began offering free shipping on larger orders, an idea which it considered and scrapped in summer 2001. Later in 2002, it reduced considerably the purchase minimums for free shipping. [8]

Another major advantage is Amazon's negative cash conversion cycle, because it collects sales payments from customers before it must pay distributors and vendors. By 2003 Amazon had 37 million customers.[9] Though growth was strong, Amazon continued to lose money until January 2002, when Amazon reported its first quarter of profitability.[10]

Barnes and Noble

Barnes and Noble's first reaction to Amazon was to design a store using America Online, which launched in 1997, nearly two years after the launch of Amazon. The site, however, was criticized as being slow and difficult to use. The site was also overloaded with orders at times, especially during the holiday season, without the technological capabilities to handle them.[11] There were also no signs of integration with retail stores.

Barnes and Noble's offline business had always been centered around low prices, in contrast to its main offline competitor, Borders, which had competed on its wide assortment of titles. The core of the strategy was scale in distribution infrastructure and administration and in-store discounts. In 1998, Bertelsmann bought a 50 percent stake in the Web site for $200 million.

The new barnesandnoble.com was first designed as a separate unit, and eventually spun off as a stand-alone separate company. The Web site's headquarters was a colorful, open, and high-tech environment, designed to imitate the feel of a pure-play company. In 1999, its IPO raised $486 million, which was used primarily to improve the Web site and fulfillment operations.[12] This relaunch of the Web site overhauled both front-end and back-end operations. The site itself was redesigned to be more like Amazon's, making ordering simpler and faster for customers. Amazon successfully sued Barnes and Noble, however, for too closely imitating its checkout technology.

In 2000, CEO Stephen Riggio began a new initiative, pushing integration between the Web site and the retail stores. Previously, customers had many complaints, including the inability to return items purchased online to the stores. One goal of the integration was to improve conversion rates of visits, and the view was that integrated marketing was the best way to achieve this. Stores began to reflect signs of integration, with the Web site advertised above counters and with salespersons assisting customers by referencing the Web site. The company also created a Readers' Advantage program that offered both in-store and online discounts to yield one price. The Web site then began allowing returns to be made to retail stores for the first time. It also installed kiosks in its retail stores. As part of the integration effort, the Web site was able to make considerable cuts in both marketing and fulfillment costs.

Barnesandnoble.com tried to create competitive advantage by venturing into digital books, wireless ordering, and reprinting out-of-print public domain books. It also provided a search service that permitted customers to find out-of-print books through a network of used book stores. Wireless ordering was dropped in 2001, but the other services remained. The digital book division began offering premium royalties to authors early in 2001, and it offered these publications to other e-retailers as well.[13] The company's strong IT capabilities allowed the company to bring such initiatives online faster than average online implementation times.[14]

Eventually, Barnes and Noble began buying back stock in its spun-off Web site. Partner Bertelsmann also began purchasing stock, and by 2002, each held 36 percent of the stock in barnesandnoble.com.[15] In July 2003, Bertelsmann cut ties with barnesandnoble.com and sold its stake back to Barnes and Noble for $164 million.[16] Revenue in 1999 was $193.7M, and it rose to $320.1M in 2000. However, the company lost $276 million that year.[17] In 2002, Barnes and Noble saw sales increase and net losses fall, leading to the company's first projections of profitability in 2003. In addition to higher revenue, the site benefited from cuts in operating expenses and more efficient shipping.[18] But its slow move into e-commerce and poor integration with its bricks and mortar operation has kept it to a small fraction of the size of Amazon.

Borders

Borders' offline strategy was built around providing a broad offering of books with a strong customer perspective. Anticipating demand was

---

Lessons Learned:

- If you can't beat them . . .
  - While Borders did not concede defeat to Amazon, it realized that by allying itself with what was the established leader in online book sales it could enhance its traditional stores through exposure to the substantial number of customers that accessed Amazon's Web site on a daily basis.
- An e-commerce leader in one industry can sometimes quickly expand into others.
  - Amazon's leadership in online book sales translated into a level of expertise and customer loyalty that permitted the company not only to expand into other types of business, but to do so with an already loyal customer base from its initial online bookstore.
- Companies must be willing to rethink a failing e-commerce strategy.
  - Barnes and Noble's decision to bring its e-commerce spinoff back into the company helped the company take full advantage of its preexisting capabilities while keeping online customers from straying to its competitors.

at the heart of a focused strategy. Borders' site initially featured much less content than Amazon and Barnes and Noble, in such areas as book reviews and customer reviews.

Borders boasted a wider range of products than its competitors, offering music and video in addition to books, with a total of 10 million products. From its beginning in May 1998, however, it failed to generate the number of visitors enjoyed by Amazon and Barnes and Noble. Borders had an email list of 1.25 million customers who received e-mail "updates" that included reviews of new releases. This list of customers and Borders' mastery of HTML-based email marketing were considered the strongest aspects of an otherwise failed venture.

Borders chose at first not to separate online revenue, or the number of visitors or products sold, in their reports. Before teaming with Amazon, Borders.com spent $100 million on its online venture. The company finally decided that it would focus its business strategy on its physical stores and permit Amazon to run the online offerings.

DISCOUNT RETAIL

Traditional discount retailers Wal-Mart, Kmart, and Target have struggled online to match their performance in physical space. As general retailers, they face competition in many categories from Amazon.com, which some have called the Internet version of Wal-Mart. Like Wal-Mart, Amazon's loyal customer base helps to offset any price differentials offered by discount retailers. They also face competition in specific product areas from specialty retailers.

All three companies made their first significant e-commerce efforts in 1999 and suffered similar technology problems while offering a range of products that paled in comparison to that of their physical stores. The Web sites have undergone a number of rounds of changes since then with Wal-Mart even taking the drastic step of temporarily shutting down its Web site.

A major question in this industry revolved around the proper strategies for targeting low-end customers online. One lesson learned by all three was that the lowest- price goods and indeed most low-dollar margin goods should be removed from the online offerings. The companies have experimented to find the right types of products to offer online.

A primary concern for these companies has been to draw its own customers online rather than focusing on attracting new customers. To this end, all three have entered, in some form, into the Internet service provider market, with Wal-Mart and Target signing deals with AOL and with Kmart attempting to offer its own service. The rationale was that many traditional customers were not yet online and facilitating their entry was the key to building online business.

Structurally, Wal-Mart and Kmart used similar strategies, establishing spinoff companies in Silicon Valley, outsourcing fulfillment, and creating separate management. Wal-Mart, however, maintained brand integration, while Kmart's Bluelight maintained the most tenuous of ties with the parent company. In contrast, Target strongly espoused integration from the start, correctly predicting that its peers would be forced eventually to bring their Web sites back into the fold.

Wal-Mart

Wal-Mart was the first mover among discount retailers, although its launch was not particularly spectacular and provided only a minor edge over its competitors. Throughout its history, the site has undergone a large number of renovations and redesigns. Its philosophy with regard to e-commerce has been one of slow and deliberate effort, believing that the company's position in the physical space gave it the freedom to experiment.[19]

In late 1999, Wal-Mart signed an agreement with AOL to create a co-branded Internet service, do cross-promotions, and coordinate marketing.[20] The first site was a limited effort, with a small SKU (stock keeping unit) count.

In 2000, the company realized the growing importance of selling online and spun off Walmart.com in a deal with venture capitalists Accel Partners. The deal was not particularly about a need for capital, as Wal-Mart could easily have financed its own site, but Accel offered specific knowledge and experience in e-commerce. By spinning off, Wal-Mart hoped to be better positioned to manage customer data, take more risks, and avoid the restrictions of corporate earnings requirements. It also intended to move quickly on the new site, in contrast to the cautious approach taken earlier. Walmart.com had a separate board of directors, although high-level Wal-Mart executives were among its members.

The spun-off Walmart.com decided to build an almost entirely new site and made significant improvements in functionality and service over the old site. Still, problems reported with the new Walmart.com were numerous, including poor navigation and biased and incomplete product information. Improvements were noted in pricing and product promotion.[21] The new site also had a much higher SKU count, of over 500,000, and super-store features such as photo processing. At the same time, it eliminated some of the lowest-price items and impulse purchases. It also changed its fulfillment providers, ending its prior arrangement with Fingerhut and switching to two other third parties.

In October 2000, Walmart.com took the highly unusual step of shutting down its Web site for redesign ahead of the holiday season. Changes focused on customer service improvements. In 2001, Wal-Mart began to shift its focus in terms of product lines, deciding to eliminate apparel because of its low margins and high shipping costs. In turn, it began to focus on higher-priced goods such as electronics and jewelry.[22] Its store redesign focused on product organization to attempt to provide more simplicity for customers.

Wal-Mart also began testing in-store kiosks, as part of an overall effort to rejuvenate the relationship between physical stores and e-commerce. It focused on drawing the customers of the physical stores online, rather than spending money on marketing efforts to draw new customers to Walmart.com.[23] At the end of 2001, just 1 percent of Wal-Mart's sales revenue came from its Web site.[24]

In 2002, Wal-Mart completed its buyback of Walmart.com stock from minority partner Accel. In an announcement, Wal-Mart described its desire to integrate its site more closely with its physical stores. Walmart.com remained a separate business unit, with site development, technology, and merchandising still handled out of its separate Palo Alto offices. In 2003, Wal-Mart site traffic was growing, and the company added checking accounts to its online payment options in response to rapidly growing Internet retail sales. The focus was to complement the physical stores by adding product categories that enhanced the Wal-Mart experience.[25]

Kmart

Bluelight.com, an independent unit of Kmart, was founded with venture capital funding in December 1999. The unit was physically separate from company headquarters, and almost one-third was owned by Softbank Venture Capital. The separate brand name drew a strong association with Kmart's traditional slogan, but the new site name was intended to distinguish it from the previous, unsuccessful site.[26]

In October 2000, Bluelight.com was launched with a much more extensive catalog, with four times as many items available and a much larger inventory than any physical stores carry. These 300,000 SKUs represented a six-fold increase from six months earlier, and included a mix of basic products and brand-image items. The launch was also accompanied by a major rollout of kiosks into 1,600 of its 2,000 physical stores. It also included an initiative to bring its physical store customers online, offering free Internet software and low-price computers.[27] The kiosks also encouraged customers to order hard-to-deliver items through the kiosk and have them delivered.

As Bluelight.com continued to be unprofitable into 2001, the company moved toward an integration strategy. In 2001, Kmart bought back the stock of Bluelight.com and completed the integration. Despite its new status as a subsidiary, Bluelight maintained separate headquarters in Silicon Valley. It also ended its fulfillment outsourcing and hired Global Sports to create a more integrated fulfillment arrangement, including customer service and customized promotions.[28]

Kmart eliminated apparel from its Web site in 2001. It hired an outside partner to handle technology and allied with a new customer service partner. In an effort to make e-commerce more profitable, it began a requirement of a $10 gross profit margin for products sold online, such as photography, jewelry, pharmacy orders, and toys.[29]

In 2002, fallout from Kmart's bankruptcy forced a number of changes in its e-commerce strategy. One was the elimination of the Internet service provider business that had been established to attract customers, as not a core competency for the company.[30] The unit also saw a major cutback in staffing, and most management functions were moved back to company headquarters. The site also began a greater focus on carrying name-brand products. The Web site was also renamed Kmart.com, after testing the two names and their associated click-through rates, and the company focused on tighter brand integration between the channels that coincided with a new marketing campaign from the parent company.[31]

Target

Target began by building its e-commerce venture essentially from scratch. Its philosophy with regard to structure was in sharp contrast to that of its competitors. Target's leaders were outspoken in their belief that the company should fully invest in e-commerce rather than selling equity to venture capitalists; they said that integration was vital to brand management in e-commerce. It identified brand management as the most important aspect of e-commerce, which was consistent with the parent company's overall strategy, which had abandoned the Dayton Hudson name in favor of Target.

Target's strategy was to use the Internet for more than consumer sales, as part of a multidimensional growth strategy. It also used the Internet for distribution functions, employee recruitment, and customer service and followed a philosophy of integrating the Internet in some way into every department. It built a marketing advantage online by having its Sunday circulars available online. At the same time, however, it narrowed its online offerings to avoid promotional price wars on items such as books and compact disks. In terms of its online sales, Target reinforced its integration strategy by having the same pricing both online and in physical stores. Like Kmart, Target was a member of the online procurement group the Worldwide Retail Exchange.

Its integration strategy eventually spawned a new Internet unit to plan strategy for Target.com and Web sites corresponding to its other store chains. Its e-commerce division, target.direct, worked toward establishing real-time coordination with suppliers that shipped directly to customers. Target outsourced fulfillment solutions to CommerceHub, whose applications were the basis for the real-time coordination. Doing so simplified the supply chain and enabled Target to sell certain items without keeping them in inventory. Its applications facilitated communication between incompatible systems in the supply chain.

In June 2000, Target formed a strategic alliance with AOL to offer a co-branded version of AOL's service. The deal included incentives to shop at Target.com, but was primarily aimed at customer loyalty and retention, rather than customer acquisition. Another Internet initiative was its deal to bring E*Trade kiosks into Target stores.

In 2001, Target signed an agreement with Amazon.com (since extended to 2008)[32] that became responsible for customer care and fulfillment for Target.com and adapted Amazon's Web site design. The deal included a per item fee from Target and a yearly payment. Target expressed confidence that the deal would strengthen the Target brand.[33] Items listed on the Amazon site were limited to a few categories and some exclusive high-end brands.

In 2002, Target.com was launched as a platform for both Target and its Marshall Field's and Mervyn's stores, again with back-end operations by Amazon. Target has maintained price consistency with its store prices, and the Amazon deal did not affect this, since there was little category overlap.[34] The price consistency allowed Target to offer its store circulars online without creating confusion over prices.

Lessons Learned:

- Pure-play competitors can be dangerous for traditional companies.
  - While Amazon started by selling books, its lack of early competition allowed the company to expand into other markets. This expansion also involved gaining substantial customer loyalty due to the company's reliability and seemingly ubiquitous presence on the Internet. Even firms with the strength of presence of Wal-Mart were forced to play catch-up with what began as a small Internet book venture, because of the expertise Amazon gained while it had little online competition.

Lessons Learned (continued):

- E-commerce should not focus on low-priced goods.
  - What a company defines as a low-price good will change from market to market. However, the reality remains for all companies that unless the margin for products can justify its use of space on a Web site at the expense of other higher-margin goods, it should not be included on a company's Web site.
- E-commerce is sometimes about stealing your own customers.
  - If a company faces the possibility of customers forgoing in-store shopping to take advantage of Internet availability, that company should prefer that customers be "lost" to their own Web site and cannibalized instead of going to the site of a competitor.
- Companies must be willing to rethink a failing e-commerce strategy.
  - Kmart was forced to shut down Bluelight.com, while Wal-Mart completely suspended online operations for a time. In both cases, these actions helped the company revitalize their e-commerce efforts and reestablish themselves as legitimate e-commerce vendors.

LUXURY RETAIL

The high-end retail industry faces many of the same questions as other retail industries, but the narrow target demographic and the high price of the goods do have significant implications for the various channels of distribution. Some of these mirror differences in the physical retail industry, and some are more specific to e-commerce. But, the differences related to both customers and products must be considered.

Wealthier online shoppers are the natural target demographic for high-end retailers, and customers with a net worth above $1 million spend twice as much as other buyers online and stay online longer per week.[35] Studies have shown that the most important aspects of a Web site for this demographic are convenience, confidence, and control.[36] These customers are less price sensitive and are willing to sacrifice the lowest price in order to be more confident in their online experience.

Buying luxury items without seeing the products in person is a major obstacle to overcome. Some companies have attempted to bridge this gap through high-technology solutions that attempt to create a virtual reality that imitates the in-store experience. These solutions have been largely unsuccessful.

Other companies have conceded that the online experience can never imitate real life and hope to attract customers despite this shortcoming. One strategy is the implementation of generous return policies that minimize the risk to the customer and permit the customer to experience the product with little effort required to return the good if unsatisfied.

Luxury items also vary greatly in their profit margins. This has affected luxury retailers' strategies with regard to size and scope of inventory. Some, imitating lower-end retailers, have attempted to provide a large catalog and to appeal to customers through breadth. Others have attempted to carve out niches for higher-margin goods and kept offerings narrow.

Nordstrom

Along with Bloomingdale's, Nordstrom was an early mover in luxury retailing online, opening its Web site in 1998. From the beginning, breadth of offerings was a key aspect of Nordstrom's strategy. It offered "hundreds of thousands" of items, the largest selection among luxury retailers, with an emphasis on shoes similar to its physical stores.[37] Nordstrom's has maintained this edge throughout its existence. Although its online offerings did not initially match its catalog offerings of two million items, the company completed an inventory convergence project that in 2003 brought the entire catalog online.

Nordstrom had strong operational know-how when it began work on its Web site but decided to go to venture capitalists to gain e-business-specific knowledge. Nordstrom.com was launched as a separate entity, with Nordstrom holding an 84 percent share and 15 percent owned by Benchmark Capital. The company hired executives from companies with expertise in direct-to-customer business.[38] In 2002, Nordstrom bought back all outstanding shares from the minority investors in the venture capital firms, eliminating one aspect in which integration was lacking. Nordstrom.com now is part of the direct sales division, which also includes the catalog business.

Nordstrom has also used e-commerce as a cost-cutting strategy, replacing the need to send out expensive catalogs to potential customers.[39] Nordstrom has been hesitant to release revenue figures, but Web and catalog business combined for $210 million, approximately 4 percent of revenue at physical stores.[40]

Like the parent company, Nordstrom.com hoped to make strong customer service the trademark of its Web site. It did not invest heavily in technology as a source of competitive advantage and had no illusions about imitating the in-store experience on the Web site.[41] Although the early stages of the site had problems with its checkout and search processes, these problems were corrected, and the site was later rated high for best design because of its large number of offerings, clear pictures, straightforward presentation, and customer service.

At the center of Nordstrom's customer service package is its return policy, which allows convenient returns of items both through the mail and to its physical stores. All returns are accepted regardless of reason, and orders are shipped with a prepared return slip. Free return shipping is given to customers who use a Nordstrom credit card.

Neiman Marcus

Since its inception, Neiman Marcus has followed a more cautious strategy than its pure-play, and even its bricks-and-clicks, competitors. Neiman Marcus opened for e-commerce on its Web site in 1999,[42] with an offering of just 500 items, although products were added continuously from the beginning. Despite the conservative inventory strategy, the company launched a blitz of online and offline marketing to introduce the site. The early site, however, had problems, including poor functionality and complaints about its small number of products. These problems were partially the result of a rush to get the site online before the holiday season.[43]

By 2000, the number of items offered had increased to 2,000, but the strategy had shifted to presentation, and specifically to technological applications to provide interactive and lifelike representations of products. Neiman Marcus introduced a gift gallery and shoe boutique on its site, both of which relied on technology to present the items on revolving pedestals. Later, the company eliminated such features, after determining that online customers were not attracted by them.[44] Later and more modest technological features have been more successful, including a tool for magnifying small details on products and a personal shopping program. The program makes available all inventory from its largest store and offers 24/7 customer assistance via chat that receives over 500 messages per week. Its search engine is also highly rated among luxury retailers.

Revenue tripled at the site in 2001 after the elimination of the technology strategy and a new focus on privacy assurance and search features. By 2002, the site featured 5,000 items; its drawing points included a bimonthly email letter that combined marketing with information fashion trends.

Neiman Marcus has at times tied its strategy to the concept of a luxury portal, in which customers could find many retailers of luxury items in addition to Neiman Marcus. Original plans envisioned eventually transforming the site itself into a portal-like destination for luxury shopping. In 2000, it signed a deal with Style.com, an online portal, to create a special co-branded site on the portal. In 2003, in an effort to stay competitive, Neiman Marcus implemented Oracle's e-business suite in an effort to better analyze store performance and consolidate purchasing.[45]

Neiman Marcus developed a more integrated structure than Nordstrom. It relied on its physical stores to provide return services and customer support; it processes orders, maintains inventories, and ships from a distribution center in Irving, Texas, that is shared with physical stores.[46] Its marketing has emphasized the company's consistent service throughout all its channels: stores, catalogs, and online.

Ashford.com

Ashford has been the most prominent of the pure-play luxury retailers and opened before traditional luxury retailers could get their business online. Few of these pure-play luxury retailers, however, lasted very long. Ashford, who became an early leader with a focus on service, went public in September 1999 and gained a good reputation by responding well to the rush of the holiday season by adding temporary staff and guaranteeing next-day delivery for most items.

Service, however, did not insulate Ashford from more established luxury retailers who were catching up. In the attempt to stay ahead, Ashford changed its sales strategy several times during its development, originally competing on price and focusing on jewelry and accessories. Later, it moved to a broader range of luxury items and ceased to attract new customers through discount pricing. It also divested Guild.com, the art sales portion of its business, to more narrowly focus on luxury retail.

It built its strategy around the retention of repeat customers, but found that its customer base was too small for this to be a sufficient strategy. Following the lead of many other successful e-businesses, it formed an alliance with Amazon, which created a flexible marketing arrangement that required little commitment from Ashford.[47]

Ultimately, however, Asford's stock price plunged because it could not generate enough revenue to be profitable. Serving a small niche market, its costs were too high, and the marketing budget required to bring in revenue was prohibitive. Its stock was on the verge of being delisted from NASDAQ as its price fell below $1. In 2001, Ashford was bought out by Global Sports, an e-commerce service provider, which had also taken over Bluelight.com.

Lessons Learned:

- Customer service is critical.
  - Identifying the needs of customers in any industry is essential to a successful customer service strategy. For companies in

---

Lessons Learned (continued):

  luxury retail, the keys to their customer service success have been liberal return policies and a wealth of information available online to help the customer in every stage of the purchase.
- Traditional companies can create an advantage with smaller customer bases.
  - Traditional companies can create a strong sense of loyalty with customers long before an e-commerce venture begins. E-commerce can then be used to strengthen this relationship by maintaining traditional company values and brand management when using the Internet. The problems of newcomers such as Ashford.com in this market point to the difficulty of obtaining new customers in the luxury market, where traditional companies have acquired significant customer loyalty over time.

GROCERS

Unlike many e-commerce industries, the potential profitability of the online grocery industry was widely questioned from the beginning. Although some grocery firms maintain a nationwide presence, the industry is highly fragmented, and different chain names often exist in different regions. For example, Giant and Stop'n'Shop are but two of the chains operated by Royal Ahold. For pure-play online companies, the question of target demographics was equally complex, as profitability seemed most promising for serving only densely populated regions with affluent populations.

Moreover, many believed that the notion of buying groceries online would never attract a large segment of the population. Shopping online would deprive customers of everything from weekly circulars to the ability to gauge the ripeness of fruit. From the grocer's standpoint, online shopping would limit impulse purchases, common in physical stores. It would also add up-front costs in an industry whose profit margins are already only 1 percent. Grocers would face many complications in distribution and delivery arising from the presence of perishable goods. Not surprisingly, then, incumbent grocers did not rush to put their business online.

Over a four-year period, the industry ultimately was organized into three general business models. The first, epitomized by early industry leader Webvan, was a pure-play business model that involved the construction of distribution warehouses in which food would be stored and orders processed. Delivery would then be made directly to customers. These companies, including HomeGrocer and HomeRuns, served selected markets and limited delivery to within a certain range of the warehouses.

The second, instituted by Tesco, Albertson's, and others, was a bricks-and-clicks model in which the Web site was integrated with physical store operations. Instead of creating separate warehouses, employees would simply use the store's stock to fill orders, which could then be either delivered to the customer or picked up at the store. The channels would complement each other through cross-promotion, and the labor costs associated with order preparation could be offset through delivery charges or through price differentials for the products.

The third, hybrid model was typified by MyWebGrocer and its numerous affiliated grocers. In this model, a generally small and upscale local grocer would contract with a Web company such as MyWebGrocer, which handled the creation and maintenance of the Web site, and forwarded orders to the appropriate local store, which then handled delivery. The grocer and Web site then would share in the delivery charges. Although these models provide a general description of the industry, the details of specific companies' business models are very important in understanding why so many online grocers failed.

Tesco

Tesco used its established brands and business strengths to build a multi-channel strategy. The company also made substantial investments in intranet and supply-chain applications as part of an overall e-commerce strategy. It viewed e-commerce as a way to reach existing customers through a new channel that would complement the existing channel of physical stores.

In 1996, Tesco tested the concept of e-commerce for groceries by launching a site that serviced customers at a single retail store. It concluded that supplying these orders should be done from physical stores rather than building warehouses. It also viewed the market as a niche market and downplayed thoughts of huge customer base expansion.

Its first major e-commerce venture was the creation of Tesco.com in 1998, a 100 percent–owned subsidiary that allowed online ordering with delivery from retail outlets. For each store, two delivery trucks were purchased.[48] Delivery charges were instituted from the beginning, under the assumption that a flat rate would encourage larger orders. In the first year, it lost more than $15 million, but forecast profits within two years, and it gradually expanded to service more and more retail locations. It continued to invest in the site and by 2000 began to sell products and services other than groceries, including a banking service.[49] Online sales represented 2 percent of company revenues, reaching $420 million. By late 2001, the supermarket began expanding into more types of goods and reached one million registered users. Many competitors were also beginning to cede the market.

In January 2000, Tesco began operating an online unit called GroceryWorks. In 2001, Tesco reached a deal with Safeway, in which Tesco would provide technical resources and intellectual property for a 35 percent stake in Safeway's online venture. In early 2002, it began online efforts in the Vancouver and Portland markets, as a test before expanding further. Safeway's model, like Tesco's, called for taking products off shelves in physical stores. Initial goals were to bring online sales up to 1 percent of revenue while avoiding losses. It is important to note that because of structural differences in the grocery markets, profits, in general, tend to be higher in the grocery industry in England than they are in the United States.[50]

Webvan and HomeGrocer

Webvan was the creation of Louis Borders (unrelated to Borders' bookstores), who envisioned profitability in online groceries through inexpensive delivery costs. The company was funded by venture capital and went public in November 1999. Webvan believed it could quickly create a large market for online shopping and invested in trying to build a brand and customer base, dismissing suggestions that sufficient demand did not exist. It also believed the industry needed a new type of organization, a company centered around logistics, but did not adequately consider the amount of time and learning required to integrate the new infrastructure. The entire belief system of the company was built around an "all or nothing" mentality pushed by Borders himself.[51]

In 1999, Webvan built the first of a series of warehouses, which attempted to leverage ten times higher productivity through technology, with an estimate of $300 million in sales each year. The first area, which may have been an error, was the hilly, traffic-filled San Francisco Bay Area market. The company believed profitability would come within a year or less. Twenty-six more warehouses were scheduled to be built at a cost of $30 million. The venture capital environment encouraged this high-speed approach, which some considered reckless. Delivery was free for larger orders, under the assumption that productivity would compensate for the labor costs. The Webvan model required 1,500 orders per day per facility to break even.[52]

HomeGrocer was a competitor whose customer base was in the Pacific Northwest. Its business model was similar, but its strategy was slower and more conservative than Webvan's. Its model also required 1,500 orders per day per facility to break even, and delivery was free for larger orders and for frequent customers.[53] In 1999, it announced a partnership with Amazon.com, and later that year brought in Citigroup executive Mary Alice Taylor as CEO in preparation for an IPO. After those plans collapsed, it was forced to chose between finding a partner and scaling back operations.[54]

In 2000, Webvan merged with HomeGrocer in an all-stock deal. At that point, the company decided to shelve further expansion in favor of integrating operations with its new partner. This included establishing a new brand in new geographic markets, integrating platforms, and making personnel decisions in light of Webvan's more labor-intensive model.[55] The company chose to stick with Webvan's more aggressive business strategy. In the process, many customers were lost because of technology problems and unfamiliarity.[56] In 2001, the merged company declared bankruptcy after $1.2 billion of spending and a loss of $130 per order. None of its facilities had ever reached its potential in terms of order processing.

D'Agostino's-MWG

After years of using telephone-based delivery, D'Agostino's began offering online services in 2001, gradually introducing it to all 23 locations in the New York area. Orders were filled at the neighborhood store rather than from a central warehouse by staff members working from a printout. Customers could indicate whether out-of-stock items could be substituted with similar items. At some locations, delivery service was available, while in others prepared orders had to be picked up at the store. Delivery charges began at $13 and were lowered to $8–10, depending on size. D'Agostino's estimates 1–3 percent of sales coming from the online channel.[57] The Web site itself was run by MyWebGrocer.com, which updated the site's prices each morning and received $6 per order for its services.[58]

MyWebGrocer, for its part, had a clientele of more than 160 grocery stores and a customer base of 40,000. Growth had been extremely rapid, both in terms of new partnerships and sales at existing locations. The company had also been building its product database with the acquisition of new partners, so that its system had a catalog of 120,000 items. MyWebGrocer left certain decisions in the hands of the individual partners, including delivery options, to maintain flexibility at both ends. It also facilitated the use of promotions and incentives from the physical stores to be transferred online.

Lessons Learned

- E-commerce can help create customer demand.
  - Recent studies have shown that attitudes toward online grocery shopping have substantially shifted. The number of regular online shoppers more than doubled between 1998 and 2000, and hesitancy toward purchases in general and perishable food purchases in particular have both shrunk drastically.[59]
- E-commerce is not always easy.
  - For the most part, these companies have been fighting against extinction rather than against each other. Competition between online grocers has been infrequent, and the stories emerging from those markets have not yet given us a clear picture as to what to expect from such competition.

OFFICE SUPPLIES

The office supplies industry online is fairly consistent with the situation in the physical space. The top companies (Office Depot and Staples) are the same, but the industry remains highly fragmented, and these companies account for less than a quarter of sales both online and offline.

Purchasing office supplies online was a fairly reasonable proposition that faced no major logistical threats. Most office supply companies already controlled some catalog business and thus were well acquainted with the needs of both individual and corporate customers. The products themselves presented no major logistical threats, nor gave any reason to think that online purchasing would be undesirable. The online channel stood to increase efficiencies and cut costs without making any major changes in the industry.

Office Depot and Staples have been the two giants in the industry, and began by following very different plans in e-commerce. Office Depot, believing strongly in e-commerce, was the first mover and followed an integration strategy, hoping to build synergies between physical stores, catalog sales, and online sales. Staples was an Internet skeptic and a late mover that decided to respond to Office Depot by spinning off its Web site as a separate unit with a tracking stock and an IPO (which never occurred).

With the collapse of the dot.com stock market, Staples folded its Web site back into the company, and its strategy now resembles that of Office Depot. Competition in the industry is now based on leveraging functional capabilities, offering services that complement office product purchases, and getting the most out of integration efforts.

Office Depot

Years before its e-commerce ventures began, Office Depot developed a real-time inventory database for its physical stores. The physical stores and catalog business were also supported by a fleet of delivery trucks.[60] The launch of the Web site came in 1998, and immediately followed an integration strategy, in which the Web site, catalog, and physical stores were to be viewed as different channels of the same company, offering the same prices and services.

Many in the company feared the integrated effort, but salespeople were offered bonuses for steering customers online, which helped build a customer base that would use multiple channels. The stores also began promoting the Web site through in-store kiosks and pitches from salespeople.

The conveniences of OfficeDepot.com to customers were numerous. The site was personalized for customers and offered tailored views for individuals and corporate customers. The site offered all products that were in the Office Depot catalog, and many more items than in most stores. Delivery was free, and customers also had the option to pick up the item from a local store.

Corporate customers had personalized pages on the Web site that automatically kept track of spending authorizations. Suppliers could also check inventory in stores and warehouses through a private extranet. To push more traditional customers online, Office Depot began expanding its Web site into other services, such as accounting and payroll in 2001. In 2002, Office Depot began offering direct mail marketing through its site, providing large numbers of customers with services.[61]

In 2002, Office Depot signed a deal with Amazon to begin selling office products through Amazon's site, in an arrangement similar to Amazon's deals with Target and other companies. Amazon processed the transactions, while Office Depot managed inventory and fulfillment, including the option to pick up merchandise at the store.

From a cost perspective, the Web site provided an alternative to printing costly catalogs, and Web transactions cost half as much as phone transactions.[62] For this reason, Office Depot offered incentives to customers to do business online. The catalog agents also used the browser-based system for order processing, which helped cut costs and increased sales by 12 percent.

In 2000, online sales approached $1 billion[63] and by 2001, they reached $1.6 billion.[64] Forty percent of major customers used the Web

site for ordering. The officedepot.com site has been continuously profitable since its launch, with continual growth. In 2002, it was the most
important online retailer behind Amazon. The company estimated that
online sales made up 14 percent of total sales in 2001, up from 3 percent
in 1999.[65] The share of customers' wallets has increased on the site, with
purchases one-third higher than other channels.

Office Depot has a large data warehouse, which helps it maintain
customer metrics and design the personalization of the Web site to
maximize purchases. This data helps cross-selling efforts online by
analyzing frequent customer purchases. It also measures metrics such
as transaction speed and download times against those of direct competitors and other similar companies' sites.

Staples

The Staples Web site was first created in 1998 and immediately
established as a separate business unit, with separate growth targets
and infrastructure, but with ties to the parent company's functional
areas such as purchasing and fulfillment. The unit was kept within
company headquarters, but distance was built through office design
and practices. Hires were mixed, with an eye on both traditional systems and innovation.

Staples began its e-commerce venture later than Office Depot. In 1999,
it began issuing stock in advance of a planned 2000 IPO. Investors'
expertise was the main basis for the alignment with venture capital. The
stock options proved to be a strong recruiting tool. In the second quarter
of 2002, the site reached profitability for the first time, though Staples
had overestimated clients' knowledge of the Internet.

The company began with three online operations, each targeted at a
different customer base. Later, the company began offering services
online in addition to office supplies, including a section of the site
dedicated to building small business. The goal was to achieve $1 billion
in revenue and acquire one million customers by 2003. The strategy
included leveraging the brand name, competitive advantages in fulfillment and service, and acquiring customers in untapped markets, especially small business.[66] The company used a marketing campaign to link
the site with the parent company's brand name.

A strength of Staples' strategy was learning about customers through
focus groups and other feedback efforts, which led to several features
on the site. The Web site included tailoring page views to customers
based on their profile in the customer database. Customers could also
assign purchases to specific cost or budget centers.[67]

Staples developed a unique system for processing returns, which
automated paperwork for returns and guaranteed quicker credits while

reducing costs. Customers could also receive information on long-term procurement in an appropriate format without disputes or problems.

Integration required connecting the Web site to the point-of-sale system, and Staples decided to implement an integration layer rather than customizing connections in different areas, thus leaving an easier task for future integration efforts. In 2001, Staples decided to merge its online and catalog functions, eliminating any more discussions of the postponed IPO. Cost savings from operations was cited as the major purpose. The online unit had failed to reach profitability, losing $11.5 million in 2000. In August 2001, Staples voted to convert its online stock into common stock, bringing the e-commerce venture back into the company.

New efforts have been aimed at small business and getting customers to use multiple channels, as customers who use both stores and the Web site purchase 2.5 times more merchandise.

Lessons Learned:

- Pre-existing IT capabilities can enhance e-commerce ventures.
  - A strong, preexisting IT strategy can help ease any cultural change the company may face with e-commerce. Such capabilities can also augment the back-end of an e-commerce venture through a previously established proper IT hierarchy within the company.
- Customer information is of tremendous value.
  - The wealth of information made available to both Office Depot and Staples through e-commerce helped them coordinate direct marketing campaigns and offers that were specifically tailored to identifiable needs of their customers.
- E-commerce can facilitate new types of business for a company.
  - Staples and Office Depot were able to move into a number of small business services due largely to their level of involvement in other business activities of their customers.

CHAPTER 8

Company Cases: B2C—Services

INTRODUCTION

Companies that provide services to customers, in addition to or instead of physical goods, face certain expectations when moving into e-commerce. Customers of traditional service companies expect that the level of service that they experience will not deteriorate for any reason (and hopefully will improve), even as a company makes a transition into e-commerce. The service expectations are typically based on a company providing some unique service to its customers, a certain level of personal interaction, or any number of other tangible and intangible benefits that customers do not want to forgo when taking advantage of a newly available e-commerce venture.

Some companies have realized that for an e-commerce strategy to work for their particular line of business, it must be coupled with a tangible real-world presence that a customer can utilize. This duality does not mean that a company can succeed by simply adding Internet-based services to the traditional services. Rather, the two channels must be complementary to provide the necessary level of service. Wells Fargo, for example, developed goals that were similar to other companies beginning an e-commerce venture, centering on the idea of both cutting costs and increasing revenue through the use of online services and transactions. However, the company also noticed that most of the people who did online research on various products offered by Wells

Fargo eventually completed their purchase at a physical branch. In this way, cross-channel promotion can often become a significant advantage to companies looking to incorporate e-commerce into their larger corporate strategy.

Another common attribute of the companies in this chapter has been their need to cannibalize or steal their own customers. Employees working for traditional aspects of a business might, understandably, resist losing customers to an e-commerce venture. However, companies have come to realize that it is better to lose traditional customers to their own e-commerce venture than to that of a competitor. Companies have dealt with this internal competition in a number of different ways, but one essential lesson is that often the employees of a company must be provided with incentives that align their personal rewards to the company goals so they do not fear the cannibalization of traditional company business into a new e-commerce venture.

In the end, the companies in this chapter have faced a number of challenges. But the lessons that ought to garner the attention of all senior executives and managers of e-commerce ventures center on the balance that must be achieved among traditional company practices and those of e-commerce ventures. The industries and companies examined in this chapter include the following by industry.

Stockbrokers
  Charles Schwab
  Merrill Lynch
  E*Trade

Consumer Banks
  Wells Fargo
  Bank of America
  Bank One-Wingspan

Pharmacies
  CVS
  Walgreens
  Rite Aid-Drugstore.com

Postal Services
  UPS
  Federal Express

STOCKBROKERS

The online brokerage industry has seen substantial competition between Internet startups and traditional brokerage firms. Brand name is a strong asset for traditional brokerage firms among large, experienced investors, but large marketing budgets and low prices have been successful in enticing many inexperienced investors to do business with Internet startups. The industry has featured a wide range of prices and levels of services, with companies following a wide variety of customer acquisition strategies.

Charles Schwab, an early mover, established a strong position as a full-service provider. Its integration strategy pervaded all areas of the company, including price consistency among trading channels and a company structure that treated e-commerce as simply an extension of its traditional business. As Merrill Lynch entered online trading long after Schwab and many Internet traders, it was forced to find new strategies to position itself against its more established competitors.

E*Trade has been the most successful of the pure-play Internet brokers without a history in the physical space. Its strategy was built around price and convenience rather than service, attracting less experienced investors. Once customer acquisition was no longer a viable basis for continued growth, E*Trade turned to diversification and, eventually, toward establishing a presence in the bricks-and-mortar space.

Online trading has moved beyond the customer acquisition strategies that dominated the first few years in the industry. Diversification, offering new services, cost cutting, and gaining a large share of customers' wallets have become increasingly more relevant to profitability.[1]

Charles Schwab

Schwab decided in 1995 to pursue Internet trading and within four months had set up a site for online trading with a fee of $29–$39 per trade depending on number of shares. It immediately noted the lower costs of operations associated with online trading.[2]

Schwab's approach was to compete not by offering the lowest prices, but by offering full service for a moderate price. Throughout its history, the site prioritized the volume of information available to customers on its Web site.[3] The company immediately understood the importance of cannibalizing its offline business, and its first major marketing campaign was directed at its own customers, which helped draw 400,000 customers online in the first year. By 1998, Schwab had integrated its online and offline services so that customers could make a trade on any channel for $29.95. In early 2000, that fee was cut in half for high-volume traders.

By the end of 1999, 67 percent of all customer trades were being executed online, and that increased to 80 percent a year later. Schwab has always had a considerably larger average account size than pure-play competitors such as E*Trade because of its significant presence in both online and traditional business.

Schwab viewed this strategy as a "clicks and mortar" strategy and treated all customers equally regardless of channel. It also invested heavily in building its brand. Schwab was targeted by both pure-play and full-service competitors and succeeded in carving out a position between the two that encompassed the advantages of each. In 2000, Schwab bought investment bank U.S. Trust to be able to offer financial advice to larger customers and compete more effectively with full-service competitors.

Schwab also chose to do most of its IT work in-house, originally because vendors were unable to meet the deadlines that Schwab established to develop its online services. As the company was convinced that exposure to back-end systems was one of the potential liabilities of e-trading, the maintenance of those systems was crucial to retaining the customers' loyalty and trust.

OneSource, a pre-Internet Schwab initiative established as a "mutual fund supermarket," represented one of the company's biggest competitive advantages because of its critical mass. Competitors such as E*Trade offered large numbers of mutual funds, but OneSource's application and the interaction between the financial advisor network and mutual funds made it somewhat less imitable.

Merrill Lynch

In 1997, when Charles Schwab and E*Trade were both experiencing 30 percent growth in online trading, Merrill Lynch still had a Web site that offered neither online trading nor any data services.[4] Vice-chairman John Steffens was an Internet skeptic well into 1998, believing that trading online was dangerous and a bad value for clients.

Later, he did an about-face, offering a free trial access to research in late 1998, in an effort to attract clients. Channel conflict and the fear of angering brokers was a major cause of this delay. Many believe the change was motivated by Schwab's passing Merrill in market capitalization, and the resulting potential loss in margins that Merrill Lynch faced. Steffens realized that full-commission brokerages were endangered and embraced the Internet with the hope of replacing commissions with new fees and assets. CIO John McKinley was a major influence in convincing Steffens to embrace online trading. His decisions in using the IT budget to develop the Web site were vital to the change in both the formulation and the implementation of the new strategy.[5]

Merrill attempted to make up for the disadvantage of being a late mover by appealing to the loyalty of its own customer base and bringing that base online. In June, 1999, Merrill Lynch began offering online trading at the same $29.95 as Schwab. The company also initiated a program called "Unlimited Advantage," which offered unlimited trading under any channel and access to research for a yearly percentage of assets.[6] Other features included a cash management account to conduct online banking, a business purchasing section, and other features directed to small business.[7]

Merrill Lynch also established a strategic goal to be the first mover in the area of being an "institutional portal" between corporate clients. It believed that focusing on the business of institutional investors provided more competitive advantage than targeting the individual investors' market that had been saturated by marketing from Schwab, E*Trade, and others. It signed deals with more than 400 retailers to sell through its portal.[8] Without an asset such as Schwab's OneSource, Merrill hoped to compete with interaction among online brokerage services and leverage its brand name.

Unlike Schwab, Merrill Lynch turned to outsourcing for its IT needs. Already behind its competitors, it could not afford to spend the time and money required to build its own competencies in this area.

E*Trade

E*Trade, which has been the most successful of the pure-play Internet brokers, became an early leader in part due to the slow strategic decisions and actions of traditional financial institutions. The company's history dates back to 1982. In 1992, E*Trade made arrangements to do trades through CompuServe and AOL, and in 1996 it opened its own Web site.

Its early strategy was to build market share through a heavy marketing and customer acquisition campaign that spent much of the company's early revenues.[9] It positioned itself as a low-cost alternative to traditional companies like Charles Schwab by offering lower commissions and lower minimum investment requirements. The Web site offered less information than its competitors and relied on price and simplicity of use to attract customers. E*Trade also chose to package and present its information differently from most of its competitors. Instead of developing its own content, it purchased content from multiple online providers, thus saving development costs and focusing on its core business of customer acquisition and retention.[10] By 2003, E*Trade received 58 percent of company revenue from online brokerage.[11]

Diversification was a priority for E*Trade throughout its history. In 1999, it invested in a new full-service online investment banking operation to gain more access to financial markets for its customers. E*Trade provided much of its online platform to the new bank in exchange for the services provided. It also bought the country's largest ATM network in 2000.[12] Other non-stock offerings included auto and life insurance and home mortgages. By 2002, banking services made up 32 percent of E*Trade sales.

In 2000, E*Trade considered and negotiated, but did not conclude, deals to be acquired by American Express or Goldman Sachs. Recognizing, however, that a presence in the physical space was vital, E*Trade shifted its strategy toward building such a foothold. In April 2001, it attempted to move into the bricks-and-clicks segment by opening its E*Trade Center in midtown Manhattan, which gave its online model a strong presence in the physical space. The store included 200 computers, a trading service area, educational seminars, and a more private area to service high-net-worth customers.

It also began opening centers in Target stores throughout 2001, first setting up kiosks in twenty stores and later in more stores. In addition to the kiosks, stores later were equipped with ATM machines and company representatives to assist customers.[13]

In 2002, E*Trade partnered with Yahoo to provide customers with financial data and access to trading through instant messaging for which it also began producing unique video content. E*Trade followed this pattern of diversifying channels throughout its history.[14]

Lessons Learned:

- A pure-play e-commerce competitor with a new idea can gain substantial market presence in a short time.
  - E-Trade was able to become an e-commerce leader among Internet stockbrokers by providing a type of service that traditional companies had not previously offered—low-cost and low-service—to attract a specific customer segment previously ignored by brokers.
- Traditional firms can use e-commerce to enhance, not replace, their traditional structure.
  - Schwab's "clicks and mortar" strategy allowed the company to couple online growth with traditional brick-and-mortar growth, ensuring that customers had access to all of the resources, both online and offline, that Schwab could make available.
- E-commerce cost savings
  - Every company needs to assess what actions will lead to the most significant cost savings through e-commerce. For brokers, the costs of online trading were substantially lower than the traditional alternative. In addition, the cost of providing research to investors online was less expensive through e-commerce.

CONSUMER BANKS

In the banking industry, convenience is a prime motivation for customers. Competing on price is possible through certain fees (or lack thereof) or rates on products such as certificates of deposit and loans. But price competition has severe limitations, especially for bricks-and-clicks banks. From the bank's perspective, costs can be reduced through online banking, as banking transactions online have been shown to have dramatic cost savings compared to traditional methods for transactions, such as tellers and ATMs.[15]

The banking industry doesn't break out numbers for e-commerce in their financial results, and profitability is generally determined through more indirect measures such as cost savings. Online customers also tend to buy proportionally more of the most profitable products. Studies have also shown that online banking deepens the customer relationship and increases customer satisfaction.

The three companies analyzed here made very different structural decisions with regard to e-commerce. Wells Fargo followed an integration strategy and treated e-commerce as a natural progression in line with its history of bank pioneering. Bank of America started with an integrated effort, but quickly moved to separate e-commerce functions, hoping to inspire innovations through a separate business unit. Later, it returned to a more integrated structure. Bank One was one of the few banks to spin off an Internet-only bank, Wingspan. It also, however, maintained a site tied to the parent company and eventually folded Wingspan back into that site.

Wells Fargo

Wells Fargo began offering online banking services in 1995. By 1998, it had nearly a half million online customers, over a million online customers by 2000, and almost 5 million by 2003. Its customers do an average of 50 percent of their banking transactions online. More than 25 percent of Wells Fargo's offline customers have moved online, and 35 percent of the company's commercial customers have enrolled online.[16]

The online division, formed in 1999, is a self-contained unit, regarded as a "total business group" within the company. The Internet is regarded as another delivery channel, not a separate line of business. The division has focused on uses of the Internet to serve all customer segments, including small business and investors. Profits for online operations are not tracked separately because of the company's belief in tight integration, but the company announced in 2002 that the division had become profitable for the first time.[17]

The Web site shares the corporate marketing slogan "Fast Then, Fast Now," drawing on the company's history of being banking pioneers. The site is promoted online through advertising and also in the branches, including having the Web address on envelopes.

Wells Fargo followed a philosophy of delivering a fully integrated online service, rather than putting out the fastest possible product online. In the interest of customer satisfaction, it prioritized functionality over speed.[18] The site integrated its offline and online operations well. Customers were automatically signed up for online service when they opened a new checking account, and online information seekers received follow-up calls from the bank. There were no additional charges for online service, except for the bill payment service, which attracted many customers despite the fee. Online orders cost 30 percent less to process on average than an offline transaction, and online customers made 17 percent fewer calls to bank call centers.

The primary purpose of the online channel is to retain customers and increase share of wallet rather than cut costs (though reduced costs is a significant benefit). For Wells Fargo, attrition rates have been half as high among online customers, who are twice as likely to make additional purchases. Further, the company's research shows that 80 percent of customers who research a product online eventually purchase it at a branch.

In late 1999, Wells Fargo expanded into services on its Web site, targeting small business with products for building small business sites. In 2000, it began targeting the middle market with similar offerings. Another important feature was the sales of home equity products, which feature ChatLive, a feature that allows customers to chat online with a banker about equity products. This feature increased purchase rates by 50 percent.[19] In 2003 alone, the number of active online customers (4.8 million) increased by 35 percent and the number of active online small business customers increased by 40 percent.

Bank of America

In 1999, Bank of America eliminated its integrated e-commerce unit, distributing many of its functions to various business units and assigning responsibilities according to the nature of the product. In 2001, it began to reintegrate functions under the leadership of a former GE executive. Its online products had become scattered throughout different divisions, and the company found that it became difficult for consumers to conduct multiple transactions online. The ultimate goal of the reorganization was a new Web portal that coordinated Internet products. Like most online banking companies, Bank of America does not report the profitability of e-commerce business. Instead it focuses on values created by online functions, including lower attrition rates, higher balances, and fewer call-center calls.

Bank of America's online banking is the most popular in America, in terms of both number of customers and number of unique visitors.[20] In 2000, Bank of America reached 2 million online customers, and that number jumped to 4 million by 2002. Customers conduct 31 percent of their banking transactions online.

Bank of America made the observation of customer behavior a key determinant of strategy and has used a series of customer polls and pilot programs to determine the programs that are important to online customers. It eliminated programs such as wireless banking and person-to-person payments because of low customer interest.

In April 2001, it entered into a partnership with Homestore.com to create an online marketplace dedicated to financial services related to home buying, financing, and improvement. In May 2002, it decided to eliminate fees for online bill payment, which had been one of its more successful online draws. This change in strategy worked. The following quarter, 30 percent more customers began using the function, which reduced costs to go along with the elimination of the fees.[21] By 2003, Bank of America was the leader in the customer adoption of online bill payment, with over 25 percent of online customers using online bill payment, and the leader in overall active online customers, followed by Wells Fargo.[22]

Bank One-Wingspan

As of 1999, Bank One's site had 350,000 online customers and was building the site by signing new marketing deals. Still, it decided to launch a stand-alone subsidiary, Wingspan, to be an Internet-only bank with no branches. The decision was based in large part on Bank One's belief about the existence of distinct customer segments. Physical branches and BankOne.com were well equipped to handle some of the segments, but Wingspan was targeted to a segment of customers who desired Bank One products but also wanted full and convenient access to a wide range of other products.[23]

Wingspan customers could use teller machines, but not Bank One branches, and the model anticipated and accepted some level of cannibalization. It also competed against its parent by offering higher rates on certificates of deposit.[24] Bank One's site offered 49 mutual funds compared to 7,000 at Wingspan. Problems with the model included that Wingspan could not deliver cash and that deposits had to be made by regular mail.

Unlike the Bank One Web site, Wingspan offered multiple vendors of mortgages, insurance, and investments.[25] It also offered lower fees and higher rates on deposits, which were possible because of lower costs associated with online accounts.[26] Still, creation and maintenance of the site and sponsoring and supporting the brand were costly. Spending for Wingspan was projected at $150 million for its first year.

In June 2001, Bank One folded Wingspan back into its other online operations, which had three times as many customers. It concluded that customers were interested in value-added services from banks, but that they wanted to maintain offline relationships.[27] The limitations of online banking, including accepting deposits and maintaining high value per account metrics, were also never solved by Wingspan. Bank One also folded Loans.com, another site that it had previously purchased and maintained as a separately branded site, back into the parent company in November 2001, citing customer comfort with the Bank One brand name as the main reason.[28]

Another important part of Bank One's e-commerce strategy had been its partnership with Microsoft in its Passport.NET program, which included banking services from Bank One as part of an overall electronic wallet Web service. Bank One saw further cost cutting from customer relationships in this program, along with cross-selling opportunities, an advertising contract, and building Bank One products in Microsoft accounting software.[29] In 2002, Bank One launched its revamped and upgraded Web site based on customer feedback and usability tests to give faster access, easier use, and more organization to its more than 1 million online customers.[30]

Lessons Learned:

- E-commerce is often, in part, about stealing your own customers
  - For each of these banks, customer demand for online services required them to pursue an e-commerce model to keep their own customers. While traditional company employees might resist, it is better for a traditional company structure to lose customers to its own online venture than to that of a competitor.
- E-commerce cost savings
  - Companies need to find ways to use e-commerce to reduce costs through methods that were never before possible. For banks, these savings were found in the reduced cost of online transactions compared to transactions through ATMs or branches.
- Customers have not been willing to accept e-commerce if it means a reduced level of service quality.
  - While Wingspan.com provided all of the online services that customers expected from an online bank, it could not provide the basic banking functions that they had come to expect.

PHARMACIES

The pharmacy industry moved more slowly online than many other industries, with only rudimentary Web sites existing in 1998. Pure-play competitors moved first, but building a trustworthy brand became a major issue that allowed traditional pharmacies to catch up despite a slow start.

A variety of security issues were prevalent in the pharmacy industry, including monitoring of prescriptions, quality of medical advice, and the safety supply chain processes for prescription filling. Addressing these matters and assuring both customers and regulators of safety was important to all competitors in this industry. Speed was also an important issue for customers: 30 percent of all prescriptions are needed immediately.[31]

CVS, Walgreens, and Rite Aid followed entirely different strategies for establishing an online pharmacy. CVS chose to acquire a pure-play competitor and take advantage of its already-established Web presence and expertise, while imposing the CVS brand name on the site. Walgreens chose an integration strategy, with its Web site fully owned and operated by the parent company. Rite Aid chose a partnership with pure-play Drugstore.com and chose not to integrate brand or management.

The companies also differed with regard to their product offerings strategy. CVS.com focused on increasing the number of products available, becoming more of a general retailer, and modeling the store to be similar to its physical stores. Walgreens chose to focus on pharmacy customers and only expanded product offerings for the sake of convenience. Rite Aid kept its focus on drugstore products, but its strategy also recognized the importance of increasing average order size. Each company also focused on offering related nonproduct features, including medical advice and prescription histories.

CVS

CVS began in e-commerce by considering building its own Web site, but shifted strategies because of concerns over internal capabilities. Instead of building its own Web site, CVS began its e-commerce venture by acquiring online pharmacy Soma.com for $30 million. Doing so gave CVS expertise in e-commerce and eliminated a major online competitor. CVS believed it would be able to rapidly expand its online presence and foster online alliances while using a strategy that included its physical stores.[32] It also hoped to leverage the CVS brand name, and thus renamed Soma.com as CVS.com. The e-commerce venture was fully owned as a subsidiary of CVS, but run by a separate management team that included input from Soma's experienced e-commerce team.

The Web site immediately expanded from Soma.com's online offerings, tripling the number of items and shifting the emphasis to higher-margin items such as over-the-counter medicines, vitamins, and health and beauty aids. The Web site also offered CVS label products, generally with much lower prices than name brands, as well as the popular photo services available in stores. CVS.com offered personalized service, including individually tailored health pages, health-management programs, and an email service for inquiries about pharmaceutical advice.[33] The site also offered next-day delivery for all online orders.

In 2000, the site was upgraded, with a number of changes focused on expanding product mix and customer service. New product offerings included cosmetics and homeopathics, which were not available in physical stores. In collaboration with Kodak, it launched the first online photo processing services.[34]

Behavior tracking was a key aspect of CVS's e-commerce strategy. As CVS quickly determined that click-through visitors who were attracted by some marketing efforts were high-cost and low-value, it switched its focus to increase profitability. By outsourcing to a database-marketing software company, it created tracking software that identified some problems in the ordering process. Solving those problems increased conversion rates and sales.[35]

Later, CVS entered into key alliances to improve both its supply chain and its ability to assist customers with medical advice. The first alliance, with pharmacy benefits management (PBM) company Merck-Medco, ensured that the CVS.com Web site would become an exclusive online supplier of prescription drugs to Merck-Medco members.[36] An alliance with WebMD drove new customers to CVS.com after receiving advice on WebMD and made CVS the exclusive pharmacy for related health channels. A third alliance, with MSN.com, enabled CVS to sell certain products on the MSN portal. In 2001, CVS took its integration strategy one step further by bringing the CVS.com management team into corporate headquarters, instead of its previous location across the country.[37]

Walgreens

Walgreens' e-commerce venture started slower than its competitors', especially with regard to actually ordering products online. In 1998, Walgreens introduced a service for online prescription refills enabling shoppers who have the number from the prescription label to reorder online and then pick up the medicine at their local store. The popularity of that service led to exploration of a more complete e-commerce service.

In 1999, Walgreens signed a deal with Peapod, to be an exclusive supplier of over-the-counter health and beauty products and several new general merchandise categories to its distribution center.[38] It also launched a full online pharmacy, funding it with its own cash reserves rather than outside investors. Its strategy was to tightly integrate the Web site with the physical retail stores. Walgreens.com was fully owned and operated by its bricks-and-mortar parent. The online pharmacy was fully integrated with the Walgreens retail pharmacy computer system, offering patients seamless service whether a prescription was filled in a store, online, or by the mail service facilities.[39]

Redesigning the site cost Walgreens $10 million, and it launched an expensive marketing campaign to advertise the new site's functionality. It also offered free shipping for a limited period. Even after the redesign, the e-commerce strategy focused on pharmacy customers, with other products and features offered as a convenience.

One site feature permitted patients to look up their prescription history in a secure, password-protected area. In line with its belief in integration, the personal profiles included all prescriptions filled both online and in stores along with purchases of over-the-counter medication.[40] The new site continued to emphasize the ability to place new and refill prescription orders online and pick them up at any physical store, and an added function allowed pre-set automated refills complete with email notification. Other features included access to Mayo Clinic health information and the ability to ask pharmacists questions online.[41]

Rite Aid

From the beginning, Rite Aid believed that online sales would only constitute a small portion of sales, so its e-commerce strategies were tentative. On its first Web site, Rite Aid only handled prescription refills, enabling shoppers who have the Rx number from the prescription label to reorder online and then pick up the medicine at their local store.[42]

Once Rite Aid realized the importance of selling online, it decided to enter into an agreement with pure-play company Drugstore.com, which was one of the first movers in the industry, instead of expanding its Web site. In the deal, Rite Aid bought a 25.3 percent equity stake in Drugstore.com, which was an ideal partner because it brought Internet capabilities and strong investors, including Amazon, thus limiting Rite Aid's investment risk.[43]

Rite Aid and Drugstore.com had separate ownership and management, but some aspects were integrated. Marketing efforts were coordinated, including the presence of the Drugstore logo on Rite Aid bags and bottle caps. The partners also had operation integration, including fulfillment, which gave Drugstore previously fettered access to pharmacy benefits management. Another aspect of integration was the ability for customers to pick up Drugstore.com prescriptions at Rite Aid locations. The two companies also established an integration team to share ideas and coordinate strategies. Still, separation of brands was maintained because Drugstore.com was founded on providing a unique customer service experience that traditional drugstores couldn't.[44] Although prescription customers were important to Drugstore's strategy, it offered additional products not simply for convenience, but to increase order size.[45]

Drugstore.com had its own distribution center that provided strong measurement and customer response systems. After the opening of the center, order size increased for subsequent orders. It also had a secure facility for handling prescription drugs. As the center is still operating well below maximum capacity, future increases in efficiency are still possible.[46]

Drugstore.com created a number of additional alliances, including fulfillment of health and beauty products for Amazon. It developed a fully integrated order system with former acquisition Beauty.com and purchased the customer list of defunct pure-play competitor PlanetRx.com., which led to a simple process of prescription transfers.[47] In 2002, Rite Aid completed selling its equity in Drugstore.com, although its partnership remained unaffected, and Rite Aid downplayed the importance of this move.[48]

Like many pure-play companies, Drugstore.com was hoping to reach profitability for the first time in 2004.[49]

Lessons Learned:

- It is never too late for a traditional company to expand into e-commerce.
  - Although these companies were late movers in e-commerce, their traditional brand strength allowed them to make up quickly for their early lack of initiative.
- E-commerce can be tailored for any industry.
  - The e-commerce side of these pharmacies has a far more limited scope than their traditional business ventures. It is perfectly acceptable, and sometimes advantageous, for the e-commerce side of a business to have an entirely different and innovative approach to the business.

POSTAL SERVICES

UPS and Federal Express dominate the e-commerce postal services industry in much the same way they do physical space. The two companies have alternated in the introduction of new technological advantage-builders, but UPS has maintained a much larger market share, in part because of the strategies of the companies in the physical space. UPS and its moderate-speed strategy has had much more functionality in e-commerce than Federal Express's high-speed services.

The companies addressed e-commerce with somewhat different structures, although both recognized that the nature of their industry meant that anything resembling a spin-off would make little sense. These companies recognized that they had much to gain by encouraging traditional customers to use the online channel.

Both companies focused on forging partnerships to encourage or mandate the use of their firm for the shipment of e-commerce purchases. Both companies also saw a major opening for advantage in creating the ability to track deliveries. In 2000, 74 percent of Web sites did not allow the tracking of orders, though that changed quickly. Customers identified tracking as a reason for repeat purchases. Another key area for e-business growth was return of goods bought online. Federal Express and UPS both provided an outsourcing opportunity for companies, a market estimated at $300 million and rapidly growing.[50]

Finally, the companies were competing in an extension of their traditional business, providing services for supply-chain management and logistics in e-commerce. This segment was seen as much more profitable than the e-commerce opportunities associated with the traditional business.

UPS

UPS was the first company to use online technologies, but Federal Express maintained its early advantage through its unique tracking system. UPS gained an advantage over Federal Express in 1999 by creating UPS Online Tools, a platform for shipment tracking that did not require proprietary software or system reconfiguration. The service also included pick-up and drop-off coordination and cost calculations.[51] UPS's large amount of spending on IT ($1 billion in 2000) helped narrow the gap. Its approach was to move deliberately into e-commerce while minimizing the risk for the parent company.[52]

By 2000, UPS handled 55 percent of all shipments for e-commerce retailers.[53] Moreover, for 49 percent of retailers, UPS was the default carrier, and many large companies such as Amazon had exclusive arrangements with UPS. It also had shipping links built into more than 100,000 sites. UPS did not separate revenue by source channels, so its metrics were based on tracking requests per day, which were in the millions.[54] More than half of shipments came from companies with online connections to UPS.

Key to the UPS strategy was repositioning the company as not only a shipper, but also an information-delivery company and a problem solver. In February 2000, it launched a subsidiary, e-Ventures, to develop new businesses and capabilities. It hoped to use its fleet of trucks and warehouses as a competitive advantage in new Internet businesses. Its e-commerce units operated semi-autonomously, with some oversight from the parent company.

The first resulting new business was UPS e-Logistics. UPS offered online logistics services years before FedEx began offering them, including tools for improving Web site functionality, reducing costs, and improving customer service. UPS also moved into handling payments for COD shipments and guaranteeing credit for smaller retailers who bought furniture and shipped it via UPS.

One contract for UPS's online logistics division consisted of handling returns for buy.com, allowing massive simplification of the process for customers. In 2000, it created a more extensive e-commerce returns service, a browser-based system that permitted customers to print return labels through UPS servers. The e-retailer paid a transaction fee and delivery charges for the service.

By 2000, the logistics division's business had grown to $1.4 billion. It also had been expanding its capabilities by acquiring two smaller logistics firms.[55] Unlike Federal Express, UPS focused on existing retailers rather than targeting nascent firms looking to set up an e-business. In December 2000, UPS partnered with eBay to provide users direct access to UPS shipping and to simplify shipping arrangements for buyers and sellers. Although previous eBay partners had offered discounts and connections, UPS was the first to integrate directly into the site,[56] and in 2003, the two companies extended their relationship and introduced a new set of shipping options to eBay customers.[57]

Federal Express

FedEx had PowerShip terminals installed in customers' mailrooms as early as 1988 for digital interaction. Federal Express was also the first shipper to allow customers to track packages via computers, as early as 1990. That tracking, however, required proprietary software.[58]

Although the proprietary nature of the software was somewhat of a disadvantage in arranging carrier contracts, FedEx offered this software to companies in syndication, allowing them to integrate it with their offerings and customize a tracking system. Federal Express did not charge a fee for the software, but instead profited by creating high switching costs for the partner company and ensuring shipments through FedEx.[59] Federal Express also attempted to gain an advantage by creating mobile devices that allowed customers to arrange shipments from anywhere.

As of 2000, Federal Express carried only 10 percent of e-commerce shipments. One major problem was that the speed offered by Federal Express was not necessarily needed in e-commerce, especially for its price. For that reason, FedEx introduced a new home delivery service in 2000 targeted to online shoppers, with lower rates, flexible delivery dates, and delivery by appointment available. It risked, however, creating confusion due to the strong association of its brand with high-speed delivery.[60]

In 1999, Federal Express forged a partnership with Netscape to become the default shipping option for all e-commerce conducted through the Netcenter portal site.[61] Later that year, it introduced the FedEx MarketPlace, which provided site users one-click access to a number of its largest customers, including HP, LL Bean, and Value America.[62]

In 2000, Federal Express introduced services designed to help e-commerce firms manage inventory and deliver packages, targeting small and medium-sized companies. Under one offering, FedEx would help retailers set up Web stores using a platform outsourced from Orbit Commerce. FedEx would benefit by inducing the retailer to use it for shipping.

Federal Express reorganized itself in 2000 in response to some of the challenges posed by e-commerce. Its four divisions focused on logistics, premium deliveries, high-speed deliveries, and low-cost deliveries. It did not, however, establish a division to specifically focus on e-commerce. Its new business units also maintained a large amount of integration in resources.[63] In 2002, FedEx enhanced its high-speed delivery division, FedEx Custom Critical, by adding features such as quoting, scheduling, tracking, and mapping to its online shipping toolkit.[64]

Lessons Learned:

- Competitive partnerships
  - Partnerships can develop into something more than simple growth for a company. The competitive nature of the partnerships pursued by both UPS and FedEx led to each company staking claim to different and new segments of the e-commerce industry.
- E-commerce can facilitate new types of business for a company
  - UPS and FedEx were both able to position themselves in the role of e-commerce facilitators and logistics providers, beyond their stereotypical shipping roles, because of their

Lessons Learned (continued)

    early experiences with incorporating e-commerce into their own strategies.

- Traditional companies can establish a tremendous advantage in e-commerce.
  - Neither UPS nor FedEx would have been able to achieve e-commerce success without the capabilities already available to them through their traditional businesses. Newcomers to the market, attempting to start from scratch with an e-commerce initiative to compete against these two companies, would have needed to raise significant start-up funding to create a shipping network with comparable capabilities and recognition to what was made available quickly by both UPS and FedEx.

CHAPTER 9

Company Cases: B2B

INTRODUCTION

The companies in this chapter play a number of different roles in the world of e-commerce, including roles that could sometimes be characterized as either retail or service-based. However, some of the most important lessons to be learned from the companies described in this chapter center on their innovations in business-to-business commerce.

The most common characteristic among the success stories in this chapter is a strong preexisting IT capability that can complement an e-commerce venture. For companies such as Dell and Cisco, e-commerce is an essential channel of business. But despite the importance of the e-commerce channel for these companies, it is still a smaller aspect of a much larger IT strategy that serves to connect all aspects of business from suppliers to shipping in an efficient manner. Whether these IT capabilities existed prior to the start of an e-commerce venture or were developed parallel to an e-commerce venture, the fact remains that a company can wisely use e-commerce to enhance a much larger IT strategy.

The success that these companies have found has also been largely due to vigilance on the part of corporate leadership regarding e-commerce. From Jack Welch's "Destroy Your Business" initiative to identify future threats to GE to Michael Dell's status as an iconic e-commerce guru, companies that operate on the scale of those found in this chapter have required not only skilled leadership, but bold leadership that has been willing to support the growth of e-commerce through all of the ups and downs of the industry.

Companies that do not have the resources or e-commerce presence of a GE or Dell have had to utilize a variety of methods to keep pace with e-commerce leaders. Strategic alliances have been critical for companies that have found themselves in this position. The Omnexus alliance, as a counter to GE's plastics division, provided a collective power to the companies involved that could not have been available to any of them individually. Though the union of HP and Compaq has faced a number of challenges since its inception, it has slowly enabled the newly formed company to begin to approach the level of e-commerce culture and proficiency found at Dell.

The companies in this chapter have faced the successes and failures of e-commerce on a much larger scale than most. Their experiences help to demonstrate the variety and acute nature of results that can develop from the implementation of an e-commerce strategy. The industries and companies examined in this chapter include the following, by industry.

Computers
  Dell
  Compaq/HP

Networking Infrastructure
  Cisco
  Lucent

Plastics
  GE Plastics
  Omnexus
  PlasticsNet.com

COMPUTERS

Successful e-commerce for the computing industry has centered on the use of technology and information as a substitute for other, more costly aspects of the industry. While the success of such substitution for various corporations has varied tremendously, the potential of e-commerce in the industry has been typified by the success of Dell in utilizing a production model that is not only lean, but also entirely dependent on online ordering, tracking mechanisms, and inventory control. This model has become so popular that Dell has provided consulting to automakers regarding the advantages of this system of manufacturing.

While the industry might be characterized as being both B2B and B2C, the majority of the business in this sector is defined as B2B. Dell, for example, derives 90 percent of its income from businesses, 10 percent from individuals.[1]

Dell is as close to a pure-play retailer as one can find in the industry and has enjoyed considerable first-mover advantage because of its early entry onto the Internet. Compaq attempted to replicate Dell's model of e-commerce and production with meager results. When these changes did not prove to be successful, Compaq turned to a merger with Hewlett Packard. While this merger may have pulled Compaq back from the brink, the newly formed HP/Compaq behemoth continues to face challenges in competition with the more efficient Dell.[2]

Dell

In 1985 Michael Dell began to build his own brand of computers. The company performed well from the outset and experienced major growth from the late 1980s to the early 1990s. In 1992, Dell posted its first loss. This loss was due largely to efforts to expand into the retail market and quality problems with its notebook computers. The problems of 1992 caused Dell to formulate two core components of its business plan: (1) Dell would exist solely as a made-to-order direct seller, and (2) Dell would not make forays into new markets until such markets were proved to be both profitable and reliable.

After the loss in 1992, Dell moved on to exclusively operate its made-to-order system. From 1992 to 1996, Dell relied upon phone, fax, and mail to receive orders while establishing the foundation of its production systems. Dell first moved into experimenting with the Internet in the early 1990s to meet market demands for online customer support and information on order tracking. At the same time Dell began to examine the possibility of creating of customized Internet mechanisms that Fortune 500 companies could use to allow their employees to directly interact with Dell for their computer needs.

Dell expanded its Web site in 1996 for ordering. Other than a high customer error rate while using the Web site's ordering mechanism (80 percent error rate at first), Dell experienced a high level of success with the venture, as online ordering grew to more than 50 percent of Dell's orders.[3] In 2002, sales through dell.com comprised 48 percent of the 22 million computers sold through the Internet. Traffic to the small business pages and small business sales of the Web site increased 300 percent between 2002 and 2003.[4]

Dell's Web site is uniquely structured so that customers can easily access only the information and products that they would likely find appealing. The ordering mechanisms are easily customizable, allowing for a wider variety of configurations of products than Dell's competitors.[5] This Web site was the industry's pioneering effort in the direct-to-customer e-business model.[6] Dell was well positioned to adopt e-commerce into its business model by its preexisting direct order format for computer sales. Without this advantage Dell's competitors, such as Compaq, have faced difficulty in trying to convert more of their business to the use of e-commerce while at the same time satisfying retailers and other intermediaries who may not benefit from the full integration of e-commerce.[7]

Further, Dell provided Premier Pages for top clients, similar to what they began to develop for Fortune 500 companies in the early 1990s. These pages were custom designed by Dell for specific customers, permitting the employees of these companies to order Dell products with minimal effort and paperwork at prenegotiated prices. These pages also provided a wide variety of other business data ranging from budgeting tools to custom technical support data and the same information available to Dell's support staff.

These Premier Pages provided Dell with a number of unique competitive advantages. By "owning" the relationship with its customers, Dell was able to also stake claim to a vast amount of information regarding a customer's IT needs and business practices. Competitors often rely upon intermediaries to collect such data from customers, which often leads to a lower quality and quantity of data.[8]

Because of its market power in the industry, provided largely by e-commerce, Dell has had substantial latitude in structuring its production model for high efficiency. Dell suppliers are responsible to maintain storehouses within 15 minutes of Dell's factories and keep the company stocked on a continual basis. The suppliers are able to perform this function thanks to real-time production and sales data provided to them by Dell free of charge. This free flow of information permits Dell to not only keep its production lines running smoothly, but also maintain a transparency that is appealing to investors and suppliers alike.[9]

This system has enabled Dell to consistently beat its competition, including:

- a 6 percent cost advantage over the competition
- a cash conversion cycle of *negative* 5 days, since they have the customers' money before they are required to pay suppliers

Compaq/HP

Compaq began in 1984 as one of the fastest-growing companies the Fortune 500 had ever seen and quickly rose to the top of the computer industry. However, Compaq did not make its first foray into e-commerce until 1998 and did not begin the practice of online sales until early 2000.

In 1998, Compaq invested in Inex, specializing in Internet portals, to emphasize the establishment of Internet marketplaces for small to mid-sized businesses. This was a complement to Compaq's desire to promote its servers with this market segment in competition with IBM and Sun.[10]

Compaq's first steps into online sales began in 2000, along with HP, Gateway, and several other smaller companies, with the creation of an electronic marketplace for its products. To facilitate this move to online sales, Compaq bought Inacom, which it renamed Custom Edge after the purchase, to provide programming for online customization of its products.

Early on, Compaq used discounts, product financing, and joint-marketing services to attempt to lure various e-commerce firms into using its server technologies. However, Compaq was fighting an uphill battle due to poor ratings of its high-end servers and customer service in comparison with competitors such as Dell and IBM.[11] Compaq faced further challenges in switching over to online sales due to difficulties in dealer relationships. In some cases, as Compaq was trying to switch to primarily online sales and a more Dell-like production mechanism, Compaq dealers' resistance led them to simply stop selling its products. During this period, Compaq faced a significant loss of customers while attempting to change not only its Web site, but all of its production facilities.[12]

With the economic slowdown, Compaq switched its strategy to focus heavily on IT services rather than hardware in 2001. Numerous analysts said that such a move would harm Compaq's brand name association with hardware and saw this as one of the causes of poor earnings in 2001.[13]

With these losses in recent memory, Compaq negotiated a merger with rival HP where HP would acquire Compaq for $25 billion to create the largest computer company in the world. Many were concerned that whereas HP was a successful company, it would be harmed by acquiring Compaq, which many saw as a damaged company without a promising business model. The move was highly contested within the HP ranks and was narrowly approved a year later only after an independent analyst gave the merger a positive recommendation at a final price of $19 billion.[14]

The merger faced significant conflicts within the two former organizations regarding management and styles of business practices. However, many believe that the biggest obstacle to this merger remained Dell, which was able to surpass the new HP to retake the top spot for computer manufacturers after only one month. Although HP and Compaq were able to generate cost savings through the merger, the merged company still faced the problems associated with an inefficient production model and the limitations of its primary source of sales being through retailers. Efforts have been made by HP to change its production model and its relationship with suppliers to more closely model that of Dell. The success of those efforts is still in question.

Lessons Learned:

- Tailor information practices to take advantage of e-commerce.
  - Integrated and effective information practices can be used to build a highly efficient supply chain that eliminates excess production and inventory, and minimizes distribution and delivery costs. Dell is highly proficient in all of these areas because of its manufacturing systems and its ability to maintain real-time information systems.
- Use e-commerce to strengthen relationships with customers.
  - Personalized service is a strong relationship-building tool in B2B e-commerce, because it provides the customer a strong incentive to continue making purchases and builds high switching costs.
- Mergers can be used to try to overcome weakness in e-commerce.
  - Companies can pursue strategic partnerships to make themselves more competitive with an e-commerce leader when other strategic or structural changes are not promising. Compaq entered the ultimate strategic partnership—a merger—with fellow computer giant Hewlett Packard in the hope of reversing its fortunes in its battle with Dell.

NETWORKING INFRASTRUCTURE

While much of the market for IT was lagging, Cisco was able to recover from an initial slide that was actually more severe than that experienced by most other companies in the industry to take its place as the industry leader. Reduced telecommunications and network spending made it increasingly difficult for companies to attract the necessary revenue. The primary goal for businesses in this industry, considering these conditions, had often been to tightly control costs while attempting to gain market share during the economic downturns.

Cisco enjoyed a significant e-commerce advantage due to its first-mover status and the scalability and seamlessness of its network and online site. It successfully linked e-commerce to every aspect of its business, including online ordering, customer service, and a free flow of information between itself and its suppliers. Further, Cisco's willingness to use acquisitions, instead of in-house solutions, to meet market needs provided the company with a unique structure compared to its competitors.

Lucent did not fare as well as Cisco over the last years. From numerous problems with accounting and disclosures and a lack of strong, consistent leadership, Lucent faced a challenge of credibility during the economic downturn. Further, the company faced a disadvantage due to its late-mover status and an inability to fully incorporate a "Cisco-like" integrated model.

Cisco

Cisco, a leading producer of routers and other packages to help control traffic and information on corporate intranets and on the Internet, was founded in 1984 and went public in 1990. In 1994, because of rapidly increasing business and demands upon its network, Cisco's UNIX legacy system failed and the company was forced to look for a new foundation for its IT systems. It chose Oracle, for its scalability, and invested $15 million to bring the project to completion. This was Cisco's largest capital investment to that point. There was no clear plan as to where this project would take the company. However, the scalability of Oracle would eventually permit Cisco to facilitate substantial online growth and seamless connections between the company's systems and its online services.[15]

In 1996, Cisco began to offer pricing configuration and order status data online. In 1997, the Web site expanded to online ordering, and in 1998, the online ordering systems were integrated with its largest customers' purchasing systems. By 1999, customer-specific business tools were available for service providers, small and medium businesses, large firms, and Cisco resellers. At this point, Cisco's largest customers could also directly access Cisco's manufacturing systems and schedule their own orders. In 2000, Cisco began to expand its market base by implementing multi-vendor solutions to integrate the ordering of related third-party products in an attempt to become a more comprehensive manufacturer. Cisco also began to venture into telecommunications.[16]

During this period, Cisco grew at an astounding rate. At one point its overall value was greater than that of GE and investors thought that its growth had no end in sight, much like the rest of the technology sector at this time.[17] However, while Cisco's competitors were beginning to notice economic indicators of a slowing market, such as rising debt levels, troubles in the bond market, and fluctuating interest rates, Cisco forged ahead with the belief that the market was continuing to grow. Cisco's viewpoint was based upon projections of its own sales rooted entirely in its own internal data.[18]

This view led to Cisco falling on especially hard times in 2001. Due to continued projections of market growth, Cisco had been driven to enter long-term commitments with suppliers to ensure that they could meet a market demand that began to overwhelm their capabilities in late 2000. When the market began to collapse, Cisco was burdened by these supplier commitments and a business model that was not lean.[19]

Cisco's ability to recover from this downturn was found largely within its e-commerce capabilities. By expanding the role of the Internet to fulfill internal functions typically performed by employees and, in turn, cutting its workforce, Cisco was able to cut costs significantly. Further, the seamlessness between Cisco's internal systems and its Web site permitted the company to provide a wider variety of benefits to its customers. One of the most noted benefits of this was complete access to Cisco's entire business model. Customers were able not only to know Cisco's general business plan, but also to access considerable data regarding Cisco's economic performance at any time. Further, Cisco began to use e-commerce to do more than just trim costs and provide services. The company also began moving into new markets, beginning with telecommunications in 2000[20] and then into broader markets, due to increased competition from other manufacturers such as Dell. Though the industry was lagging, Cisco reemerged as the industry leader by turning profits in a time of tremendous industry losses. In 2003, Cisco spent $100 million on three Web-related projects, including a consolidation of its databases to improve forecasting. In 2002, Cisco achieved $2.1 billion in savings by utilizing the Web.[21]

Cisco's business model was one of a virtual manufacturer in a business-to-business framework. The company received 90 percent of its orders from the Web and then employed contract manufacturers to produce the order.[22] Cisco never developed its own manufacturing capabilities because it did not believe it had the time to do so with the rapid growth that the company experienced.[23] Further, this model of acquiring capabilities through acquisitions and alliances had been the basis of much of Cisco's success. Contracting and acquiring different capabilities from others had allowed Cisco to become more flexible than its competitors while keeping responsibilities and costs to a minimum.

Cisco enjoyed a number of advantages through the establishment of its ordering and service departments online, including reduced selling costs, 24/7 availability, speed, completely downloadable software for tremendous savings on shipping costs, and global expansion without the bricks and mortar of other businesses. Perhaps one of the most important advantages of these online capabilities was accuracy and efficiency. Without some of the challenges of human errors and the higher related costs for human labor, Cisco had been able to streamline its business practices significantly.[24]

Lucent

Lucent designs and manufactures public and private networks, communications systems, and other microelectronic components. This AT&T spin-off got its start in 1996 with its separation from AT&T, while taking Bell Labs and about 100,000 employees with it. By January of 2000, Lucent had become the most widely held stock in the United States with its stock rising twelve-fold since the spin-off, and was one of the five largest U.S. companies based on market capitalization. Also at this time Lucent began to see the beginning of its troubles, and despite a strong market position it issued its first profit warning for the quarter. Since that time, the performance of Lucent has been characterized by continuous losses.[25]

From 2000 to 2003, Lucent was plagued by the Securities and Exchange Commission and the Department of Justice with continuous questions about its accounting practices and several investigations. The company's business performance was also very troubled. Since 2000, Lucent cut more than two-thirds of its workforce and was forced to spin off and sell businesses to raise cash. In 2001, Lucent saw its credit rating reduced to junk status.[26]

In 2002, though profits were elusive, Lucent took major steps to cut costs. This included moving away from "revolutionary" network services to providing more enterprise-oriented business solutions, a reduced focus on R&D, and an emphasis on e-commerce solutions.[27]

Despite a new emphasis on becoming more "Cisco-like," Lucent still faced a number of challenges to its new business plan. Market credibility was severely lacking, and promises of visible progress were not met. Further, the overall market was recovering slowly and was not especially conducive to Lucent's recovery.

However, most important, Lucent simply began working to cut costs too late. Cisco's early-mover advantage had permitted the company to gain considerable market share while cutting costs. Lucent also faced difficulty in trying to emulate Cisco's example. A number of Lucent's acquisitions had to be sold off because they did not contribute significantly to Lucent's business plan.

Lessons Learned:

- Acquisitions for innovation and growth
  - Obtaining technology capabilities through acquisitions is a creative way of addressing operational needs without interfering with an integration strategy or confronting the hidden costs associated with outsourcing.

Lessons Learned (continued)

- Online customization
  - Customizing to meet customer needs online is not only more efficient online, but also dramatically improves accuracy.
- Don't follow blindly.
  - An industry leader or first-mover may have built an advantage that precludes switching by customers, but more important, the model may not be easily imitable. Blindly emulating strategy without considering whether your company can match the strategy, systems, structure, and culture will likely lead to failure.

PLASTICS

In the plastics industry, producers, manufacturers, and distributors have turned to e-commerce to reduce the costs associated with their supply chains. Public marketplaces were popular in the early years of B2B, with their focus on transparency and full information. Private exchanges, however, have become one of the dominant business models in B2B industries, as public marketplaces have been unable to provide the privacy and value-added features sought by customers.[28] Private exchanges have also proven more capable of providing flexibility, customization, and higher savings.

GE was the early e-commerce mover in the plastics industry, building on the capabilities of its established company Polymerland to roll out the first private exchange. PlasticsNet was its first major pure-play competitor, a public marketplace that tried to beat GE by bringing together the largest number of participants and becoming a one-stop shop for all goods and services related to the industry. Omnexus, a conglomerate of five major industry members, was not formed until 2000, but hoped to compete through critical mass and value-added services, but in a private exchange format.

For both exchange models, critical mass was one of the keys to building a successful exchange. To be desirable to customers, there must be enough members to ensure adequate supply and demand. Since critical mass poses a "chicken and egg" problem, obtaining commitments up front had been vital to the creation of a viable business model.[29]

Another challenge for these exchanges was dealing with competing channels. PlasticsNet, as a pure-play, did not face this issue, but GE and Omnexus did. GE had full integration between Polymerland's online and non-Internet functions, while Omnexus's members had no such integration. Pricing was also a challenge in the channel relationships.

Suppliers in B2B were hesitant to put their lowest prices online, fearful of being undercut and being forced to offer those prices through other channels. Another issue was that while these exchanges created the potential for channel conflict with phone and in-person channels for selling, brokers were unlikely to be eliminated entirely.

GE Plastics

GE Plastics had long been a technology leader both within the company and in the industry. GE Polymerland.com was created in 1997, two years after its product catalog was first posted online. The operation had been a key aspect of GE's plastics division before it went online. The Web site only provided a new channel and did not change existing relationships.

GE ensured that it would reach critical mass by involving customers in the planning process and obtaining feedback on the Web site's design. When customers requested the ability to order products according to internal part numbers, GE implemented this quickly. Other capabilities included customized accounts, past purchase accessibility, frequent-purchase templates, and research and design tools.

In 1999, the site became the focus of the unit in response to CEO Jack Welch's Destroy Your Business (DYB) exercise. DYB was a company-wide initiative that encouraged business units to formulate the manner in which a hypothetical online competitor could threaten GE's business. It recognized that cannibalizing its traditional business might be a necessary reaction to the e-commerce boom. Its DYB team was housed in new office space designed to enhance creativity.[30] Welch kept constant pressure on the units, inquiring as to the status of the exercise, but allowed them flexibility to break all company rules outside of core principles. GE did not, however, create separate compensation systems.[31] It staffed its team with both insiders and outsiders, but sought innovators rather than e-commerce experience.

GE Plastics realized that its processes were working well for smaller customers, but not as well for large customers. The Internet provided a single interface through which it could serve both equally well. It also realized that its site could be vulnerable to a competitor with strong community features and smart technology.

GE Plastics became a benchmark division within GE as a model of how to do e-commerce effectively. GE's goal for the site was to reduce costs and help customers streamline purchasing. GE Polymerland was the model for GE's other online ventures, which provided $1 billion in cost savings in 2001. Ninety-five percent of orders through this channel require no human interaction.[32] In 2001, GE enabled customers to link their internal systems to Polymerland. For customers with incompatible software, GE offered a solutions service to make them compatible. GE's online sales increased significantly, starting from $10 million in 1998 and growing to $4 billion in 2002.[33]

GE had previously rejected the notion of cooperating with or participating in PlasticsNet, in the belief that it would lose competitive advantages drawn from its brand, customer service, and fulfillment capabilities. GE was also asked to join the Omnexus consortium, but declined, not wanting to have an additional intermediary between GE and its customers.[34]

Omnexus

Omnexus was founded in 2000 by five large companies in the plastics industry: Dow, DuPont, BASF, Bayer, and Celanese. The $50 million exchange was established as a supplier-driven source for injection molding, a major plastics product. Launched in 2000, it intended to build critical mass quickly by being supplier-driven, thus ensuring available inventory. That, however, did give the exchange a bias.[35] The site included search capabilities that included drawings and a full accounting of technical aspects of all its machinery.

Revenue from the site came from a transaction fee system that included many parameters, including different fee schedules based on size, frequency of transactions, and inclusion of services. Still, the company's business plan was based more on cost savings than on these fees.

Following its American launch, plans were made to launch a European equivalent, and expansion into Asia followed in 2002. By 2001, it had 10,000 participating members and represented as much as an 80 percent market share for some products.

Online billing and payment services were already available by 2001, and connectivity was furthered through a partnership with IQMS Software. It also planned to expand heavily into value-added services related to the plastics industry with a willingness to take on logistics partners to become a one-stop shop for industry members. Finally, it provided downloadable software that a prospective company could use to estimate its cost savings from using the site.

In 2001, it began operating below budgeted costs and building up its transaction rates with a goal of reaching monthly liquidity of $100 million by 2002. Omnexus did not try to reach this goal by acquiring many new customers; rather, it focused on converting and automating existing relationships with buyers and suppliers.[36]

Omnexus offered not only plastics, but also primary and auxiliary equipment and maintenance, repair, and operating supplies. It also differentiated itself by allowing customers to host their own enterprise resource planning solutions through the site.[37] It attempted to compete with GE by offering a fully integrated supply chain and the ability to purchase from many companies in one location.[38]

PlasticsNet.com

PlasticsNet was established as a B2B exchange designed to link suppliers, processors, and manufacturers in the plastics industry. In 1996, it began engaging industry members with an informational Web site in a discussion of the benefits of B2B e-commerce. The push for this dialogue came from technologists in the parent company, Commerx, which began to have an increased role in strategy.[39] It also started with an aggressive marketing and recruiting campaign that included hiring managers from GE and other industry leaders.

The business model was an attempt to provide one-stop shopping for goods and services in the plastics industry. In 1997, PlasticsNet launched its first procurement system after having lined up enough suppliers, processors, and manufacturers. The profits from the exchange were to come both from transaction fees and from the sales of related services.

In 1998, the site began offering more options, including tiered pricing, data formats for invoices, and shipping estimates. It partnered with Schneider Logistics to provide the last of these services, which resulted in marked improvements in procurement times for most companies. In addition to the standard selling functions, the site also included an auction function for excess inventory and used machinery and an area in which one-time offers and specially priced offerings could be made.

PlasticsNet attempted to build an advantage through the many information features of its site. Through a partnership with MatWeb, the site featured a materials database that gives specific product information. It also included a supplier directory that covers nearly every product in the industry and a technical forum to help users discuss products and services and exchange advice.

After an attempted IPO failed to materialize, Commerx began to rethink the PlasticsNet model. The trend toward private exchanges had become obvious, and Commerx began repositioning PlasticsNet as a services company rather than a marketplace.[40] In 2001, Commerx sold PlasticsNet.com to VerticalNet, believing that the exchange was no longer compatible with its new business model, which focused on software and other supply chains solutions.

Lessons Learned:

- IT Leaders should not take e-commerce for granted.
  - Companies that hold traditional leadership positions in technology must act boldly to maintain that advantage in

Lessons Learned (continued)

e-commerce. GE's understanding of e-commerce led to its DYB
initiative, which prepared the company well enough to not
only maintain that advantage, but build on it.
- Strategic alliances can help laggard companies to achieve profitability in an industry dominated by an early mover.
  - The companies taking part in Omnexus understood GE's advantage, and when their attempts to lure GE into an exchange
were spurned, they developed their large partnership, hoping
to take advantage of scale and offer more diverse services.
- Companies must be willing to reshape an e-commerce strategy.
  - The online exchange model, which is primarily present in B2B
industries, is still evolving, and requires constant reevaluation
by companies doing business in the industry. GE may have
anticipated the Omnexus model in its DYB exercise, but the
threat of new forms of competition requires continued vigilance of companies that could possibly profit by moving into
the industry.

CHAPTER 10

Achieving Success in E-Commerce

The e-commerce experiment has finally grown out of its infancy. The mistakes that corporations made during a time of acute growth and expansion for this new channel of acquisition and distribution have been extensively noted by the media and both the successes and failures are analyzed in this book. But have we learned the right lessons from these missteps? Some people still believe in the lofty e-commerce dreams of the late 1990s, as evidenced by the stock gains by a few core e-commerce firms. On the other hand, some companies and investors have simply given up on e-commerce as being too costly or unreliable.

We know that these extreme positions are untenable for senior managers if they wish their companies to continue to compete with others who have already begun to use technology to improve their internal operations and to reach out to customers and other businesses using e-commerce. While it is a disadvantage for those that have not already established an e-commerce strategy, it is not insurmountable. Late movers such as Barnes and Noble and Walgreens have proven that even a delayed dedication to e-commerce can lead a company to e-commerce success.

The company cases in the previous three chapters provide extensive examples that numerous different circumstances have surrounded e-commerce success stories. However, it is not just the circumstances in which a company finds itself that leads to e-commerce success. If such circumstances were the only factor, Wal-Mart's e-commerce reincarnation would not have been needed following its difficult entry into e-commerce. Instead, e-commerce success, in the past and for the future, depends on a commitment to the four primary characteristics of e-commerce introduced in chapter 1 on leadership, strategy, structure, and systems (Exhibit 10.1).

All of the issues discussed in this book, ranging from online product selection to IT competency, rely on this foundation of principles, which is essential to the success of the formulation and implementation of an e-commerce strategy. The particulars of an e-commerce strategy for any company must be customized to meet the needs of the company and its customers. However, these four sets of characteristics are common to all companies and must be considered not only to ensure the success of an e-commerce venture, but also to ensure the compatibility of that success with the traditional aspects of a company, its industry, and its consumer base.

LEADERSHIP

Commitment at the top is essential to any successful e-commerce venture, and the communication and actions related to that commitment are critical to e-commerce success. The commitment is also demonstrated by bringing the CIO into the senior management team and providing the appropriate recognition and compensation to demonstrate appreciation for the hands-on leadership and critical importance of the company's e-commerce initiative. But most important, cooperation and a common vision among senior company leaders are needed not only to ensure that the company shows a strong public commitment to

Exhibit 10.1
Characteristics of Successful E-Commerce Companies

Leadership	Strategy
1. Commitment at the top	1. Well-positioned online brand
2. Thorough competitive analysis	2. Online friendly offerings
3. Significant financial investment	3. Reliable customer service
4. Cultural transformation	4. Cross-channel coordination
Structure	Systems
1. Internal investment	1. Modernized internal processes
2. Integrated management teams	2. Incentive-laden HR practices
3. IT know-how from within	3. Aligned performance measures
4. Strategic partnerships	4. Improved customer management

e-commerce, but also to ensure that this commitment is effectively executed.

E-commerce leadership also requires special attention to the relative position of a company in comparison to industry leaders when implementing an e-commerce initiative. Two considerations when making this analysis are the company's relative position based on e-commerce competence and the company's position based on financial commitment. A determination of relative e-commerce competence and capabilities provides guidance as to the areas a company must improve to strengthen e-commerce market position. Financial analyses help to ensure that a company has the resources to effectively launch an e-commerce initiative and also that it is not overpaying for particular e-commerce aspects. It also can identify how the e-commerce strategy can provide a competitive advantage and can provide the initial analysis for the ultimate examination of the prospective and actual payoffs of e-commerce investments. These are important inputs to e-commerce success.

The result of the leadership requirements and activities outlined in this book should be the creation of a company culture that is conducive to the introduction and cultivation of successful e-commerce integration. As with the traditional aspects of commerce, e-commerce related leadership should serve to create a framework and impetus that enable a company to move e-commerce from just a good idea to a significant creation of value for the business.

STRATEGY

Multi-channel coordination and effectiveness are critical components of the formulation and implementation of an e-commerce initiative. Effectiveness, in particular, serves to find ways to make e-commerce simpler for a company both financially and strategically by promoting continuing evaluations of opportunities for a company to look both inside and outside to create competitive advantage.

Multi-channel coordination and effectiveness serve to enable a company to establish itself in e-commerce with a well-positioned online brand and online friendly offerings, two characteristics that are essential to the success of an e-commerce initiative. Online brand management requires steps ranging from naming issues to the coordination of a bricks-and-clicks strategy, but one important purpose of brand management for an online enterprise centers around building awareness of that company's online presence. Once that awareness is established, companies must build on the awareness with programs to retain customers with excellent service and product selections. Smaller companies can use e-commerce to expand their offerings beyond what they could possibly achieve in a bricks-and-mortar business environment, while larger companies may want to limit their offerings to focus on products with the highest margins. In short, an online presence alone does not increase profitability and must be carefully managed to achieve success.

An Internet presence affords a company the opportunity to provide customized products more efficiently. To achieve higher levels of online customer service, both commoditized and unique solutions can be utilized. Companies can personalize Web pages to more closely meet the particular needs of any customer or choose to simply pursue a standardized approach to e-commerce without immediate modification for the customer. These choices represent significant opportunities for a company to meet the needs of its customers in ways that are simple, yet effective. Companies also make other strategic and tactical choices related to customer service such as the level of interaction in the online service exchange. This can range from a basic listing of frequently asked questions to a fully interactive messaging service between customers and the company. While it can generally be said that more is better when it comes to meeting the needs of customers, the Internet permits companies to make a much wider array of choices than before in providing superior customer service and to carefully analyze the potential and actual payoffs of these choices.

STRUCTURE

One common mistake made in early e-commerce initiatives was for companies to look for solutions to all of their Internet needs from external sources. When there were IPOs and spin-offs, there was often a lack of both control and coordination. Not only did managers and employees quickly notice it, so did customers. Service often suffered, and so did the success of the e-commerce venture. Companies also often found that the venture capitalists or other alliances could not provide the assistance, guidance, and capabilities necessary for success. Though IPO stock prices rose rapidly, they often fell just as quickly as profits failed to materialize.

A company's e-commerce initiative should be based on working from within the company whenever possible and only looking outside for partnerships and alliances when the advantages are clear and significant. These may include advantages such as procurement of a particular savings mechanism or access to a new group of customers. Such alliances should not be used to substitute for deficiencies in aspects of a company that should be core competencies. However, they can be used to reinforce particular systems or gain short-term advantage over competitors. But, the goal should be a full integration of e-commerce throughout the organizational structure even if the strategy is to accomplish this in stages using a partial corporate integration or business unit integration initially.

SYSTEMS

Modernizing internal processes throughout a company is an essential component of any e-commerce strategy. Whether addressing demand and supply chain management or customer data-mining efforts, companies must identify the systems that can be markedly improved with the aid of e-commerce in a way that promotes networking and information sharing across the company. Companies also need to ensure that HR practices are properly adjusted to promote the implementation and acceptance of e-commerce-inspired changes to company systems through incentives and other means.

An e-commerce leader must ensure that the systems used throughout the company to measure performance are modified as necessary to meet the arrival of e-commerce. Preexisting accountability measures and IT solutions do not lose their relevance with the arrival of e-commerce; instead, they are given new life with the opportunities made possible by Internet connections to partner companies.

Perhaps the most significant systems changes associated with e-commerce relate to customer management. Improved service practices can evolve with e-commerce through an increase in information available to customers and facilitated with Internet-enabled connections throughout company operations.

MEASURING THE PAYOFFS
OF E-COMMERCE INVESTMENTS

In addition to the effective formulation and implementation of an e-commerce strategy, companies also need realistic measures to evaluate the success of an e-commerce initiative. Beyond the fantasy-like business practices surrounding early e-commerce, a company wishing to implement an e-commerce solution today faces the responsibility of creating an e-commerce initiative that is not only appealing, but a clear creator of value. For too long, IT and e-commerce were seen as value destroying rather than value creating. Senior corporate managers focused on reducing IT costs rather than creating value through IT and e-commerce. The measures developed in this book are essential in ensuring that the implementation of the four characteristics just listed actually leads to the increase in profitability forecast through the development of an e-commerce initiative. Senior e-commerce and IT managers must demonstrate the value and payoffs of e-commerce investments to business unit and corporate leaders. This will also provide the opportunity to obtain increased internal resources for e-commerce initiatives.

FUTURE OF E-COMMERCE

Because of the prolific expansion of the Internet and related technologies during the tech boom of the late 1990s and early 2000s, companies began to consider the possible saturation of business-related technology in the market. But, the use of the Internet and e-commerce in business operations is just in its infancy.

Moore's Law, claiming that computer processing power will double about every 18 months, seems to continue to hold true and appears to have strong footing to carry on into the foreseeable future. Although computing power does not make headlines in the same way that it did during the race to reach processing speeds above 1 GHz, advances are still being made that will continue to contribute to business opportunities in numerous ways.

Mobile technology continues to improve in convenience and versatility thanks to increased processing power, expanded cellular capabilities, and the WiFi revolution, all of which are contributing to the presence of the Internet in our homes, our offices, and our pockets. As the Internet moves into these new environments, businesses will need an Internet presence and an Internet strategy flexible enough to adapt to advances in technology and the opportunities presented by those advancements.

Beyond these new markets for business that are emerging from new technologies, the maturation of the Internet is creating new markets out of previously existing, and sometimes illicit, technologies. Technologies ranging from mp3s, to digital movie services, to Internet-based book availability and beyond are beginning to be viewed as viable business opportunities by large companies such as Apple and Disney, in addition to smaller companies making their first forays into legal versions of these popular forms of technology. Such business innovations were not based on increases in bandwidth or new forms of technology alone. Rather, they were driven by consumer demand for legal alternatives to meet their needs.

The companies that have met this demand have discovered a new channel for making money, but they also demonstrate that companies can afford to wait for a time before venturing into new varieties of e-commerce. While Napster faced a backlash from the entertainment industry because of its revolutionary file-sharing capabilities, the experimentation and vision of Napster founder Shawn Fanning opened the door for many companies to find legal methods to meet the demand for file-sharing that Napster had created. Opportunities and consumer demand similar to this can be found across the Internet, but only those companies that have at least a minimum level of commitment and expertise in e-commerce will be able to turn these opportunities into profit centers.

CONCLUSIONS

What should CEOs and other senior managers do today? In the end, the requirements of e-commerce are not especially profound or revolutionary. Instead, successful e-commerce requires a company to adhere to traditional business principles and good sense instead of allowing the easier and less orderly business practices of the dot.com bubble to take over. This new technology may be among the most important development in decades. It certainly has and will have a major impact on business. Companies that have not made significant forays into e-commerce need to do so soon. The investments and commitments must be made according to fundamental concepts and principles of good business, and the payoff of potential e-commerce investments must be established. E-commerce can be among the most important value creation activities for most businesses. The key is in the implementation. This book provides an examination of the successes and failures of the early entrants into e-commerce and provides guidance as to the characteristics and measures of e-commerce success.

Notes

CHAPTER 1

1. For further information on this example, see the Stockbrokers case studies in chapter 8.
2. For more about change management, see John Kotter, "Leading Change: Why Transformation Efforts Fail," *Harvard Business Review,* March-April 1995, 59–67.
3. For further information on these examples, see the Luxury Retail and Bookstores case studies in chapter 7.
4. For further information on this example, see the Bookstores case studies in chapter 7.
5. For further information on this example, see the Postal Services case studies in chapter 8.
6. For further information on this example, see the Bookstores case studies in chapter 7.
7. For further information on this example, see the Stockbrokers case studies in chapter 8.

CHAPTER 2

1. Rakesh Khurana, *Searching for a Corporate Savior: The Irrational Quest for Charismatic CEOs* (Princeton, NJ: Princeton University Press, 2002).
2. Larry Hooper, "2002 Top 25 Executives: John Chambers," *CRN,* November 18, 2002.
3. "The Comeback Kids: E-biz Has Returned with a Vengeance. Meet the 25 Men and Women Who Got Things Clicking," *BusinessWeek,* September 29, 2003.

4. Henry Lucas, *Strategies for Electronic Commerce and the Internet* (Cambridge: MIT Press, 2002), 142.

5. Michael Earl and David Feeny, "How to Be a CEO for the Information Age," *MIT Sloan Management Review* 41(2): 11–23.

6. "Comeback Kids."

7. Russ Banham, "The Power of 3," *Chief Financial Officer-IT*, Spring 2003, 40–45.

8. Lucas, *Strategies for Electronic Commerce and the Internet*, 142.

9. Heather Green, "Special Report: The Web," *BusinessWeek*, November 24, 2003.

10. For more on CEO-CIO collaboration, see Glen Rifkin and Joel Kurtzman, "Is Your E-Business Plan Radical Enough" *MIT Sloan Management Review*, 43(3): 91–95.

11. For more on first-mover advantage, see Michael Porter, "Strategy and the Internet," *Harvard Business Review* 79(2): 63–78; and George Day, Adam Fein, and Gregg Ruppersberger, "Shakeouts in Digital Markets: Lessons from B2B Exchanges," *California Management Review* 45(2): 131–150.

12. Further information on these examples can be found in the case studies in Part II.

13. Mauro Guillen, "What Is the Best Global Strategy for the Internet" *Business Horizons*, May–June 2002, 39–40.

14. For more on a global perspective, see Subramanian Rangan and Ron Adner, "Profits and the Internet: Seven Misconceptions," *MIT Sloan Management Review*, 42(4): 44–53.

15. Earl and Feeny, "How to Be a CEO for the Information Age," 11–23.

16. John Kotter, "Leading Change: Why Transformation Efforts Fail," *Harvard Business Review*, March–April 1995, 59–67.

CHAPTER 3

1. Michael Porter, "Strategy and the Internet," *Harvard Business Review,* March 2001, 64.

2. Michael Porter, "What Is Strategy?" *Harvard Business Review* 74(6): 61–78.

3. For an excellent discussion of the fundamental considerations in strategy, see Porter, "What Is Strategy?" 73.

4. Nicholas Carr. "IT Doesn't Matter," *Harvard Business Review,* May 2003, 9–12.

5. Lynda Applegate and Meredith Collura, "Overview of E-Business Models." *Harvard Case Teaching Note*, August 30, 2000, pp. 17–18.

6. Marc J. Epstein, "Organizing Your Business for the Internet Evolution," *Strategic Finance,* July 2000, 60.

7. Jennifer Mack, "Business.com: The $7.5 million domain," *ZDNet News*, December 1, 1999. Online at http://zdnet.com.com/2100-11-516999.html.

8. Leslie Willcocks and Robert Plant, "Pathways to E-business Leadership: Getting from Bricks to Clicks," *MIT Sloan Management Review*, Spring 2001, 53–54.

9. Ranjay Gulati and Jason Garino, "Get the Right Mix of Bricks and Clicks," *Harvard Business Review,* May/June 2000, 107–114.

10. Epstein, "Organizing Your Business for the Internet Evolution," 58.

11. Gulati and Garino, "Get the Right Mix of Bricks and Clicks," 113–114.

12. Subramanian Rangan and Ron Adner, "Profits and the Internet: Seven Misconceptions," *MIT Sloan Management Review*, 42(4): 44–53.

13. John de Figuereido, "Finding Sustainable Profitability in Electronic Commerce," *MIT Sloan Management Review*, 41(4): 41–52.

14. Ibid.

15. Thomas Eisenmann and Alastair Brown, "Online Retailers," *Harvard Business School Case*, December 11, 2000.

16. Paul Gillin, "Schwab impresses," *Computerworld*, October 20, 1997; 31(42): 49.

17. Charles Haddad, "Office Depot's E-Diva," *BusinessWeek e.biz*, August 6, 2001, EB 24.

18. Faith Keenan, "The Price Is Really Right," *BusinessWeek,* March 31, 2003, 70.

19. Heather Green, "Special Report: The Web," *BusinessWeek*, November 24, 2003.

20. "Amazon.com Case Study," Information Society Standardization System, 2000. Online at http://www.isss-awareness.cenorm.be/home/Home_frame.htm.

21. Willcocks and Plant, "Pathways to E-business Leadership," 55.

22. N. Venkataraman, "Five Steps to a Dot-Com Strategy: How to Find Your Footing on the Web," *MIT Sloan Management Review*, Spring 2000, 23–26.

23. Roger Hallowell, "Service on the Internet: The Effect of Physical Scalability," *Harvard Business School Case*, October 23, 2002.

24. Henry Lucas, *Strategies for Electronic Commerce and the Internet* (Cambridge: MIT Press, 2002).

25. John Hagel III and John Seely Brown, "Your Next IT Strategy," *Harvard Business Review,* October 2001, 108.

26. Jeanne Harris and Jeffrey Brooks, "Why IT Still Matters," *Accenture Research Note: IT Value,* June 19, 2003, 3–4

27. N. Venkataraman, "Five Steps to a Dot-Com Strategy," 16.

28. Heather Green, "Special Report: The Web," *BusinessWeek*, November 24, 2003.

CHAPTER 4

1. Michael Porter, "Strategy and the Internet," *Harvard Business Review* 79(2): 77.

2. Ranjay Gultati and Jason Garino, "Get the Right Mix of Bricks and Clicks," *Harvard Business Review* 78(3): 107–114.

3. Ibid., 113–114.

4. N. Venkataraman, "Five Steps to a Dot-Com Strategy: How to Find Your Footing on the Web," *MIT Sloan Management Review* 41(3): 20.

5. Ron Leuty, "Wells Fargo Hits the Middle with E-Commerce Pitch," *San Francisco Business Times,* March 10, 2000, 3.

6. Ajit Kambil, Erik Eselius, and Karen Monteiro, "Fast Venturing: The Quick Way to Start Web Businesses," *MIT Sloan Management Review* 41(4): 57–58.

7. Marc J. Epstein, "Organizing Your Business for the Internet Evolution," *Strategic Finance,* July 2000, 59–60.

8. Venkataraman, "Five Steps to a Dot-Com Strategy," 21.

9. Ibid., 20.

10. Jerome Barthelemy, "The Hidden Costs of IT Outsourcing," *MIT Sloan Management Review* 42(3): 67.

11. Kambil, Eselius, and Monteiro, "Fast Venturing," 60.

12. Barthelemy, "The Hidden Costs of IT Outsourcing," 60.

13. James Brian Quinn, "Outsourcing Innovation: The New Engine of Growth," *MIT Sloan Management Review* 41(3): 16–17.

14. Judith Mottl, "IT Outsourcing Gives Staples the Tools to Grow," *Informationweek*, May 15, 2000, p. 112.

15. Barthelemy, "The Hidden Costs of IT Outsourcing," 67.

16. Ibid.

17. John Hagel III and John Seely Brown, "Your Next IT Strategy," *Harvard Business Review* 79(10): 110.

CHAPTER 5

1. Robert Simons, "Control in an Age of Empowerment," *Harvard Business Review*, March-April 1995, 80–88.

2. Further information on this topic can be found in the Office Supplies and Bookstores case studies in chapter 7.

3. Mohanbir Sawhney, "Don't Homogenize, Sychronize," *Harvard Business Review*, July-August 2001, 102.

4. Henry Lucas, *Strategies for Electronic Commerce and the Internet* (Cambridge, MIT Press, 2002).

5. Anitesh Barua, Prabhudev Konana, Andrew Whinston, and Fang Yin, "Driving E-Business Excellence," *MIT Sloan Management Review* 43(1): 36–44.

6. More information on this topic can be found in the Computers case studies in chapter 9.

7. More information on this topic can be found in the Online Grocery Stores case studies in chapter 7.

8. Heather Green, "Special Report: The Web," *BusinessWeek*, November 24, 2003.

9. Ibid.

10. Ibid.

11. Sari Kalin, "It's Not Easy Being B2B," *CIO*, October 1, 1999. Online.

12. For relevant discussion on these systems, see Michael Earl and Bushra Khan, "E-Commerce Is Changing the Face of IT," *MIT Sloan Management Review* 43(11): 64–72.

13. Preston Cameron, "For Good Measure," *Strategic Finance*, July 2000.

14. Hilary Rosenberg, "Mad to Measure," *ECFO*, Fall 2001, 29–36.

CHAPTER 6

1. For example, see Paul A. Strassmann, *Information Payoff: The Transformation of Work in the Electric Age* (New Canaan, CT: Information Economics Press, 1985); *The Business Value of Computers: An Executive's Guide* (New Canaan, CT: Information Economics Press, 1990); *The Squandered Computer: Evaluating the Business Alignment of Information Technologies* (New Canaan, CT: Information Economics Press, 1997); Sarv Devaraj and Rajiv Kohli, *The IT Payoff: Measuring the Business Value of Information Technology Investments* (Upper Saddle River, NJ: Financial Times, Prentice-Hall, 2002); Chuck Lenatti, "Grinding Away on ROI," *CFO IT*, Summer 2003, 23–29.

2. Strassmann, *Information Payoff, The Business Value of Computers,* and *The Squandered Computer.*

3. For example, see Marc J. Epstein and Bill Birchard, "Applying the Balanced Scorecard," *Management Accounting Guideline, Society of Management Accountants of Canada*, 1999.

4. For more on causal linkages, see Marc J. Epstein and Robert Westbrook, "Linking Actions to Profits in Strategic Decision Making," *MIT Sloan Management Review*, Spring 2001.

5. For more on accountability, see Marc J. Epstein and Bill Birchard, *Counting What Counts: Turning Corporate Accountability Into Competitive Advantage* (Reading, MA: Perseus Books, 1999).

6. For more information on the measurement of IT and e-commerce investments, see Devaraj and Rajiv Kohli, *The IT Payoff*; and M. Khosrow-pour, "Does Corporate America Know How to Measure Payoff in Information Technology Investment?" *Document Management—Executive Strategies*, January 2000.

7. Bob Violino, "Payback Time for E-Business," *Internet Week*, May 2000, 4.

8. For more on complete and controllable measures, see Marc J. Epstein and Jean-François Manzoni, "Implementing Corporate Strategy: From Tableaux de Bord to Balanced Scorecards," *European Management Journal*, April 1998, 16(2): 190–203.

9. For more information on e-commerce and demand and supply chain management, see Harriet Engle, Peter Heckmann, and Dermont Shorten, "Capturing the Value of Supply Chain Management," *Strategy and Business*, June 26, 2003.

10. For more information on cost savings, see Kip Krumwiede, Kevin Stocks, and Monte Swain, "10 Ways E-Business Can Reduce Costs," *Strategic Finance*, July 2003, 25–29.

11. Heather Green, "Special Report: The Web," *BusinessWeek*, November 24, 2003.

CHAPTER 7

1. Henry Lucas, *Strategies for Electronic Commerce and the Internet* (Cambridge: MIT Press, 2002), 98.

2. Molly Prior, "Amazon to Operate Borders.com" *DSN Retailing Today*, May 1, 2001; 40(9): 6.

3. Kevin Werbach, "Syndication: The Emerging Model for Business in the Internet Era," *Harvard Business Review* 78(3): 91–92.

4. "Amazon.com Case Study," Information Society Standardization System, 2000. Online at http://www.isss-awareness.cenorm.be/home/Home_frame.htm.

5. Jessica Wohl, "Amazon, Toys R Us Plan Online Toy Stores," *Reuters*, August 10, 2002. Online.

6. Ted Kemp, "Borders Hands Off E-Commerce Operations to Amazon," *Internet Week*, April 11, 2001.

7. Saul Hansell, "Bertelsmann to Let Amazon.com Run CDNow," *New York Times*, November 26, 2002; 6.

8. Keith Regan, "Amazon's Free-Shipping Gamble: Will Rivals Ante Up?" *E-Commerce Times*, January 24, 2002.

9. Thomas Broening, "Reprogramming Amazon," *BusinessWeek*, December 22, 2003, 82–86.

10. Susannah Patton, "Barnesandnoble.com fights back," *CIO*, September 15, 2001, 4.

11. Ibid., 2–5.

12. Ibid., 6.

13. Nora Macaluso, "Barnesandnoble.com Expands E-Book Efforts," *E-Commerce Times*, January 4, 2001.

14. Patton, "Barnesandnoble.com fights back," 8.

15. Jim Milliot, "B&N, B'mann buy up B&N.com shares," *Publishers Weekly*, November 11, 2002; 249(45): 12.

16. Ryan Naraine, "Barnes & Noble in Takeover Bid for BN.com," *Earthwebnew.com*, November 7, 2003. Online at http://news.earthweb.com/finanews/article.php/3105761.

17. Ted Kemp, "Borders Hands Off E-Commerce Operations to Amazon," 1.

18. Jim Milliot, "B&N.com sales rise 5.9%," *Publishers Weekly*, October 28, 2002; 249(43): 13.

19. Molly Prior, "Wal-Mart: Store-site Synergies Open On-line Opportunities," *DSN Retailing Today*, June 4, 2001; 40(11): 68.

20. Mike Troy, "Wal-Mart, AOL Form Alliance of Giants," *Discount Store News*, January 3, 2000; 39(1): 48.

21. Laurie Heller. "Quest for Web Success Begins Anew with Dot.com Venture," *DSN Retailing Today*, June 5, 2000; 39(11): 131–132.

22. Jon Swartz, "Retailers Discover Leap to Web's a Doozy," *USA Today*, December 18, 2001, B.03.

23. Prior, "Wal-Mart: Store-site Synergies Open On-line Opportunities," 68.

24. Swartz, "Retailers Discover Leap to Web's a Doozy," B.03.

25. Erin Joyce, "Your Checks Are Good at Walmart.com," *Ecommerce-guide. com*, July 23, 2003. Online at http://ecommerce.Internet.com/news/news/article/0,3371,10375_2239011,00.html.

26. Prior, "Wal-Mart: Store-site Synergies Open On-line Opportunities," 2.

27. Anne D'Innocenzio, "Bricks-and-Mortar Retailers Are Becoming Competitive Online," *St. Louis Post-Dispatch*, November 2, 2000, C1, 2.

28. Prior, "Wal-Mart: Store-site Synergies Open On-line Opportunities," 2.

29. Swartz, "Retailers Discover Leap to Web's a Doozy." B.03, 3.

30. Lorene Yue, "Kmart to Pull Out of Internet Business as Part of Restructuring," *Knight Ridder Tribune Business News*, September 18, 2002, 1.

31. Jenny Strasburg, "Kmart turns off Bluelight.com," *San Francisco Chronicle*, June 20, 2002, B3; 1.

32. Ina Steiner, "Amazon.com Extends Ecommerce Agreement with Target to 2008," *AuctionBytes.com*, August 15, 2003. Online at http://www.auctionbytes.com/cab/1abn/yø3/mø8/1°15/Sø1.

33. Regan, "Amazon's Free-Shipping Gamble," 1–2.

34. Prior, "Wal-Mart: Store-site Synergies Open On-line Opportunities," 2.

35. Paul Greenberg, "Luxury E-Trailers Face Cyber Challenges," *E-Commerce Times*, June 5, 2000, p. 2. Online at http://www.ecommercetimes.com/perl/story/3475.html.

36. Ann Zimmerman, "Just Show Us the Stuff and Forget the Flash," *Wall Street Journal Europe*, April 19–21, 2002, 2.

37. Jennifer Couzin, "Saks Shops for Customers Online," *The Industry Standard*, August 28, 2000, p. 2. Online at http://www.thestandard.com/article/display/0,1151,17829,00.html.

38. Ajit Kambil, Erik Eselius, and Karen Monteiro, "Fast Venturing: The Quick Way to Start Web Business," *MIT Sloan Management Review* 41(4): 61.

39. Carol Tice, "Streamlined Online Operation Promises Profits," *Puget Sound Business Journal*, July 13, 2001, 3.

40. Couzin, "Saks Shops for Customers Online," 2.

41. Zimmerman, "Just Show Us the Stuff and Forget the Flash," 3.

42. Rob Spiegel, "Neiman Marcus Launches 'Affluent Platform' on the Web," *E-Commerce Times*, October 18, 1999, 1. Online at http://www.ecommercetimes.com/perl/story/1476.html.

43. Chet Dembeck, "Do Luxury Retailers 'Get' E-Commerce?" *E-Commerce Times*, November 5, 1999, 1. Online at http://www.ecommercetimes.com/perl/story/1667.html.

44. Zimmerman, "Just Show Us the Stuff and Forget the Flash," 1.

45. "Neiman Marcus: Using Oracle for a Competitive Advantage," *E-Businessiq.com*, October 13, 2003. Online at http://ebusinessiq.com/special%20interests/e-commerce/122--ebusinessIQ%20e-comm.html.

46. Beth Cox, "Doing E-Commerce in Style," *Internet News.com*, September 15, 2000, 2. Online at http://www.Internetnews.com/ec-news/article.php/461311.

47. Paul Greenberg, "Do Luxury E-Tailers Stand a Chance?" *E-Commerce Times*, January 9, 2001, p. 3. Online at http://www.ecommercetimes.com/perl/story/6549.html.

48. John Frederick Moore, "Why Peapod Is Striving: First-Failure Advantage," *Business 2.0*, August 14, 2001, 2. Online.

49. Leslie Willcocks and Robert Plant, "Pathways to E-business Leadership: Getting from Bricks to Clicks," *MIT Sloan Management Review* 42(3): 54.

50. Christopher Heun, "Grocers Count on IT to Keep Cash Registers Ringing," *InformationWeek*, December 24, 2001, 2. Online.

51. Miguel Helft, "What a Long, Strange Trip It's Been for Webvan," *The Industry Standard*, July 23, 2001, 9.

52. Linda Himelstein, "Commentary: Webvan Left the Basics on the Shelf," *BusinessWeek*, July 23, 2001, 2.

53. Margaret Kane, "Tesco Aims Where Webvan Flamed," *CNet News*, January 14, 2002, 2. Online.

54. Mike Flynn, "Drayton: HomeGrocer model viable," *Puget Sound Business Journal*, August 24, 2001, 2.

55. Lori Enos, "Webvan to Delay Expansion," *E-Commerce Times*, September 22, 2000. Online, 1.

56. Helft, "What a Long, Strange Trip It's Been for Webvan," 1.

57. Terry Pristin, "Ordering Groceries in Aisle 'www'," *New York Times*, May 4, 2002, 1.

58. Heun, "Grocers Count on IT to Keep Cash Registers Ringing," 2. Online.

59. Lori Enos, "Report: Net Grocers Gaining Ground," *E-Commerce Times*, March 20, 2001. Online, 1–2.

60. Ranjay Gulati and Jason Garino, "Get the Right Mix of Bricks and Clicks," *Harvard Business Review*, May/June 2000, 108.

61. Charles Haddad, "Office Depot's E-Diva," *BusinessWeek e.biz*, August 6, 2001, EB 24.

62. Gulati and Garino, "Get the Right Mix of Bricks and Clicks," 109.

63. Clinton Wilder, "Profile: Office Dept Inc: E-commerce Pays Off for Office Depot," *InformationWeek*, September 11, 2000, 1.

64. Katherine R. Clark, "Multi-Channel Retailers Gain Ground among Top 50 E-Retailers, Retail Forward Study Reports," *Retailforward.com*, July 31, 2002. Online at http://www.retailforward.com/freecontent/pressreleases/press48.asp.

65. Haddad, "Office Depot's E-Diva," p. EB 23; and Bob Violino, "E-Business 100: Office Depot Builds Winning Strategy on the Web," *InformationWeek*, December 13, 1999, 2.

66. Gillian Morris, "Staples.com," *Harvard Business School Case*, December 19, 2000, 2–3.

67. Debby Young, "Staples' E-Business Staples," *Line 56*, May 15, 2001, 2. Online at http:// www.line56.com/print/default.asp?ArticleID=2561.

CHAPTER 8

1. Lisa Meyer, "Will Online Brokerages Get Swallowed?" *Red Herring*, August 25, 2000.

2. Henry Lucas, *Strategies for Electronic Commerce and the Internet* (Cambridge: MIT Press, 2000), 135.

3. Paul Gillin, "Schwab Impresses," *Computerworld*, October 20, 1997; 31(42): 49–51.

4. Ibid., 50.

5. Lucas, *Strategies for Electronic Commerce and the Internet*, 141–142.

6. Ibid., 142.

7. Mary Hillebrand, "Merrill Lynch Joins Online Trading Party," *E-Commerce Times*, June 1, 1999.

8. Lucas, *Strategies for Electronic Commerce and the Internet*, 144.

9. Lisa Meyer, "Will Online Brokerages Get Swallowed?" *Red Herring*, August 25, 2000.

10. Kevin Werbach, "Syndication: The Emerging Model for Business in the Internet Era," *Harvard Business Review*, May/June 2000; 78(3): 85-93.

11. Davide Dukcevich, "Ameritrade Vs. E*Trade," *Forbes.com*, January 12, 2004. Online at http://www.forbes.com/2004/01/12/cx_dd_0112mondaymatchup _print.html.

12. Sam Jaffe, "Why E*Trade Isn't Just Another Online Hawker of Stocks," *BusinessWeek*, March 24, 2000.

13. "ETrade Hits the Big Apple with 'Super-Store,'" *Internet News.com*, April 4, 2001.

14. Keith Regan, "ETrade-Yahoo! Pact Opens Door for IM E-Commerce," *E-Commerce Times*, April 1, 2002.

15. Stephanie Miles, "What's a Check? After Years of False Starts, Online Banking is Finally Catching On," *Wall Street Journal*, October 21, 2002, R5.

16. Brett Bush, "Wells Fargo: Fast Then, Fast Now," *Digitends*, February 2, 1998; Ron Leuty, "Wells Fargo Hits the Middle with E-commerce Pitch," *San Francisco Business Times*, March 10, 2000, 3; and Louise Lee, "Wells Fargo: Blazing a Trail Online," *Business Week*, March 20, 2002.

17. Laura Mandaro, "Parsing Wells' Success Driving Customers to Web," *American Banker*, April 20, 2002, 1.

18. Amanda Fung, "Wells Finds Integration Key to Web Banking," *American Banker*, December 11, 2001; 166(236): 16A.

19. Mandaro, "Parsing Wells' Success Driving Customers to Web," 2.

20. Steve Bills, "Online Banking: B of A Makes Its Case," *American Banker*, April 11, 2002; 167(69): 1.

21. Priya Malhotra, "How Some Banks Gave E-Services Shot in the Arm," *American Banker*, October 28, 2002, 1.

22. "Online Banking Adds Up," www.bizjournals.com, April 21, 2003. Online at http://www.bizjournals.com/sanjose/stories/2003/04/21/daily12.html.

23. Peter Weill and Michael Vitale, *Place to Space: Migrating to e-Business Models* (Boston: Harvard Business School Press, 2001), 67–68.

24. Chet Dembeck, "Bank One Gets It," *E-Commerce Times*, August 27, 1999.

25. "Bank One: Nothing But Net," *BusinessWeek*, August 2, 1999.

26. Delroy Alexander, "Net-only Bank's Wings Clipped: Bank One to End Failing Wingspan," *Chicago Tribune*, June 29, 2001; 3.1. 2.

27. Paul Greenberg, "E-Banks: Learning the Hard Way," *E-Commerce Times*, July 6, 2001.

28. "Another Dot.com Fizzles Out," *Bank Systems and Technology*, November 2001; 38(11): 32.

29. Chris Costanzo, "Bank One: Passport Is 'Special' Because Microsoft Backs It," *American Banker*, March 27, 2002; 167(59): 1–3.

30. BankOne.com, "Bank One Launches Next Generation of Easy-To-Use bankone.com," June 18, 2002. Online at http://www.shareholder.com/one/news/20020618-82917.cfm.

31. Ranjay Gulati and Jason Garino, "Get the Right Mix of Bricks and Clicks," *Harvard Business Review* 78(3): 112.

32. Gary Gately, "CVS Pharmacy Writes Prescription for Online Expansion," *E-Commerce Times*, May 19, 1999, 1. Online at http://www.ecommercetimes.com/perl/printer/47/.

33. Susan Reda, "E-Commerce Puzzle: Where Are the Drug Stores?" *Stores*, April 1998, p. 2. Online at http://www.stores.org/archives/apr98cover.html.

34. Michael Johnson, "CVS Pioneers Online Service," *Drug Store News*, January 15, 2001; 23(1): 1.

35. Brendan Maher, "Prescription for CVS.com," *Target Marketing*, February 2001; 24(2): 1–2.

36. Joanna Pearlstein, "CVS, Merck Team Up to Own Consumer Drug E-commerce," *Red Herring*, October 8, 1999, 1. Online at http://www.redherring.com/insider/1999/1008/new-cvs.html.

37. Liz Parks, "CVS.com to Upgrade Mix and Customer Service," *Drug Store News*, April 24, 2000; 22(6): 3.

38. Andy Wang, "Peapod and Walgreens Enter Online Drug Market," *E-Commerce Times*, March 11, 1999, 1. Online at http://www.ecommercetimes.com/news/articles/990311-4.shtml.

39. Chet Dembeck, "Walgreen Co. Launches Revamped Web Site," *E-Commerce Times*, October 28, 1999, 1. Online at http://www.ecommercetimes.com/perl/story/1584.html.

40. Mary Hillebrand, "Walgreens to Escalate Online Drug War," *E-Commerce Times*, June 28, 1999, 2. Online at http://www.ecommercetimes.com/perl/story/667.html.

41. Christopher Saunders, "Walgreens.com Launches First Marketing Campaign," *Internet News.com*, February 12, 2001, 1. Online at http://www.Internetnews.com/IAR/article.php/585551.

42. Reda, "E-Commerce Puzzle: Where Are the Drug Stores?" 2.

43. Gulati and Garino, "Get the Right Mix of Bricks and Clicks," 111–112.

44. Ibid.

45. Marlene Piturro, "Drugstore.com: All Work and No Profit," *Strategic Finance*, November 2002; 84(5): 6.

46. Chris Hauser, "Drugstore.com Blazes the Internet Irail," *Modern Materials Handling*, February 2001; 56(2): 2.

47. Piturro, "Drugstore.com: All Work and No Profit."

48. Monica Soto, "Rite Aid Sells Stake in Online Pharmacy Drugstore.com," *Knight Ridder Tribune Business News*, May 7, 2002; 1, 1–2.

49. Piturro. "Drugstore.com: All work and no profit," 4.

50. James Christie, "FedEx and UPS to Wrangle Online," *Red Herring*, June 16, 2000, p. 2. Online at http://www.redherring.com/industries/2000/0616/ind-fedex061600.html.

51. Andy Wang, "Peapod and Walgreens Enter Online Drug Market," *E-Commerce Times*, March 11, 1999, 1. Online at http://www.ecommercetimes.com/news/articles/990311-4.shtml.

52. Dembeck, "Walgreen Co. Launches Revamped Web Site," 2.

53. Charles Haddad, "Big Brown's Big Coup," *BusinessWeek e.biz*, September 19, 2000, 1.

54. Sean Robinson, "E-commerce Delivers Growth in Shipping Industry," *Puget Sound Business Journal*, May 12, 2000, 1.

55. Christie, "FedEx and UPS to Wrangle Online," 3.

56. Keith Regan, "EBay and UPS Unveil Shipping Pact," *E-Commerce Times*, December 20, 2000, 1. Online at http://www.ecommercetimes.com/perl/printer/6205.

57. "UPS & eBay Extend Relationship, Expand Online Shipping Options," June 23, 2003. Online at http://pressroom.ups.com/pressreleases/archives/archive/0,1363,4319,00.html.

58. Haddad, "Big Brown's Big Coup," 2.

59. Kevin Werbach, "Syndication: The Emerging Model for Business in the Internet Era," *Harvard Business Review* 78(3): 92–93.

60. Sandeep Junnarkar, "FedEx slows down to move at Internet speed," *CNET News*, June 29, 2000, p. 1. Online at http://news.com.com/2102-1017-242612. html.

61. Andy Wang, "FedEx and Netscape Build Shipping Portal," *E-Commerce Times*, April 8, 1999, 1. Online at http://www.ecommercetimes.com/perl/printe/3087.

62. Linda Rosencrance, "FedEx Creates Online Shopping Marketplace." *Computerworld*, November 22, 1999; 33(47): 1.

63. Tom Kaneshige, "Expedient Precision." *Upside*, June 2000; 12(6): 209–213.

64. BusinessWire, "FedEx Custom Critical Enhances Online Shipping Toolkit," March 6, 2002. Online at http://www.findarticles.com/cf_dls/MOEIN/2002_March_6/83526469/pl/article/jhtml.

CHAPTER 9

1. Peter Weill and Michael Vitale, *Place to Space: Migrating to e-Business Models* (Boston: Harvard Business School Press), April 2001.

2. Paul McDougall, "Profile: Compaq Computer Corp.—Compaq Takes Direct Approach to Profitability," *InformationWeek*, September 11, 2000.

3. Henry C. Lucas, Jr., *Strategies for Electronic Commerce and the Internet* (Cambridge: The MIT Press, 2002), 103–123.

4. Dell.com, "New Industry Data Shows Dell Continues to Lead in Serving Customers through Internet Commerce," October 20, 2003. Online at http://www.www1.us.dell.com/content/topics/global.aspx/corp.pressoffice.

5. Morten Hansen, Nitin Nohria, and Thomas Tierney, "What's Your Strategy for Managing Knowledge?" *Harvard Business Review* 77(2): 112.

6. Weill and Vitale, *Place to Space: Migrating to e-Business Models*.

7. Lester C. Thurow, "Does the 'E' in E-Business Stand for 'Exit'?" *MIT Sloan Management Review* 42(2): 112.

8. Weill and Vitale, *Place to Space: Migrating to e-Business Models*.

9. Lucas, *Strategies for Electronic Commerce and the Internet*, 103–123.

10. Jim Davis, "Compaq Revamps E-commerce Strategy," *CNET News.com*, May 18, 1999.

11. Tim Ouellette, "Compaq Takes a Hit," *Computerworld*, November 22, 1999.

12. Thurow, "Does the 'E' in E-Business Stand for 'Exit'?"

13. Todd R. Weiss, "Compaq to Pursue Services," *Computerworld*, July 2, 2001.

14. Ian Fried, "HP-Compaq Merger: Worth the Wait?" *CNET News.com*, September 2, 2002.

15. Lucas, *Strategies for Electronic Commerce and the Internet*, 103–123.

16. Weill and Vitale, *Place to Space: Migrating to e-Business Models*.

17. Stephen Lawson, "Cisco Takes Aim at New Competitors," *IDG News Service*. January 8, 2003.

18. Scott Berinato, "What Went Wrong at Cisco," *CIO Magazine*, August 1, 2001.

19. Ibid.

20. Weill and Vitale, *Place to Space: Migrating to e-Business Models*.

21. "Cisco's Savvy Overhaul: Here's How the Networking Giant Has Put Itself Back in the Catbird Seat," *BusinessWeek*, November 24, 2003.

22. Lucas, *Strategies for Electronic Commerce and the Internet*, 103–123.

23. Tony Rizzo, "The Fallacy of Emulating Cisco," The Product Development Institute, 2000.

24. Weill and Vitale, *Place to Space: Migrating to e-Business Models*.

25. Matt Richtel, "Lucent's Results a 'Speed Bump,' " *International Herald Tribune*, July 25, 2003.

26. Jonathan Moules, "Making Tough Calls at Lucent," *Financial Times*, July 17, 2003.

27. Lou Hirsh, "Can Lucent Regain Its Footing?" *E-Commerce Times*, May 23, 2002.

28. Clay Boswell, "Private Exchanges Promise an Inside Line to Greater Efficiency," *Chemical Market Reporter* 260(9): 141.

29. Steven Kaplan and Mohanbir Sawhney, "E-Hubs: The New B2B Marketplaces," *Harvard Business Review* 78(3): 102.

30. Christopher Bartlett and Meg Glinska, "GE's Digital Revolution: Redefining the E in GE," *Harvard Business School Case*, May 29, 2002, 7.

31. Marc J. Epstein, "Organizing Your Business for the Internet Evolution," *Strategic Finance*, July 2000, 60.

32. Alex Frangos, "Plastics: General Electric Has an Online Marketplace That Works; What's Its Secret?" *Wall Street Journal*, May 21, 2001, 2.

33. Demir Barlas, "GE Plastics: Embracing Technology and Change Turns Mainline Manufacturer from Visionary into Runaway Business Leader," *Line56.com*, October 11, 2002. Online at www.line56.com/articles/default.asp?NewsID=4086.

34. Bartlett and Glinska, "GE's Digital Revolution: Redefining the E in GE," 7–12.

35. Brian Moran, "Powerhouses Partner in Atlanta," *Atlanta Business Chronicle*, July 28, 2000, 23(8): 1.

36. Bo Glasgow, "Omnexus on solid footing in its second year," *Chemical Market Reporter*, November 26, 2001; 260(20): 15.

37. "Plastics Industry Delves into E-commerce," *Beverage World*, July 15, 2000; 119, 1692, 1.

38. Frangos, "Plastics: General Electric Has an Online Marketplace That Works," 4.

39. Mark Leon, "Commerx CTO Sees Great Future in Plastics," *InfoWorld*, June 19, 2000; 22(25): 44.

40. Richard Karpinski, "Independent Exchanges Seek Shelter," *B to B*, October 23, 2000; 85(17): 3.

Bibliography

Adams, Chris and Neha Kapashi. "Managing with Measures." *Cranfield University School of Management*: 2–24.

Alexander, Delroy. "Net-only Bank's Wings clipped: Bank One to End Failing Wingspan." *Chicago Tribune*, June 29, 2001, sec. 3. 1.

"Amazon.com Case Study." Information Society Standardization System, 2000. Online. http://www. isss-awareness.cenorm.be/home/ Home_frame.htm.

Anonymous. "Another Dot.com Fizzles Out." *Bank Systems and Technology*, November 2001, 38(11): 32.

Anonymous. "Borders, Amazon.com Strengthen Ties." *Chain Store Age*, June 2002, 78(6): 95.

Anonymous. "Cisco's Savvy Overhaul: Here's How the Networking Giant Has Put Itself Back in the Catbird Seat." *BusinessWeek*, November 24, 2003.

Anonymous. "The Come Back Kids: E-Biz Has Returned with a Vengeance. Meet the 25 Men and Women Who Got Things Clicking." *BusinessWeek*, September 29, 2003.

Anonymous. "Kmart Installs 3,500 Shopping Kiosks in Stores Nationwide." *Direct Marketing* 63(12): 11.

Anonymous. "Late Online Starter Goes the Distance." *Drug Store News* 24(4): 36.

Anonymous. "Plastics Industry Delves into E-commerce." *Beverage World* 119(1692): 16.

Anonymous. "Retailers Eye Real-time Supply Chains." *Frontline Solutions* 2(9): 58–59.

Anonymous. "Target Direct at the Core of E-commerce Strategy." *DSN Retailing Today* 40(7): 48.

Applegate, Lynda and Meredith Collura. "Overview of E-Business Models." Harvard Case #9-801-172, August 30, 2000.

Auchard, Eric. "Office Depot Offers Direct Mail Marketing via Web." *Reuters*, February 5, 2002. Online.

Aufreiter, Nora, Pierre-Yves Ouillet, and Mary-Kate Scott. "Marketing Rules." *Harvard Business Review* 79(2): 30-31.

Banham, Russ. "Malice in Wonderland." *Executive Chief Financial Officer*, Fall 2000, 34–40.

Banham, Russ. "The Power of 3." *Chief Financial Officer-IT*, Spring 2003, 40-45.

BankOne.com. "Bank One Launches Next Generation of Easy-to-Use bankone.com." June 18, 2002. Online. http://www.shareholder.com/one/news/20020618-82917.cfm.

"Bank One: Nothing But Net." *BusinessWeek*, August 2, 1999.

Bannan, Karen. "Helping Businesses Evaluate Their Internet Presence." *New York Times*, June 12, 2002.

Barlas, Demir. "GE Plastics: Embracing Technology and Change Turns Mainline Manufacturer from Visionary into Runaway Business Leader." Line56. com, October 11. 2002. Online. www.line56.com/articles/default.asp?NewsID=4086.

Barthelemy, Jerome. "The Hidden Costs of IT Outsourcing." *MIT Sloan Management Review* 42(3): 60-69.

Bartlett, Christopher and Meg Glinska. "GE's Digital Revolution: Redefining the E in GE." *Harvard Business School Case*, May 29, 2002.

Barua, Anitesh, Prabhudev Konana, Andrew Whinston, and Fang Yin. "Driving E-Business Excellence." *MIT Sloan Management Review* 43(1): 36–44.

Berinato, Scott. "What Went Wrong at Cisco." *CIO*, August 1, 2001. Online.

Berthon, Pierre, James Hulbert, and Leyland Pitt. "Brand management prognostications." *MIT Sloan Management Review* 40(2): 53–65.

Bills, Steve. "Online Banking: B of A Makes Its Case." *American Banker* 167(69): 1.

Boswell, Clay. "Private Exchanges promise an Inside Line to Greater Efficiency." *Chemical Market Reporter* 260(9): F14.

Bradley, Peter, et al. "Wal-Mart to Use Third Party for E-commerce." *Logistics Management and Distribution Report* 38(9): 26.

Broening, Thomas. "Reprogramming Amazon." *BusinessWeek*, December 22, 2003, 82–86.

Brynjolfsson, Erik, and Glen L. Urban. *Strategic for E-Business Success*. San Francisco: Jossey-Bass, 2001.

Burger, Katherine. "Strategic IT Investments Still on Track." *Insurance and Technology* 26(8): 23.

Bush, Brett. "Wells Fargo: Fast Then, Fast Now." *Digitends*, February 2, 1998. Online. http://www.digitrends.net/marketing/13639_8664.html

BusinessWire. "FedEx Custom Critical Enhances Online Shipping Toolkit." March 6, 2002. http://www.findarticles.com/cf_dls/MOEIN/2002_March_6/83526469/pl/article/jhtml.

Byrne, John. "Caught in the Net." *BusinessWeek*, August 27, 2001, pp. 114–115.

Cameron, Preston. "For Good Measure." *Strategic Finance*, July 2000, 63–66.

Carr, Nicholas. "IT Doesn't Matter." *Harvard Business Review*, May 2003, 9–12.

Chabrow, Eric. "Who Calls the Shots? A New Management Matrix Emerges." *Informationweek*, March 6, 2000 (776): 72.

Chabrow, Eric, and Mary Hayes. "Facing an IT Future." *Informationweek*, June 18, 2001, 842, 39–46.

Christiansen, Clay and Michael Overdorf. "Meeting the Challenge of Disruptive Change." *Harvard Business Review* 78(2): 66–76.

Christie, James. "FedEx and UPS to Wrangle Online." *Red Herring*, June 16, 2000. Online. http:///www.redherring.com/industries/2000/0616/ind-fedex061600.html.

Coltman, Tim, et al. "E-Business: Revolution, Evolution, or Hype?" *California Management Review*, Fall 2001, 44(1): 57–86.

Clark, Katherine R. "Multi-Channel Retailers Gain Ground among Top 50 E-Retailers, Retail Forward Study Reports." Retailforward.com, July 31, 2002. Online. http://www.retailforward.com/freecontent/pressreleases/press48.asp.

Costanzo, Chris. "Bank One: Passport Is 'Special' Because Microsoft Backs It." *American Banker* 167(59): 1.

Couzin, Jennifer. "Saks Shops for Customers Online." *The Industry Standard*, August 28, 2000. Online. http://www.thestandard.com/article/display/0,1151,17829,00.html.

Cox, Beth. "Doing E-Commerce In Style." *Internet News.com*, September 15, 2000. Online. http://www.internetnews.com/ec-news/article.php/461311.

Cunningham, Michael J. *B2B: How to Build a Profitable E-Commerce Strategy*. Cambridge: Perseus Publishing, 2001.

Curry, James, and Martin Kenney. "Beating the Clock: Corporate Responses to Rapid Change in the PC Industry." *California Management Review* 42(1): 8–36.

Datz, Todd. "Strategic Alignment." *CIO Magazine*, August 15, 2002.

Davis, Jessica. "Restructure Your Business: Put IT in the Center of Your E-commerce Plans." *InfoWorld* 22(48): 90.

Davis, Jim. "Compaq Revamps E-commerce Strategy." *CNET News.com*, May 18, 1999.

Day, George, Adam Fein, and Gregg Ruppersberger. "Shakeouts in Digital Markets: Lessons from B2B Exchanges." *California Management Review* 45(2): 131–150.

de Figuereido, John. "Finding Sustainable Profitability in Electronic Commerce." *Sloan Management Review* 41(4): 41–52.

DeKare-Silver, Michael. *Streamlining: Using New Technologies and the Internet to Transform Performance*. Hampshire, U.K.: Palgrave Publishing, 2002.

Dell.com. "New Industry Data Shows Dell Continues to Lead in Serving Customers through Internet Commerce." October 20, 2003. Online. http://www.www1.us.dell.com/content/topics/global.aspx/corp.pressoffice.

Dembeck, Chet. "Bank One Gets It." *E-Commerce Times*, August 27, 1999.

Dembeck, Chet. "Walgreen Co. Launches Revamped Web Site." *E-Commerce Times*, October 28, 1999. Online. http://www.ecommercetimes.com/perl/story/1584.html.

Dembeck, Chet. "Do Luxury Retailers 'Get' E-Commerce?" *E-Commerce Times*, November 5, 1999. Online. http://www.ecommercetimes.com/perl/story/1667.html.

Dembeck, Chet. "Wal-Mart Spins Off E-Commerce Operations." *E-Commerce Times*, January 7, 2000. Online. http:///www.ecommercetimes.com/perl/story/2250.html.

Dembeck, Chet. "Why Webvan Will Win the Online Grocery War." *E-Commerce Times*, April 19, 2000. Online.

Dembeck, Chet, and Paul Greenberg. "UPS Forms New E-Commerce Subsidiary." *E-Commerce Times*, February 7, 2000. Online. http://www.ecommercetimes.com/perl/story/2440.html.

DeMers, John. "Online Groceries Give It Another Try." *Houston Chronicle*, May 20, 2002.

Devaraj, Sarv, and Rajiv Kohli. *The IT Payoff: Measuring the Business Value of Information Technology Investments*. Financial Times. Upper Saddle River, NJ: Prentice Hall, 2002.

D'Innocenzio, Anne. "Bricks-and-Mortar Retailers Are Becoming Competitive Online." *St. Louis Post-Dispatch*, November 2, 2000, C1.

Diorio, Stephen. "Challenges of Online Branding." *Businessline*, July 4, 2002.

Downes, Larry, and Chunka Mui. *Unleasing the Killer App: Digital Strategies for Market Dominance*. Boston: Harvard Business School Press, 1998.

Driver, Anna. "Kmart Reevaluating BlueLight Slogan, Web Site." *Reuters*, April 9, 2002. Online.

Dukcevich, Davide. "Ameritrade vs. E*Trade." Forbes.com, January 12, 2004. Online. http://www.forbes.com/2004/01/12/cx_dd_0112mondaymatchup_print.html.

Earl, Michael, and David Feeny. "How to Be a CEO for the Information Age." *MIT Sloan Management Review* 41(2): 11–23.

Earl, Michael, and Bushra Khan. "E-Commerce Is Changing the Face of IT." *MIT Sloan Management Review* 43(1): 64–72.

"E-Commerce Executive Steps Down at Ford." *New York Times*, July 4, 2002.

"E-Commerce Success Story: Charles Schwab.com." *E-Commerce Times*, September 3, 2002. Online. http://www.ecommercetimes.com/success_stories/success-schwab.shtm.

Eid, Riyad, Myfanwy Trueman, and Abdel Moneim Ahmed. "A Cross-Industry Review of B2B Critical Success Factors." *Internet Research: Electronic Networking Applications and Policy*, 2002; 12(2): 110–123.

Eisenmann, Thomas, and Alastair Brown. "Online Retailers." Harvard Case #801306, December 11, 2000.

Engle, Harriet, Peter Heckmann, and Dermont Shorten. "Capturing the Value of Supply Chain Management." *Strategy and Business*, June 26, 2003.

Enos, Lori. "Webvan to Delay Expansion." *E-Commerce Times*, September 22, 2000. Online.

Enos, Lori. "Report: Net Grocers Gaining Ground." *E-Commerce Times*, March 20, 2001. Online.

Enos, Lori. "Luxury Site Ashford.com Warned by Nasdaq." *E-Commerce Times*, April 20, 2001. Online. http://www.ecommercetimes.com/perl/story/9109.html.

Epstein, Marc J. "Organizing Your Business for the Internet Evolution." *Strategic Finance*, July 2000, 56–60.

Epstein, Marc J., and Bill Birchard. "Applying the Balanced Scorecard." *Management Accounting Guideline, Society of Management Accountants of Canada*, 1999.

Epstein, Marc J., and Bill Birchard. *Counting What Counts: Turning Corporate Accountability Into Competitive Advantage*. Cambridge: Perseus Publishing, 2000.

Epstein, Marc J., and Jean-François Manzoni. "Implementing Corporate Strategy: From Tableaux de Bord to Balanced Scorecards." *European Management Journal*, April 1998, 16(2): 190–203.

Epstein, Marc J., and Robert Westbrook. "Linking Actions to Profits in Strategic Decision Making." *MIT Sloan Management Review*, Spring 2001.

"E*Trade Adds Insurance to Its Web Site." *Houston Chronicle*, October 12, 1998.

"E*Trade Hits the Big Apple with 'Super-Store.'" *Internet News.com*, April 4, 2001. Online. http://www.internetnews.com/fina-news/print.php/733571.

"E*Trade Launches E-Commerce Investment Bank." *E-Commerce Times*, January 12, 1999. Online. http://www.ecommercetimes.com/perl/story/472.html.

Evans, Philip, and Thomas Wurster. "Getting Real about Virtual Commerce." *Harvard Business Review* 77(6): 85–94.

Evans, Philip, and Thomas Wurster. *Blown to Bits: How the New Economics of Information Transforms Strategy.* Boston: Harvard Business School Press, 2000.

Farmer, Melanie Austria, and Greg Sandoval. "Webvan Delivers Its Last Word: Bankruptcy." *CNet News*, July 9, 2001. Online.

Farrell, Diana, Terra Terwilliger and Allen Webb. "Getting IT Spending Right This Time." *McKinsey Quarterly*, 2003; 2.

Feeny, David. "Making Business Sense of the E-Opportunity." *MIT Sloan Management Review* 42(2): 41–51.

Fitter, Fawn. "Retail: Minding the Store." *Computerworld*, June 28, 1999, 33, 26, CW55-CW56.

Flynn, Mike. "Drayton: HomeGrocer Model Viable." *Puget Sound Business Journal*, August 24, 2001.

Frangos, Alex. "Plastics: General Electric Has an Online Marketplace That Works. What's Its Secret?" *Wall Street Journal*, May 21, 2001, R20.

Fried, Ian. "HP-Compaq Merger: Worth the Wait?" *CNET News.com.* September 2, 2002.

Fung, Amanda. "Wells Finds Integration Key to Web Banking." *American Banker* 167(236): 16A.

Garner, Rochelle. "In & Out of IT." *Computerworld*, March 15, 1999, 33(11): 51.

Gately, Gary. "CVS Pharmacy Writes Prescription for Online Expansion." *E-Commerce Times*, May 19, 1999. Online. http://www.ecommercetimes.com/perl/printer/47/.

Gilbert, Alorie. "BlueLight finds fulfillment outside Kmart's walls." *InformationWeek*, May 21, 2001; (838): 20.

Gillin, Paul. "Schwab impresses." *Computerworld*, October 20, 1997, 31(42): 49–51.

Glasgow, Bo. "Omnexus on Solid Footing in its Second Year." *Chemical Market Reporter*, November 26, 2001; 260(20): 15.

Glazer, Rashi. "Winning in Smart Markets." *MIT Sloan Management Review*, Summer 1999.

Glover, Steven, Stephen Liddle, and Douglas Prawitt. *E-Business: Principles and Strategies for Accountants.* Upper Saddle River, NJ: Prentice-Hall, 2002.

Goold, Michael, and Campbell, Andrew. *Designing Effective Organizations: How to Create Structured Networks.* San Francisco: Jossey-Bass, 2002.

Green, Heather. "Special Report: The Web." *BusinessWeek*, November 24, 2003.

Greenberg, Paul. "Luxury E-Tailers Face Cyber Challenges." *E-Commerce Times*, June 5, 2000. Online. http://www.ecommercetimes.com/perl/story/3475.html.

Greenberg, Paul. "Do Luxury E-Tailers Stand a Chance?" *E-Commerce Times*, January 9, 2001. Online. http://www.ecommercetimes.com/perl/story/6549.html.

Greenberg, Paul. "Blending E-Commerce and Street Smarts." *E-Commerce Times*, April 13, 2001. Online. http://www.ecommercetimes.com/perl/story/8905.html.

Greenberg, Paul. "Internet Drugstores Need A New Prescription." *E-Commerce Times*, June 28, 2001. Online. http://www.ecommercetimes.com/perl/printer/11567/.

Greenberg, Paul. "E-Banks: Learning the Hard Way." E-Commerce Times, July 6, 2001. Online. http://www.newsfactor.com/perl/story/11754.html.

Guillen, Mauro. "What Is the Best Global Strategy for the Internet?" *Business Horizons*, May-June 2002, 39–40.

Gulati, Ranjay, and Jason Garino. "Get the Right Mix of Bricks and Clicks." *Harvard Business Review*, May/June 2000; 78(3): 107–114.

Haddad, Charles. "Big Brown's Big Coup." *BusinessWeek e.biz*, September 18, 2000.

Haddad, Charles. "Office Depot's E-Diva." *BusinessWeek e.biz*, August 6, 2001, EB 22–24.

Hagel, John, III. "Edging into Web Services." *McKinsey Quarterly*, November 2002, 5–13.

Hagel, John, III. *Out of the Box: Strategies for Achieving Profits Today and Growth Tomorrow through Web Services*. Boston: Harvard Business School Press, 2002.

Hagel, John, III, and John Seely Brown. "Your Next IT Strategy." *Harvard Business Review* 79(10): 105–113.

Halkias, Maria. "Neiman Marcus Encouraged by Online Sales of Furniture." *Knight Ridder Tribune Business News*, October 24, 2002.

Halkias, Maria. "Retailers Find a Few Ideas That Click on the Internet." *Knight Ridder Tribune Business News*, October 24, 2002. Online.

Hall, Robert E. *Digital Dealing: How e-Markets are Transforming the Economy*. New York: W.W. Norton and Company, 2001.

Hallowell, Roger. "Service on the Internet: The Effect of Physical Scalability." Harvard Case 802146, October 23, 2002.

Hamel, Gary. *Leading the Revolution*. Boston: Harvard Business School Press, 2000.

Hamel, Gary. "Smart Mover, Dumb Mover." *Fortune*, September 3, 2001, 191–193.

Hamel, Gary. "Is This All You Can Build with the Net? Think Bigger." *Fortune*, April 30, 2001, 134–138.

Hamm, Steve. "Sizing Up Your Payoff." *BusinessWeek e.biz*, October 29, 2001, EB 24–25.

Hansell, Saul. "In Rewritten Internet Fables, the Late Bird Gets the Worm." *New York Times*, December 27, 2001.

Hansell, Saul. "Bertelsmann to Let Amazon.com Run CDNow." *New York Times*, November 26, 2002, 6.

Hansell, Saul. "A Retailing Mix: On Internet, in Print, and in Store." *New York Times*, December 14, 2002.

Hansen, Morten, Nitin Nohria, and Thomas Tierney. "What's Your Strategy for Managing Knowledge?" *Harvard Business Review* 77(2): 106–116.

Harris, Jeanne, and Jeffrey Brooks. "Why IT Still Matters." *Accenture Research Note: IT Value*. June 19, 2003, 34.

Hartman, Amir, and John Sifonis. *Net Ready: Strategies for Success in the E-conomy*. New York: McGraw-Hill, 2000.

Hauser, Chris. "Drugstore.com blazes the Internet trail." *Modern Materials Handling*, February 2001, 56(2): 79.

Heilig, Julia, et al. (2001). "Assessing the E-Commerce Strategies of Grocers." Working Paper.

Helft, Miguel. "What a Long, Strange Trip It's Been for Webvan." *The Industry Standard*, July 23, 2001.

Heller, Laurie. "Quest for Web Success Begins Anew with Dot.com Venture." *DSN Retailing Today*, June 5, 2000; 39(11): 131–132.

Heun, Christopher. "Grocers Count on IT to Keep Cash Registers Ringing." *InformationWeek*, December 24, 2001. Online.

Hillebrand, Mary. "Merrill Lynch Joins Online Trading Party." *E-Commerce Times*, June 1, 1999. Online. http://www.ecommercetimes.com/perl/story/434.html.

Hillebrand, Mary. "Walgreen's to Escalate Online Drug War." *E-Commerce Times*, June 28, 1999. Online. http://www.ecommercetimes.com/perl/story/667.html.

Himelstein, Linda. "Commentary: Webvan Left the Basics on the Shelf." *BusinessWeek*, July 23, 2001.

Hirsh, Lou. "Pure-Play Drugstore Faces Real World Challenges." *E-Commerce Times*, May 19, 1999. Online. http://www.newsfactor.com/perl/story/14391.html

Hirsh, Lou. "Can Lucent Regain Its Footing?" *E-Commerce Times*. May 23, 2002.

Hof, Robert, and Steve Hamm. "How E-Biz Rose, Fell, and Will Rise Anew." *BusinessWeek*, May 13 2002, 64–72.

Hoffman, Donna, and Thomas Novak,. "How to Acquire Customers on the Web." *Harvard Business Review* 78(3): 179–188.

Hooper, Larry. "2002 Top 25 Executives: John Chambers." *CRN*, Nov. 18, 2002.

Hoque, Faisal. *The Alignment Effect: How to Get Real Business Value Out of Technology*. Upper Saddle River, NJ: Financial Times, Prentice Hall, 2002.

Jaffe, Sam. "Why E*Trade Isn't Just Another Online Hawker of Stocks." *BusinessWeek*, March 24, 2000.

Jap, Sandy D., and Jakki J Mohr. "Leveraging Internet Technologies in B2B Relationships." *California Management Review*, 44(4): 24–38.

Jayachandra, Y., and Gita Melkote. *Future Prospect: Envisioning E-Business in 2020*. New Delhi: Tata McGraw-Hill, 2003.

Johannes, Laura, and John Hechinger. "Buyback Plan for Staples.com Raising Some Eyebrows." *Wall Street Journal*, March 23, 2001.

Johnson, Lauren Keller. "New Views on Digital CRM." *MIT Sloan Management Review*, Fall 2002, 10.

Johnson, Michael. "CVS pioneers online service." *Drug Store News*, January 15, 2001, 23(1): 46.

Joyce, Erin. "Your Checks Are Good at Walmart.com." *Ecommerce-guide.com*, July 23, 2003. Online. http://ecommerce.internet.com/news/news/article/0,3371,10375_2239011,00.html.

Junnarkar, Sandeep. "FedEx Slows Down to Move at Internet Speed." *CNET News*, June 29, 2000. Online. http://news.com.com/2102-1017-242612.html.

Kaiser, Rob. "Commerx Sells Unit, Highlights Software Service." *Chicago Tribune*, February 23, 2001, 3.2.

Kalin, Sari. "It's Not Easy Being B2B." *CIO*, October 1, 1999. Online.

Kambil, Ajit, Erik Eselius, and Karen Monteiro. "Fast Venturing: The Quick Way to Start Web Businesses." *MIT Sloan Management Review* 41(4): 55–67.

Kane, Margaret. "Tesco Aims Where Webvan Flamed." *CNet News*, January 14, 2002. Online.

Kanellos, Michael, et al. "Dell Still Tough to Beat in PC Market." *CNET News*, September 4, 2001. Online.

Kaneshige, Tom. "Expedient precision." *Upside*, June 2000; 12(6): 209–213.

Kanter, Rosabeth Moss. "The Ten Deadly Mistakes of Wanna-Dots." *Harvard Business Review* 79(1): 91–100.

Kaplan, Peter. "U.S. Commerce Dept. Report Says Internet Use Growing." *Reuters*, February 5, 2002. Online.

Kaplan, Steven, and Mohanbir Sawhney. "E-Hubs: The New B2B Marketplaces." *Harvard Business Review* 78(3): 97–103.

Karpinski, Richard. "Independent Exchanges Seek Shelter." *B to B*, October 23, 2000; 85(17): 46

Kary, Tiffany. "Solid Dell Helps Steady Techs." *CNET News*, November 16, 2001. Online.

Keen, Jack M., and Bonnie Digrius. *Making Technology Investments Profitable: ROI Road Map to Better Business Cases.* Hoboken: John Wiley & Sons, 2003.

Keenan, Faith, and Timothy Mullaney. "Let's Get Back to Basics, Folks." *BusinessWeek e.biz*, October 29, 2001, EB 26–28.

Keenan, Faith, Stanley Holmes, and Jay Greene. "A Mass Market of One." *BusinessWeek*, December 2, 2002, 68–72.

Keenan, Faith. "The Price Is Really Right." *BusinessWeek*, March 31, 2003, 62–67.

Kemp, Ted. "Borders Hands Off E-Commerce Operations to Amazon." *Internet Week*, April 11, 2001. Online. http://www.internetweek.com/story/INW20010411S0003.

Kenny, David, and John Marshall. "Contextual Marketing: The Real Business of the Internet." *Harvard Business Review* 78(6): 119–127.

Khosrow-pour, M. "Does Corporate America Know How to Measure Payoff in Information Technology Investment?" *Document Management: Executive Strategies* X, 1, January 2000.

Khurana, Rakesh. *Search for a Corporate Savior: The Irrational Quest for Charismatic CEOs.* Princeton: Princeton University Press, 2002.

Kirkpatrick, David. "The Internet Is Dead—Long Live the Internet." *Fortune*, December 10, 2001, 239–241.

Kissler, Gary. "e-Leadership." *Organizational Dynamics*, Fall 2001; 30(2): 121–133.

"Kmart Completes Takeover of Web Unit." *New York Times*, August 1, 2001.

"Kmart files Chapter 11." *CNN/Money*, January 22, 2002. Online.

Knowledge @ Wharton. "Borders, Barnes & Noble take separate paths to profits." CNET News.com, September 4, 2000. Online. http://new.com/2100-1017-245231.html?tag=rn.

Kotter, John. "Leading Change: Why Transformation Efforts Fail." *Harvard Business Review*, March-April 1995; 59–67.

Krumwiede, Kip, Kevin Stocks, and Monte Swain. "10 Ways E-Business Can Reduce Costs." *Strategic Finance*, July 2003, 25–29.

Laaretz, Jurgen, Alexander Scherdin, Dante Caferelli, and Klemens Hjartar. "Evolve Your Architecture." *CIO*, September 15, 2000. Online.

Laseter, Tim, Barrie Berg, and Martha Turner. "What Fresh Direct Learned from Dell." *strategy + business*, issue 30.

Lawson, Stephen. "Cisco Takes Aim at New Competitors." *IDG News Service*, January 8, 2003.

LeClaire, Jennifer. "The Rebirth of the Online Grocery." *E-Commerce Times*, August 6, 2002. Online.

Ledbetter, James. "Is Borders Closing the Book on E-commerce?" *The Industry Standard*, November 12, 1998. Online. http://www.thestandard.com/article/display/0,1151,2507,00.html.

Lee, Hau, and Seungjin Whang. "Winning the Last Mile of E-Commerce." *MIT Sloan Management Review* 42(4): 54–62.

Lee, Louise. "Wells Fargo: Blazing a Trail Online." *BusinessWeek*, March 20, 2002.

Lee, Louise. "Online Grocers: Finally Delivering the Lettuce." *BusinessWeek*, April 28, 2003, 67.

Leibs, Scott. "Fewer Banks, More Competition." *CFO.com*, September 1, 2001. Online. http://www.cfo.com/article/1,5309,4816%7C%7CA%7C3%7C,00.html.

Lenatti, Chuck. "Grinding Away on ROI." *CFO IT*, Summer 2003, 23–29.

Leon, Mark. "Commerx CTO sees great future in plastics." *InfoWorld*, June 19, 2000; 22(25): 44.

Lerouge, Cindy. "From Bricks to Clicks: How to Lay Foundation: Planning Your E-commerce Path to Profitability, Part II." *Strategic Finance*, December 2000.

Lerouge, Cindy, and Angela Picard. "A Blue-Print for Bricks to Clicks: How to Plan Your E-commerce Path to Profitability." *Strategic Finance*, November 2000.

Leuty, Ron. "Wells Fargo Hits the Middle with E-commerce Pitch." *San Francisco Business Times*, March 10, 2000.

Levin, Rich. "Profile: Sears, Roebuck, and Co: After Slow Start, Sears Leaps into E-retailing." *Informationweek*, September 11, 2000, (803): 352.

Levinson, Meredith. "Destructive Behavior." *CIO*, July 15, 2000. Online.

Liss, Kenneth. "IT Links for Boundaryless Companies." *HBS Working Knowledge*, July 10, 2000.

London, Simon. "The future means getting personal." *Financial Times*, December 13, 2002.

Lucas, Henry. *Strategies for Electronic Commerce and the Internet*. Cambridge: MIT Press, 2002.

Luftman, Jerry, and Tom Brier. "Achieving and Sustaining Behavior: IT Alignment." *California Management Review*, Fall 1999; 42(1): 109–122.

Lumpkin, G. T., Scott Droege, and Gregory Dess. "E-Commerce Strategies: Achieving Sustainable Competitive Advantage and Avoiding Pitfalls." *Organizational Dynamics*, Spring 2002; 30(4): 325–340.

Macaluso, Nora. "Barnesandnoble.com Expands E-Book Efforts." *E-Commerce Times*, January 4, 2001. Online. http://www.ecommercetimes.com/perl/story/6468.html.

Mack, Jennifer. "Business .com: The $7.5 million Domain." *ZDNet News*. December 1, 1999. Online: http://zdnet.com/2100-11-516999.html.

Mahadevan, B. "Business Models for Internet-based E-commerce: An Anatomy." *California Management Review*, Summer 2000; 42(4): 55–69.

Maher, Brendan. "Prescription for CVS.com." *Target Marketing*, February 2001; 24(2): 28.

Mahoney, Michael, and Jon Weisman. "Is the Sun Setting on E-Bookstores?" *E-Commerce Times*, January 11, 2001. Online. http://www.ecommercetimes.com/perl/story/6632.html.

Malhotra, Priya. "How Some Banks Gave E-Services Shot in the Arm." *American Banker*. October 28, 2002; 167(206).

Mandaro, Laura. "Parsing Wells' Success Driving Customers to Web." *American Banker*, April 30, 2002; 167(82): 1.

Marchand, Donald, William Kettinger, and John Rollins. "Information Orientation: People, Technology, and the Bottom Line." *MIT Sloan Management Review*, Summer 2000; 41(4): 69–80.

Marlin, Steven. "Wells Fargo Inks Two Online Payment Deals." Bank *Systems and Technology Online*, August 7, 2002. Online. http://www.banktech.com/story/whatsNews/BNK20020807S0002.

Maruca, Regina Fazio. "Retailing: Confronting the Challenges that Face Bricks-and-Mortar Stores." *Harvard Business Review* 77(4): 159–168.

Maruca, Regina Fazio. "Are CIO's Obsolete?" *Harvard Business Review* 78(2): 55–63.

McAfee, Andrew. "The Napsterization of B2B." *Harvard Business Review*, November-December 2000; 2–3.

McDougall, Paul. "Profile: Compaq Computer Corp.: Compaq Takes Direct Approach to Profitability." *InformationWeek*, September 11, 2000, (803): 282.

McIntosh, Jay. "U.S. E-Tailing Enters a New Phase." *Global Online Retailing Report*, 2000.

McWilliams, Gary. "Retailing: People Who Need People." *Wall Street Journal*, February 12, 2001, R20.

"Measuring the Productivity Impact of IT Investments." *Knowledge @ Wharton*. Online.

Meyer, Lisa. "Will online brokerages get swallowed?" *Red Herring*, August 25, 2000. Online. http://www.redherring.com/investor/2000/0825/inv-onlinebroker082500.html.

Miles, Stephanie. "Bluelight.com Web Store Is in Jeopardy without Resources to Compete with Rivals." *Wall Street Journal*, January 23, 2002, B6.

Miles, Stephanie. "What's a Check? After Years of False Starts, Online Banking is Finally Catching On." *Wall Street Journal*, October 21, 2002, R5.

Milliot, Jim. "B&N, B'mann buy up B&N.com shares." *Publishers Weekly*, November 11, 2002; 249(45): 12.

Moore, John Frederick. "Why Peapod Is Striving: First-Failure Advantage." *Business 2.0*, August 14, 2001. Online.

Moran, Brian. "Powerhouses Partner in Atlanta." *Atlanta Business Chronicle*, July 28, 2000; 23(8): 1A.

Morris, Gillian. "Staples.com." Harvard Case 800305, December 19, 2000.

Morrow, James. "UPS Unveils E-Commerce Returns Program." *E-Commerce Times*, September 21, 2000. Online. http://www.ecommercetimes.com/perl/story/4348.html.

Moschella, David. *Customer-Driven IT: How Users are Shaping Technology Industry Growth*. Boston: Harvard Business School Press, 2003.

Mottl, Judith. "IT Outsourcing Gives Staples the Tools to Grow." *Informationweek*, May 15, 2000; (786): 112–116.

Moules, Jonathan. "Making Tough Calls at Lucent." *Financial Times*, July 17, 2003.

Mullaney, Timothy. "Break Out The Black Ink." *BusinessWeek*, May 13, 2002, 74–76.

Mullaney, Timothy, and Heather Green,. "The e-Biz: It Wasn't All Hype. For Companies as well as Consumers, E-commerce Is Hotter Than Ever." *Businessweek*, May 12, 2003, 60–68.

Murphy, Patricia. "Why WingspanBank Couldn't Stay Aloft: Great Idea, Poor Implementation, Analysts Conclude." *Bank Technology News*, September 2001; 14(9): 7–8.

Myers, Randy. "E-Tailers and Space Invaders." *CFO Asia*, May 2000. Online.

"MyWebGrocer.com: Bagging Customers in a Difficult Sector." Intel Business Computing Case Study, 2002.

Naraine, Ryan. "Barnes and Noble in Takeover Bid for BN.com." *Earthwebnew.com*, November 7, 2003. Online. http://news.earthweb.com/finanews/article.php/3105761.

"Neiman Marcus: Using Oracle for a Competitive Advantage." *E-Businessiq.com*, October 13, 2003. Online. http://ebusinessiq.com/special%20interests/e-commerce/122—ebusinessIQ%20e-comm.html.

Neuborne, Ellen. "Break It to Them Quickly." *BusinessWeek e.biz*, October 29, 2001, EB 10.

"Online Banking Adds Up." *www.bizjournals.com*, April 21, 2003. Online. http://www.bizjournals.com/sanjose/stories/2003/04/21/daily12.html.

Orr, Andrea. "Bluelight.com Fight to Survive as Kmart Reorganize." *Reuters*, January 22, 2002. Online.

Orr, Andrea. "Jury Still Out on Strength of Online Holiday Sales." *Reuters*, January 3, 2002. Online. http://dailynews.yahoo.com/h/nm/20020122/wr/retail_kmart_bluelight_dc_1.html.

Ouellette, Tim. "Compaq takes a hit." *Computerworld*, November 22, 1999, 33(47): 70–73.

Pack, Todd. "Revamped Wal-Mart Site Could Bring Stores' Dominance Online." *Los Angeles Times*, November 23, 2000, C1.

Parks, Liz. "CVS.com to Ugrade Mx and Customer Service." *Drug Store News*, April 24, 2000; 22(6): 8.

Parks, Liz. "Chains Utilize Web sites as an Aid, Rather Than Business Model." *Drug Store News*, July 23, 2001; 23, 9, 42.

Patton, Susannah. "Attention Online Shoppers." *CIO*, October 1, 2000. Online.

Patton, Susannah. "Barnesandnoble.com Fights Back." *CIO*, September 15, 2001.

Pearlstein, Joanna. "CVS, Merck team up to own consumer drug e-commerce." *Red Herring*, October 8, 1999. Online. http://www.redherring.com/insider/1999/1008/new-cvs.html.

Peterson, Kim. "Safeway Division Begins Online Ordering, Home Delivery Services." *E-Commerce Times*, August 22, 2002. Online.

Piturro, Marlene. "Drugstore.com: All Work and No Profit." *Strategic Finance*, November 2002; 84(5): 40–44.

Porter, Michael. "What Is Strategy?" *Harvard Business Review* 74(6): 61–78.

Porter, Michael. "Strategy and the Internet." *Harvard Business Review* 79(2): 63–78.

Pottruck, David S., and Terry Pearce. *Clicks and Mortar: Passion-Driven Growth in an Internet Driven World*. San Francisco: Jossey-Bass, 2000.

Prahalad, C. K., and Gary Hamel. "The Core Competence of the Corporation." *Harvard Business Review*, May-June 1990; 79–90.

Prior, Molly. "Bricks-and-Clicks Model Shows Promise for Mass." *DSN Retailing Today*, November 20, 2000; 39(22): 6.

Prior, Molly. "Amazon to Operate Borders.com." *DSN Retailing Today*, May 1, 2001; 40(9): 6.

Prior, Molly. "Wal-Mart: Store-site Synergies Open On-line Opportunities." *DSN Retailing Today*, June 4, 2001; 40(11): 68.

Prior, Molly. "Dot.com Buyouts Foretell End of Spinoff Strategy." *DSN Retailing Today*, August 6, 2001; 40(15): 6.

Prior, Molly. "BlueLight Signs Global Sports to Extended E-commerce Pact." *DSN Retailing Today*, September 3, 2001; 40(17): 6.

Prior, Molly. "Target Plans 'Common' Site as Part of New Amazon Deal." *DSN Retailing Today*, April 8, 2002; 41(7): 10.

Pristin, Terry. "Ordering Groceries in Aisle 'www'." *New York Times*, May 4, 2002.

Puente, Maria. "Online Experience Is Now a Much Better Fit." *USA Today*, December 4, 2002, E 02.

Quick, Rebecca. "Returns to Sender: Having a Physical Store Is a Big Advantage When It Comes to Dealing with Dissatisfied Customers." *Wall Street Journal*, July 17, 2000; R8.

Quinn, James Brian. "Outsourcing Innovation: The New Engine of Growth." *MIT Sloan Management Review* 41(4): 13-28.

Rangan, Subramanian, and Ron Adner. "Profts and the Internet: Seven Misconceptions." *MIT Sloan Management Review* 42(4): 44-53.

Reda, Susan. "E-Commerce Puzzle: Where Are the Drug Stores?" *Stores*, April 1998. Online. http://www.stores.org/archives/apr98cover.html.

Regan, Keith. "EBay and UPS Unveil Shipping Pact." *E-Commerce Times*, December 20, 2000. Online. http://www.ecommercetimes.com/perl/printer/6205.

Regan, Keith. "Can Barnesandnoble.com Avoid the Amazon Alliance Buzzsaw." *E-Commerce Times*, April 30, 2001. Online. http://www.newsfactor.com/perl/story/9319.html.

Regan, Keith. "Amazon Signs In-Store Pickup Deal with Circuit City." *E-Commerce Times*, August 20, 2001. Online. http://www.ecommercetimes.com/perl/story/12922.html.

Regan, Keith. "Amazon and Target Forge E-Tail Partnership." *E-Commerce Times*, September 12, 2001. Online.

Regan, Keith. "Survival of the Internet's Sneakiest Grocer?" *E-Commerce Times*, December 13, 2001. Online

Regan, Keith. "Amazon's Free-Shipping Gamble: Will Rivals Ante Up?" *E-Commerce Times*, January 24, 2002. Online. http://www.ecommercetimes.com/perl/story/15966.html.

Regan, Keith. "E*Trade-Yahoo! Pact Opens Door for IM E-Commerce." E-Commerce *Times*, April 1, 2002. Online. http://www.ecommercetimes.com/perl/story/17038.html.

Reichheld, Frederick, and Phil Schefter. "E-Loyalty: Your Secret Weapon on the Web." *Harvard Business Review* 78(4): 105–113.

Richtel, Matt. "Lucent's results a 'speed bump'." *International Herald Tribune*. July 25, 2003.

Rifkin, Glenn, and Joel Kurtzman. "Is Your E-Business Plan Radical Enough?" *MIT Sloan Management Review* 43(3): 91–95.

Rizzo, Tony. "The Fallacy of Emulating Cisco." The Product Development Institute, 2000.

Robinson, Sean. "E-commerce delivers growth in shipping industry." *Puget Sound Business Journal*, May 12, 2000.

Roman, Monica (2001). "Putting the Bricks over the Clicks." *BusinessWeek*, August 6, 2001, 36.

Rose, Barbara. "Web Startup's New Industrial Marketplace." *Crain's Chicago Business*, February 7, 2000; 23(6): 4.

Rosen, Kenneth, and Amanda Howard. "E-Retail: Gold Rush or Fool's Gold?" *California Management Review*, Spring 2000; 42(3): 72–100.

Rosenberg, Hilary. "Mad To Measure." *ECFO*, Fall 2001, 29–36.

Rosencrance, Linda. "FedEx Creates Online Shopping Marketplace." *Computerworld*, November 22, 1999; 33(47): 18.

Ross, Jeanne W., and Cynthia M. Beath. "Beyond the Business Case: New Approaches to IT Investment." *MIT Sloan Management Review*, Winter 2002.

Saliba, Claire. "Royal Ahold Wants 100 Percent of Peapod." *E-Commerce Times*, July 16, 2001. Online.

Sandoval, Greg. "As Net Fraud Grows, So Do E-tailers' Fears." *CNET News*, October 5, 2001. Online.

Sandoval, Greg. "Target spins off e-commerce group." *CNET News*, February 1, 2000. Online. http://news.com.com/2100-1017-236378.html?legacy=cnet.

Saunders, Christopher. "Walgreens.com Launches First Marketing Campaign." *Internet News.com*, February 12, 2001. Online. http://www.internetnews.com/IAR/article.php/585551.

Sawhney, Mohanbir. "Don't Homogenize, Sychronize." *Harvard Business Review*, July-August 2001; 100–108.

Sawhney, Mohanbir, and Emannela Pandell. "Communities of Creation: Managing Distributed Innovation in Turbulent Markets." *California Management Review*, 42 (4) (Summer 2000).

Schwartz, Ephraim and Dan Briody. "Putting a Price on IT Savvy." *InfoWorld*, May 22, 2000, 22(21): 134.

Sealey, Peter. "How E-Commerce Will Trump Brand Management." *Harvard Business Review* 77(4): 171-176.

Selden, Larry, and Geoffrey Colvin. "Will Your E-Business Leave You Quick or Dead?" *Fortune*, May 28, 2001, 112–124.

Semler, Ricardo. "How We Went Digital Without a Strategy." *Harvard Business Review*, September–October 2000, 51–58.

Seybold, Patricia B.. *Customers.com: How to Create a Profitable Business Strategy for the Internet and Beyond*. New York: Times Books, 1998.

Shank, John K., John Dunleavy, and Donald Peterson. "Real Options Analysis for Evaluating E-Business Opportunities." *Strategic Cost Management*, D8.

Siegel, David. *Futurize Your Enterprise: Business Strategy in the Age of the E-Customer*. New York: John Wiley and Sons, 1999.

Simons, Robert. "Control in an Age of Empowerment." *Harvard Business Review*, March-April 1995, pp. 80–88.

Sindrich, Jackie, and Michael Erman. "No Sure Way Seen to Keep Kmart Blue Light Shining." *Reuters*, January 3, 2002. Online.

Sklar, David. "Building Trust an Internet Economy." *Strategic Finance*, April 2001, 22–25.

Sliwa, Carol. "Kmart Moves to Catch Up on IT." *Computerworld*, July 31, 2000, 34(31): 115.

Slywotzky, Adrian J., et al. "The Future of Commerce." *Harvard Business Review*. January-February 2000, 3-10.

Soto, Monica. "Rite Aid Sells Stake in Online Pharmacy Drugstore.com." *Knight Ridder Tribune Business News*, May 7, 2002, 1.

Sparks, Debra. "The Prodigal Dot-Coms' Return." *BusinessWeek*, June 4, 2001, 92.

Spector, Robert. *Anytime, Anywhere: How the Best Bricks-and-Clicks Businesses Deliver Seamless Service to their Customers*. Cambridge: Perseus Publishing, 2002.

Spiegel, Rob. "Study: Internet Pharmacies Are Expensive and Unsafe." *E-Commerce Times*, October 4, 1999. Online. http://www.ecommercetimes.com/perl/story/1351.html.

Spiegel, Rob. "Neiman Marcus Launches 'Affluent Platform' on the Web." *E-Commerce Times*, October 18, 1999. Online. http://www.ecommercetimes.com/perl/story/1476.html

Spooner, John. "Ex-Compaq Exec to Drive Dell Services." *ZDNet News*, January 14, 2002. Online.

Sriram, Ram, and Gopal Krishnan. "The Value Relevance of IT Investments on Firm value in the Financial Services Sector." October, 15, 2001. Unpublished.

Stackpole, Beth. "Apps of Steel." *CIO*, October 15, 2000. Online.

Stedman, Craig. "Wal-Mart CIO Leaves Retailer an IT Leader." *Computerworld*, March 6, 2000; 34(10): 4.

Steiner, Ina. "Amazon.com Extends Ecommerce Agreement with Target to 2008." *AuctionBytes.com*, August 15, 2003. Online. http://www.auctionbytes. com/cab/1abn/yø3/mø8/1$15/Sø1.

Stellin, Susan. "Online Customer Service Found Lacking." *New York Times*, January 3, 2002.

Stevenson, Reed. "Amazon, Office Depot Launch Online Store." *Reuters*, September 6, 2002. Online.

Stoiber, John. "Maximizing IT Investments." *CIO*, July 15, 1999. Online.

Strasburg, Jenny. "Kmart Turns Off Bluelight.com" *San Francisco Chronicle*, June 20, 2002, B3.

Strassmann, Paul A. *Information Payoff: The Transformation of Work in the Electric Age*. New Canaan, Conn.: Information Economics Press, 1985.

Strassmann, Paul A. *The Business Value of Computers: An Executive's Guide*. New Canaan, Conn.: Information Economics Press, 1990.

Stressman, Paul A. *The Squandered Computer: Evaluating the Business Alignment of Information Technologies*. New Canaan, Conn.: Information Economics Press, 1997.

Strom, Stephanie, and Saul Hansell. "A Bright Spot in a Bleak Holiday Retailing Season." *New York Times*, December 19, 2001.

Swartz, Jon. "Retailers Discover Leap to Web's a Doozy." *USA Today*, December 18, 2001, B.03

"Target, Amazon in E-Commerce Deal." *Reuters*, September 11, 2001. Online.

Tedeschi, Bob. "Proposed Deal Could Help Both Retailers' Web Sites." *New York Times*, May 14, 2002.

Tedeschi, Bob. "Amazon Expected to Sell Apparel." *New York Times*, July 1, 2002.

Thurow, Lester. "Does the 'E' in E-business Stand for 'Exit'?" *MIT Sloan Management Review* 42(2): 112.

Tice, Carol. "Streamlined Online Operation Promises Profits." *Puget Sound Business Journal*, July 13, 2001; 21(10): 32.

Tice, Carol. "Federated Is Curtailing E-commerce Endeavors." *Puget Sound Business Journal*, February 15, 2002l; 22(42): 17.

Tjan, Anthony. "Finally, a Way to Put Your Internet Portfolio in Order." *Harvard Business Review* 79(2): 76-85.

Travers, Rod. "E-Culture." *CIO*, September 15, 2000. Online.

Troy, Mike. "Wal-Mart, AOL Form Alliance of Giants." *Discount Store News*, January 3, 2000; 39(1): 48.

UPS. "UPS and eBay Extend Relationship, Expand Online Shipping Options." June 23, 2003. Online. http://pressroom.ups.com/pressreleases/archives/ archive/0,1363,4319,00.html.

Urban, Glen; Fareena Sultan, and William Qualls. "Placing Trust at the Center of Your Internet Strategy." *MIT Sloan Management Review* 42(1): 39–48.

Venkataraman, N. "Five Steps to a Dot-Com Strategy: How to Find Your Footing on the Web." *MIT Sloan Management Review* 41(3): 15–28.

Venkataraman, N., and John Henderson. "Real Strategies for Virtual Organizing." *MIT Sloan Management Review* 40(1): 33–48.

Violino, Bob. "E-Business 100: Office Depot Builds Winning Strategy on the Web." *InformationWeek*, December 13, 1999.

Violino, Bob. "Payback Time for E-Business." *Internet Week*. May 2000, 4.

Vogelstein, Fred. "Mighty Amazon." *Fortune*, May 26, 2003, 60–74.

Wahlgren, Eric. "E*Trade Is No One-Trick Dot-Com." *BusinessWeek*, January 28, 2002.

Wang, Andy. "Peapod and Walgreens Enter Online Drug Market." *E-Commerce Times*, March 11, 1999. Online. http://www.ecommercetimes.com/news/articles/990311-4.shtml.

Wang, Andy. "FedEx and Netscape Build Shipping Portal." *E-Commerce Times*, April 8, 1999. Online. http://www.ecommercetimes.com/perl/printer/3087.

Weill, Peter, and Michael Vitale. *Place to Space: Migrating to e-Business Models*. Boston: Harvard Business School Press, 2001.

Weill, Peter, Mani Subramani, and Marianne Broadbent. "Building IT Infrastructure for Strategic Agility." *MIT Sloan Management Review*, Fall 2002, 57–65.

Weisman, Jon. "Global Sports To Buy Ashford.com." *E-Commerce Times*, September 14, 2001. Online. http://www.ecommercetimes.com/perl/story/13540.html.

Weiss, Todd. "Compaq to Pursue Services." *Computerworld*, July 2, 2001; 35(27): 21.

Werbach, Kevin. "Syndication: The Emerging Model for Business in the Internet Era." *Harvard Business Review* 78(3): 85–93.

"What Webvan Could Have Learned from Tesco." *Strategic Management*, from Knowledge@Wharton. Online, October 10, 2001.

Whitaker, Barbara. "Online Shopping Is Up and Prices Can Still Be Down." *New York Times*, December 8, 2002.

Wieder, Tamera. "E-commerce Benchmarking." *Computerworld*, August 2000, 58.

Wilder, Clinton. "Profile: Office Depot Inc.: E-commerce Pays Off for Office Depot." *InformationWeek*, September 11, 2000, 803, 360.

Willcocks, Leslie, and Robert Plant. "Pathways to E-business Leadership: Getting from Bricks to Clicks." *MIT Sloan Management Review* 42(3): 50–59.

Wise, Richard, and David Morrison. "Beyond the Exchange: The Future of B2B." *Harvard Business Review* 78(6): 86–96.

Wohl, Jessica. "Amazon, Toys R Us Plan Online Toy Stores." *Reuters*, August 10, 2002. Online.

Wolf, Alan. "'Marts Buy Back E-commerce Units." *TWICE*, August 6, 2001; 16(18): 19.

Young, Debby. "Staples' E-Business Staples." *Line56*, May 15, 2001. Online. http://www.line56.com/print/default.asp?ArticleID=2561.

Yue, Lorene. "Kmart to Pull Out of Internet Business as Part of Restructuring." *Knight Ridder Tribune Business News*, September 18, 2002, p. 1.

Zach, Michael H. "Managing Codified Knowledge." *Sloan Management Review*. Summer 1999.

Zeller, Thomas, and David Kublank. "Focused E-tail Measurement and Resource Management." *Business Horizons*, January–February 2002, pp. 53–60.

Zeng, Ming, and Werner Reinartz. "Beyond Online Search: The Road to Profitability." *California Management Review*, Winter 2003; 45(2): 107–130.

Zimmerman, Ann. "Just Show Us the Stuff and Forget the Flash." *Wall Street Journal Europe*, April 19–21, 2002.

Index

About the Author

MARC J. EPSTEIN is Distinguished Research Professor of Management, Jones Graduate School of Management, Rice University. He is also visiting professor and Hansjoerg Wyss Visiting Scholar in Social Enterprise at the Harvard Business School. He previously held positions at Stanford Business School and INSEAD (the European Institute of Business Administration). A specialist in corporate strategy, governance, and performance management, he is the author or coauthor of twelve books (including *Counting What Counts* and *Measuring Corporate Environmental Performance* and over 100 academic and professional papers. He currently serves as editor in chief of the journal *Advances in Management Accounting*, and consults to leading corporations and governments around the world.